LLEWELLYN'S
2016
HERBAL
ALMANAC

© 2015 Llewellyn Publications is a registered
trademark of Llewellyn Worldwide Ltd.

Cover Design: Kevin R. Brown
Editing: Jennifer Ackman

Cover images:
shutterstock.com/121518688/© mart,
71500606, 161042336, 56477956/© Kovalevska,
128760839©Julia-art

Interior Art: © Fiona King

You can order annuals and books from
New Worlds, Llewellyn's catalog. To request
a free copy, call toll free: 1-877-NEW WRLD
or visit ww

ISBN 97
Llewelly
2143 \
Woodbu

Contents

Herb Crafts

Herb History, Myth, and Lore

Moon Signs, Phases, and Tables

Introduction to
Llewellyn's Herbal Almanac

More and more people are using herbs, growing and gathering them and studying them for their enlivening and healing properties. Whether in the form of a refreshing herbal tonic, a critter-friendly garden, or a new favorite recipe, herbs can clearly enhance your life.

In the 2016 edition of the *Herbal Almanac*, we once again feature innovative and original thinkers and writers on herbs. We tap into the practical, historical, and enjoyable aspects of herbal knowledge—using herbs to help you reconnect with the earth, enhance your culinary creations, and heal your body and mind. The thirty articles in this almanac will teach you everything from making your own love charms to using flower and vibrational essences to improve your health. You'll also learn how to identify poisonous and non-poisonous mushrooms, create your own shade garden, and serve up a culinary concoction that'll wow the crowds. Enjoy!

Note: The old-fashioned remedies in this book are historical references used for teaching purposes only. The recipes are not for commercial use or profit. The contents are not meant to diagnose, treat, prescribe, or substitute consultation with a licensed health-care professional. Herbs, whether used internally or externally, should be introduced in small amounts to allow the body to adjust and to detect possible allergies. Please consult a standard reference source or an expert herbalist to learn more about the possible effects of certain herbs. You must take care not to replace regular medical treatment with the use of herbs. Herbal treatment is intended primarily to complement modern health care. Always seek professional help if you are suffering from an illness. Also, take care to read all warning labels before taking any herbs or starting an extended herbal regimen. Always consult medical and herbal professionals before beginning any sort of medical treatment—this is particularly true for pregnant women. Herbs are powerful things; be sure you are using that power to achieve balance.

Llewellyn Worldwide does not participate in, endorse, or have any authority or responsibility concerning private business transactions between its authors and the public.

Growing
and
Gathering
Herbs

Grow Your Own Herbs and Spices: Ten Easy Steps to Success

By Jill Henderson

A kitchen without herbs is like a carnival without rides—boring! Cooking with freshly picked or dehydrated herbs turns plain, everyday food into exciting gourmet fare. And you just can't beat the price! In fact, growing your own kitchen herbs is one of the easiest and most rewarding pastimes you will ever engage in—and it's terribly addictive, too.

If you are already familiar with growing flowers and vegetables, adding herbs to your repertoire should be a breeze. For those new to gardening or growing herbs, the following guidelines will go a long way to help you grow your own flavorful and healthful herbs and spices. You will no doubt enjoy the experience, and everyone who sits at your table will thank you for it!

Step 1—Start Annual Herbs at Home

Seeds

Many, but not all, culinary herbs begin their lives as seeds. This is particularly true for annual herbs like dill, basil, and cilantro. Understanding how to get those small packages of life to unfurl their greenness is a relatively simple matter. If you want to grow quality herbs, begin by purchasing quality seeds from a reputable seed house or nursery. Not only are you guaranteed good seed, but the instructions for starting the seeds are printed right on the package. Later on you can learn how to save your own annual herb seeds, which can save you a ton of money year after year.

First-time herb gardeners should begin by using easy seed-starting trays designed to offer the gardener control of the microenvironment that seeds need to germinate. They also provide excellent drainage and easy removal of young seedlings. These kits should include a plastic sheet of individual plant cells with drainage holes, a flat without drainage holes, and a clear dome to cover the whole works. The quality and reusability of these trays varies by retailer, but even the cheapest ones (usually around six dollars) can be reused at least once.

Starting Medium

There are many types of potting soils and soilless potting mixes from which to choose, and each brand promises fantastic results. However, any soilless mix that does not contain fertilizer will do. Added fertilizer prompts herbs to grow leggy. This means that the seedlings have grown too fast, have become long and slender, and often fall over because their cell structures have not grown strong enough to support them. Rarely do leggy plants recover and grow normally again. So avoid fertilizers and don't worry; nature is a wonderfully ingenious thing. All the nutrition that your newly emerging herbs will need to get off to a good start has been built into the seeds themselves by Mother Nature.

Step 2—Seedlings Need Lots of Love

Plentiful, high-quality light is crucial to the proper development of young herbs. Before you plant a single seed, take a close look at how much light the young plants will receive from natural sources. If your nursery receives less than six hours of bright, direct sunlight each day, you will need to provide some type of artificial light. This can be as simple as a single fluorescent bulb suspended over the flats, or as high-tech as multispectrum grow lights set up on adjustable chains or stands.

Keep in mind that plants will always lean toward natural sunlight regardless of the quality of an artificial source. Quality light from all directions helps prevent leggy seedlings, which is one of the worst things to have happen early on in the process. For this reason, it is very important to turn trays of seedlings receiving natural light from a window one-quarter of a turn in the same direction at least once a day. Any time your schedule and outdoor temperatures allow it, place your seedlings in a bright but shady, sheltered spot so they can become accustomed to outside conditions early on.

Warmth

Herb seeds sown indoors need consistent temperatures in order to germinate properly. Warm-season herbs such as basil, sage, and oregano require temperatures of around 70°F (21°C), while cool-season herbs such as dill, cilantro, and parsley require as little as 60°F (16°C). Soil temperature can swing wildly depending on the time of day, the average indoor temperature, and the proximity to sources of cold air, such as a window. The safest, most effective way to regulate soil temperature is by using a heating mat. These specialized flexible rubber mats are designed to provide steady, controlled heat to the bottom of the starting tray, warming the soil, not the air. Some of the more expensive mats have adjustable temperature control dials, making them quite versatile. If you are growing multiple flats of seedlings, purchasing several mats can get to be quite a price burden. Since most seeds germinate within fourteen days, and seedlings need slightly cooler temperatures to grow well, you can alternate the use of one heating mat between multiple flats planted seven to fourteen days apart.

Moisture

Germinating seeds need very little moisture. One of the most common mistakes made by those starting seeds indoors is overwatering. Waterlogged soils smother seeds, and those that do germinate often wind up dying from damping-off. This soilborne fungal infection attacks the stems of young seedlings, causing them to rot at or below the soil line. Infected seedlings often show signs of damping-off by severe wilting that is not resolved by watering. In fact, watering only makes the situation worse and eventually the seedlings will collapse and die. Once infected there is no stopping this disease. The best cure is prevention.

I have read and tried countless methods of moistening soil for seed germination, from immersing the bottoms of seed trays in water, to mixing water and soil in a large container until the soil is as damp as a wrung-out sponge. Both methods work, but to be quite honest, I have found nothing more effective, controllable, or tidy as using a spray bottle filled with water. Fill the seed cells with soilless mix and spray each cell twice. Plant the seed and then gently spray once or twice more. Check the soil moisture daily, spritzing as needed.

Step 3—Make It Easy! Start with Nursery-Grown Plants

Sometimes starting herbs from seed is not only unfeasible, but also impossible. Certain herbs such as bay, rosemary, and true French tarragon cannot be propagated from seed and must be reproduced vegetatively. This also applies to bulbous or rhizomatous herbs such as garlic, ginger, turmeric, and horseradish. If you do not have these plants growing in your garden already, go ahead and spend the money to buy them. You won't regret the quality if you purchase them from a reputable nursery. Otherwise, just ask a gardening friend if they have any plants to share.

Regardless of how you get them, be sure to carefully inspect each plant before bringing it home. You want a plant that is healthy, strong, and green. Avoid potted plants that are overly large for the container and those in bloom. Plants like these are often root- or pot-bound, meaning that the roots have run out of room to grow, and are now winding around and around inside the pot until they become a tangled mess. Look for roots protruding from the drainage holes, and ask to inspect the root ball before you decide to purchase. Often these plants are completely salvageable if the root ball is broken up before planting, but sometimes they just dwindle and die.

Like most plants, herbs grow very quickly and rarely last long in their propagation pots. Be prepared to repot or plant nursery stock as soon as possible. And don't underestimate the needs of the herbs that you start at home from seed, either. Plan to repot or plant these six to eight weeks after germination.

Step 4—A Spot of Sun

Once your seedlings are up and running and you've purchased the potted herbs you need to fill in the gaps, it's time to plant! While herbs are relatively simple to grow, it is important to understand the needs of each herb, and under what conditions they will thrive.

It is often suggested that herbs need full sun to do well, but the truth is that most herbs will thrive when given as little as six hours of direct sunlight. In fact, there are a lot of herbs that will not only tolerate partial shade, but will thrive in it. And herbs like bay and ginger may even die if grown in full sun. If you live in an area with very hot summers, a little afternoon shade will do wonders.

Step 5—Good Soil versus Healthy Soil

While it is well known that many of the dryland and Mediterranean herbs like rosemary and sage naturally grow in soils that most garden plants disdain, it doesn't mean that herbs don't need "good" soil. While hardy perennial herbs can withstand adverse conditions such as drought, heat, and low soil fertility, most will actually grow best in soils with average fertility and excellent drainage.

Indeed, fertility is not usually the problem in the case of slow or poorly formed herbs—drainage is. Heavy soils greatly reduce air movement in the soil, creating conditions favorable to root rot and other diseases. If the soil in your garden is poorly drained or is heavy clay, try raising the beds using stones, concrete blocks, or landscape timbers to create planting areas that naturally drain more quickly. In the same vein, mixing compost, shredded leaves, and other organic material into the soil prior to planting will improve drainage and increase overall soil fertility all in one shot.

Step 6—The Lowdown on Using Fertilizers

Unless you live on a rock pile, the average garden will have soil that is sufficient for growing the most common herbs. As already mentioned, over-fertilization leads to spurts of exaggerated growth that is prone to legginess. Besides that, herbs that are over-fertilized often have less flavor and less medicinal value than their unfertilized counterparts.

Simply applying compost around your plants once a year will provide them with just the right amount of quality nutrients to keep them healthy and growing strong all year. If your herbs grow poorly, direct your focus on improving soil structure through the addition of organic matter or well-rotted compost. If you feel that your herbs need a little pick-me-up during stressful summer months, spray the leaves with water-soluble fish emulsion and kelp. Kelp is a fantastic source of trace minerals, and when applied to the leaves every other week, can help prevent the formation of fungal diseases that affect the leaves.

If using a preformulated fertilizer, select one that is low in phosphorus (P), which stimulates plants to bloom. For leafy herbs like basil, blooms are not what you are aiming for. On the other hand, herbs grown for their seeds can be side-dressed with bone meal to help promote fruitful blossoms. In general, high-nitrogen fertilizers produce excessive amounts of leafy growth weak in flavor and should be avoided.

Step 7—Proper Watering and Drainage

Another misconception about herbs is that they require a lot of water. The truth is that most herbs do better on as little as one inch of water every two weeks, even during the driest parts of summer. On the other hand, if your soil drains too quickly or you are growing in pots, you will likely need to water more often. For these situations, try adding a small amount of powdered water gel to the soil before planting. This gel absorbs water and slowly releases it to plant roots as they need it, resulting in less watering and happier herbs.

Step 8—Mulch, Mulch, Mulch!

I cannot say enough about the benefits of mulching. Mulch keeps soil cool and moist during hot summer months, smothers weeds, and keeps soilborne organisms from splashing onto the leaves. In the winter, a thick layer of mulch keeps soil temperatures from fluctuating radically, preventing nasty freeze-and-thaw cycles that can heave well-established plants right out of the ground and kill them.

Anything that covers the soil can be used as mulch, including rocks, pea gravel, compost, shredded leaves, pine needles, grass, hay, straw, or bark. While landscaping fabric or row covers can be used as mulch, natural materials are much more attractive. They also break down slowly over time, improving soil texture, moisture retention, drainage, and fertility.

Step 9—Multiply Your Holdings

Once perennial herbs have reached their mature size—usually one to two years—it is easy to use them to propagate lots of new plants that can be replanted in the garden, held over as standby plants in case of loss, and shared or traded with other gardeners for new and interesting cultivars.

Root Division

Almost any mature perennial herb can be divided into two or more new plants with little effort through a process known as root division. The tools you need might include a shovel or sharp spade, a small knife, a pair of scissors, and, if you plan on potting up your new herbs, several sizes of pots, a bag of potting mix, and plant markers.

The number of new plants you can obtain from the original depends on the size and vigor of the parent plant. Most can at least be cut in half. Use a strong, swift thrust of a sharp spade right down the center of the plant, either while still in the ground or after the entire plant has been lifted. Just remember that each division must have a healthy network of roots attached to a viable stem or stems in order to survive.

Layering

Layering is another method of propagation that involves rooting actively growing stems while they are still attached to the parent plant. Layering is most successful when applied in the spring or early summer. Select long, flexible stems and bend them gently to the ground, taking care not to break them where they meet the parent plant. Strip off all but the top-most leaves, and bury the majority of the stem under several inches of soil. Use a rock to pin the stem firmly to the ground, and cover lightly with dirt and mulch, leaving the leafy portion of the stem protruding two to three inches (5 to 8 cm) above the soil. Stems layered in the spring or early summer are often well-rooted by fall and can then be cut from the parent plant and transplanted elsewhere.

Stem Cuttings

Rooting stem cuttings is often faster than layering and more productive than divisions. Start by selecting young, actively growing stems at least six inches (15 cm) long, and cut them from the parent plant with a very sharp pair of scissors. Strip the leaves from the lower two-thirds of the stem, and dip the cut end in rooting hormone. Plant the cutting in predrilled holes at least three inches (8 cm) deep in a large flat or pot filled with moist, soilless potting mix. Space the cuttings four to six inches (10 to 15 cm) apart in all directions. Place the flat in a lightly shaded area, and loosely cover to increase humidity. Be sure to keep the soil moist, but not soggy, until the stems begin to root, usually around six to eight weeks.

Once the small herbs begin to grow new leaves, allow the soil to dry slightly between waterings and move the flat into a sunnier area for two or more weeks before transplanting to larger pots or into the garden.

Step 10—Get Growing!

If you've ever wanted to try your hand at growing your own culinary herbs, now is the time to begin! Start with the herbs you use most in your kitchen, and add more variety as time and space allow. Annual herbs like parsley, dill, basil, and cilantro are easily incorporated into an existing vegetable garden. And perennial herbs such as rosemary, sage, and oregano can be grown in large pots or tucked in among established beds of flowers and shrubs. In no time your kitchen will be a vibrant carnival of beautiful colors and extraordinary flavors—and no one will ever miss the rides.

Happy gardening!

Jill Henderson *is an artist, author, and world traveler with a penchant for wild edible and medicinal plants, culinary herbs, and nature ecology. She has written three books, including* The Healing Power of Kitchen Herbs: Growing and Using Nature's Remedies, A Journey of Seasons: A Year in the Ozarks High Country, *and* The Garden Seed Saving Guide: Seed Saving for Everyone.

A lifelong organic gardener and seed saver with a passion for sustainable agriculture and local food production, Jill presents workshops to teach gardeners about the detrimental impacts of bioengineered food crops and how to grow and save open-pollinated and heirloom seeds.

Jill also writes and edits Show Me Oz *(ShowMeOz.wordpress .com), a weekly blog filled with gardening and seed-saving tips, homesteading wisdom, edible and medicinal plants, nature, and* more. She is a regular contributor to Llewellyn's Herbal Almanac, Acres USA, and the Permaculture Activist.

In her spare time, Jill is a professional artist specializing in custom pet portraits and wildlife art. You can view some of her work at ForeverPetPortraits.wordpress.com. Jill and her husband, Dean, live and work in the heart of the rugged Ozark Mountains.

Barley: An Ancient Grain for Modern Healthy Lifestyles

⤞ By James Kambos ⤝

Harvest approaches with its bustling day,
The wheat tans brown and barley bleach-
es grey.

—from "August" in *The Shepherd's Calendar* by John Clare, 1827

Barley was probably the first cereal grain cultivated by the human race. Barley grains believed to be 5,000 years old have been found in Egypt; however, experts believe barley has been cultivated for at least 8,000 to 10,000 years. Its origin remains a mystery. Some believe barley originated in Ethiopia, but others think its cultivation began in the Fertile Crescent region, an area comprising modern-day Syria,

Turkey, and Iraq. English and Dutch settlers introduced barley to North America during the 1600s.

The introduction of barley as a regular, stable food source allowed our ancient ancestors to settle in one place instead of being only hunters and gatherers. This led to one of the greatest achievements in human history: the beginning of agriculture as we know it today. Ancient civilizations held barley in high regard spiritually as well as nutritionally. Ancient Egyptians included barley in various forms as part of religious ceremonies. Roman and Greek soldiers included barley in their diets to ensure strength and stamina, and today more and more studies are proving that barley is indeed one of the healthiest foods.

Barley Facts

Cultivated barley (*Hordeum vulgare*) is the fourth-largest grain crop in the world. Only wheat, rice, and corn have larger yields. Barley, along with all grains, holds a unique position in the plant kingdom. It is a grass, which also makes it an herb. But it can also be considered a crop, a grain, and a cereal too. Barley is grown around the world; Canada, the United States, Russia, Australia, and Germany are the major producers. In the United States, more than half the states grow barley.

In Europe, barley was a major part of most diets through the Middle Ages. Wheat products were quite expensive, so barley flour was also a major ingredient in bread baking. Unfortunately, barley became known as a "peasant food" and its use began to decline. That's a pity because it's so nutritious. Soon after this period, barley became used mostly as a food for livestock in many areas of the world.

During the second half of the twentieth century in the United States, 65 percent of the barley produced was still used for livestock food. However, the most recent statistics say that number has dropped to about 51 percent. I hope this means that this super-healthy grain is being discovered by more cooks.

Today, human consumption of barley seems to be increasing. It can be found in cereals, soups, salads, crackers, confections, and certain pastas. One of the major uses of barley is barley malt, which is used primarily in the production of beer. To make barley malt, the kernels are soaked and aerated, and when the kernels begin to sprout, they're slowly heated. This process increases the amount of sugars and starch, and is an amazing step in the production of beer.

Types of Barley

The two major barley products you'll find in stores are hulled barley and pearled barley.

Hulled barley is also known as whole grain barley. This type has been processed just enough to remove only the inedible, tough outer layer, or hull. It is extremely nutritious and has a more pronounced nutty flavor. It does take longer to cook, and it doesn't absorb as much water during cooking, so as a result it's chewier.

Pearled barley is the variety you'll most likely find in the supermarket. It's usually found on the same shelf as rice and dried beans. It's more processed than hulled barley because it's been polished, or pearled. It's not a whole grain since the bran and endosperm have been removed. Although it isn't considered to be as nutritious as the hulled variety, pearled barley is still a very wholesome grain. It cooks more quickly and is the type used in most recipes.

Other forms of barley include barley flakes and barley flour. Barley flakes make a good breakfast cereal. Just cook them as you would oatmeal on the stove or in the microwave. They don't absorb as much water, so what I do is simply drain off the excess water and flavor them as I would oatmeal. Brown sugar, dried or fresh fruit, and cinnamon are good ideas.

If you want to bake with barley flour, keep in mind that you must mix it with wheat flour. Barley flour is lower in gluten, so if you try using only barley flour, your baked goods will not rise properly. For yeast breads, barley flour should make up no more than one-fourth the total amount of flour used. For quick breads, you should use about half barley flour and half wheat flour.

Health Benefits of Barley

It's no exaggeration when I say that barley is a remarkable food with many health benefits. Many researchers and health professionals have added it to the list of "super foods." The only mystery is why Americans have been so slow to embrace this ancient grain as a part of a healthy diet. As studies continue, hopefully this will change.

Introducing barley to your diet can help reduce the risk of cardiovascular disease, colon cancer, diabetes, and even arthritis. Here are some specific health benefits.

Let's start with heart disease. Hulled and pearled barley both contain a water-soluble fiber known as beta-glucan. This substance is now believed to lower "bad" cholesterol (LDL), triglycerides, and overall cholesterol. Studies reveal that beta-glucan helps to reduce the amount of cholesterol absorbed by the intestinal tract.

Barley also contains a good amount of niacin. This important B vitamin is known to raise "good" cholesterol (HDL) and helps remove the unhealthy low-density lipoprotein (LDL). This is another way barley improves heart health.

The large amount of insoluble fiber found in barley also helps maintain a healthy colon. This fiber promotes regular bowel movements, which help remove toxins from the body more quickly. Also, the fiber found in barley serves as food for the healthy bacteria found in the large intestine. This enables beneficial bacteria to grow, which reduces disease-causing bacteria, promoting overall good health.

As a low-glycemic grain, barley is helpful to diabetics. Barley has the ability to slow starch digestion, which prevents blood sugar levels from rising too quickly.

A serving of barley is also rich in the trace mineral copper. This can help the flexibility of bones and joints, which may ease the symptoms of rheumatoid arthritis.

These are only a few samples of barley's health benefits. Now it's easy to see why those ancient Roman and Greek soldiers ate their barley!

In the Kitchen with Barley

Barley is a healthy substitute for rice and pasta, and it's easy to prepare. Here are three recipes you might like to try. I've included a basic barley recipe suitable as a side dish, a salad recipe, and a vegetable soup recipe. You can make larger amounts of the basic recipe, divide into one-cup portions, and freeze or refrigerate for one week. Then thaw and use as you wish in recipes. For these recipes, please use regular-cooking pearled barley, *not* quick-cooking barley, which I've found to be too mushy in consistency.

Basic Barley Recipe

2½ cups water or your favorite broth

1 teaspoon salt (optional)

1 cup pearled barley, rinsed

In a medium saucepan, bring water or broth and salt to a boil. Add barley, stir, and return to boil. Reduce heat to low, then cover and simmer for about 40 minutes or until barley is tender and most of the liquid is absorbed. Makes about 3 cups.

Mint and Dill Barley Salad

This is a nice salad for summer. It goes well with fish, chicken, or beef. I serve this salad chilled, but the dressing and barley should be tossed together while the barley is still warm to allow the barley to absorb the flavor.

Salad:

2 ½ cups water

1 teaspoon salt

1 teaspoon olive oil

1 cup pearled barley, rinsed

10–12 cherry tomatoes, sliced in half

⅓ cup pitted kalamata olives, rinsed

2 green onions, chopped, with white and green parts

Dressing:

⅓ cup red wine vinegar

3–4 tablespoons olive oil

1 tablespoon grated parmesan cheese

4–5 fresh mint leaves, chopped

1 teaspoon dried dill

Fresh ground black pepper to taste

In a medium saucepan, combine the water, salt, and olive oil, and bring to a boil. Add barley, and return to a boil. Stir, then cover and simmer for about 40 minutes or until the water is absorbed. While the barley cooks, prepare and measure your tomatoes, olives, and onions, and set aside. For the dressing, put all the ingredients into a small bowl, and whisk until the vinegar and olive oil look frothy, then set aside.

When the barley is cooked, transfer it to a large mixing bowl, toss gently with the dressing, and cool slightly. Next, add the rest of the salad ingredients, and gently mix with the barley/dressing mixture. I let the salad cool, then cover and refrigerate for at least 1 hour. This recipe makes 6–8 side-dish-size portions.

Hearty Barley Vegetable Soup

On a cold winter day, this is the perfect soup to have simmering on the stove. It's easy to prepare. Serve it with crusty bread or crackers and cheese.

2 tablespoons olive oil

1 large onion, chopped

1 garlic clove, minced

1 medium carrot, peeled and sliced

1 celery stalk, with leaves chopped

1 14.5-ounce can diced tomatoes with juice

1 bay leaf

1 teaspoon dried basil

½ cup pearled barley, rinsed

2 14-ounce cans vegetable broth

4 cups water

1 cup frozen mixed vegetables

Optional: 1 small potato, peeled and cubed; a small turnip, peeled and cubed; or a small zucchini, chopped

Heat oil in a large soup pot. Add the onion, garlic, carrot, and celery, and sauté in the oil until the onion is soft. Next, add the tomatoes with their juice, the bay leaf, and the basil. Stir in the barley. Pour in the vegetable broth and the water, and bring to a boil. Turn heat to low, cover, and simmer, stirring occasionally. After 45 minutes, stir in the mixed vegetables, and cover and simmer 15 minutes longer. If you use any of the optional ingredients, add them to the soup during the last 30 minutes of cooking. The soup should be ready in 1 hour. After sitting, the soup will thicken and will taste better the next day. Refrigerate leftovers. Makes 6–8 servings.

As you can see, barley isn't just for soup. It can also be used in stews, or—this is really good—used as a stuffing mixture for green peppers and tomatoes.

If you choose to purchase barley in bulk, be sure that the supplier keeps it in a covered container and that it's dry. At home, store barley tightly sealed. It will stay fresh six to nine months at room temperature. Uncooked barley can also be refrigerated for longer periods.

Barley in Magic and Folklore

Since barley is such an ancient crop and was so important to the survival of the human race, it became linked to magic, religion, and folklore.

In magic, barley is considered to be a feminine herb ruled by Venus. It's associated with love, fertility, and healing magic. Barley was so highly revered by the ancients that it soon became the focus of early religious cults. These early religions honored agriculture, but more specifically, grains—especially barley. The early goddesses of the Eastern Mediteranean and Mesopotamia weren't just grain goddesses, they were probably barley goddesses.

Centuries later, due to barley's importance as a food and as an ingredient in the making of alcoholic beverages, barley also became part of British folklore. The best example of this is "John Barleycorn," an old folk ballad of the British Isles. It was probably sung before the reign of Elizabeth I, and many versions exist.

In the ballad, barley takes on human characteristics as John Barleycorn, and the agricultural cycle of the year is told. The ground is plowed, seed is planted, and then, in his prime, John Barleycorn is cut down and, of course, harvested. He returns not only as a crop, but he is also transformed into beer and wine.

The tale has both Pagan and Christian connections. In it is the story of reincarnation as well as resurrection, and I'm sure John Barleycorn is related to nature spirits such as the Wicker Man and the Green Man.

We may never know all the messages hidden in "John Barleycorn," but the story still has a deep emotional impact on people even today.

Conclusion

There was a time when barley was so important that barley grains were laid end-to-end as a unit of measure for length. And there was a time when barley was used as an important trade item for other goods. Those days are gone forever, but barley is beginning to get the recognition it deserves. Barley is now becoming more important as a key ingredient to a healthier lifestyle. Scientific studies are beginning to approve claims that the soluble fiber found in barley, beta-glucan, does help to lower cholesterol and improve heart health.

Barley—it's healthy, low in fat, high in fiber, and inexpensive.

It's a super-herb.

For More Information

Visit barleyfoods.org for more information. This is a great website and is regularly updated.

James Kambos *writes from his home in southern Ohio. He's also an artist who paints in the American primitive style. He raises many herbs and wildflowers in his garden.*

Herbal Healing for the Land: Permaculture and the Herb Garden

⤞ By Clea Danaan ⤝

Herbs are plants that contain strong oils producing distinct smells and containing constituents that have certain properties used for healing. We usually think of using these properties in healing through teas, essential oils, and tinctures. Herbs can also be invited to contribute their healing properties as whole plants, not just to the gardener, but to the garden. Thinking of how plants contribute to the garden itself is a way to develop a conscious relationship with plants that benefits you while also offering a little healing energy to the land.

A school of design called *permaculture* can offer us tools for thinking about this conscious relationship with plants. Permaculture comes from the words permanent and agriculture. It is a farming, gardening, and architectural design discipline that draws on the laws of ecology to inform its choices. Permaculturists seek to design and execute living environments that interact in sustainable and complex ways that are larger than the sum of their parts. Permaculture goes beyond organic, for it is not just about inputs and outputs as a traditional garden or farm is, but is about dynamic relationships occurring across multiple planes of space and through time. The philosophy goes beyond growing plants and includes the animals, people, and activities that interact with a space as well.

A permaculture system includes plants that offer multiple uses, such as food and healing, or food and nutrient accumulation (more on this later). It also calls for plants to fit different niches in an ecosystem, growing at different heights, for instance, and in different capacities throughout the whole system. Herbs are one kind of plant that can, therefore, be used in many ways in a permaculture design, because they each have many uses and can be grown in different ways.

Multiple Purposes

In traditional gardening, farming, or landscaping we tend to grow a plant for a single use. We grow tomatoes, carrots, or peaches so we can eat them. We plant grass to walk on. We cultivate roses for their attractive smell and also for their beauty. Even when a plant is grown for two reasons, such as roses, usually they are grown as single specimens with little thought to other plants around them. Plants are grown, in other words, to please people. In permaculture, we consider that the garden is a community of plants, bacteria, animals, and more, including but not limited to people. For this reason we choose plants that have multiple purposes, which might include:

- Beauty
- Food for people
- Food for animals
- Flowers for bees
- Shade
- A wind break
- A nitrogen fixer
- A nutrient accumulator
- A ground cover that holds in moisture
- Medicine
- A barrier to deer

Every plant offers at least two purposes, and in permaculture we take advantage of as many uses as possible. For instance, you might grow comfrey (a big player in permaculture) for its medicinal properties, which include healing gastric ulcers, bronchitis, and external wounds, among other things; as a pretty purple flower that blooms for much of the summer, which bees like, at about two or three feet tall in the middle of a garden bed; and as a nutrient accumulator, which means that the deep roots pull up minerals and nutrients from the soil, depositing them on the surface of the soil as the leaves fall off or die back in winter.

Greater Than the Sum of These Parts

By designing the landscape with multiple uses in mind, we create an ecosystem that is greater than the sum of its parts.

Nutrient accumulators, like comfrey, help rebuild soil after it is depleted by other plants. By planting it near heavy feeders, like tomatoes, for instance, we create a relationship among plants that aren't just plants growing on their own for a single purpose. By planting relationships instead of single plants, we create a garden, its parts, and what might be thought of as the harmonics of those parts. In music, a harmonic is an overtone or section of a musical wave that fits within the base tone. When you hit a guitar string, for instance, you can hear the base tone, and often you can also hear a higher frequency tone that is the harmonic of that base tone. In a garden, when you create harmonics by resonating different plants purposes, you get the results (food, beauty, nutrients) and the harmonic of those results. You get complex relationships that are more than just the two energies you put into the system. You get that "hum" that you hear over the tones of a guitar. In a garden you can't always name this harmonic, but you can see it in the results. The synergy among plants grown for multiple purposes creates further new relationships.

Herbs in the Permaculture Garden

Herbs are big players in the permaculture garden because they intrinsically offer so many uses: beauty, medicine, bug repellent, nutrient accumulators, etc. Therefore, by using herbs throughout the garden you invite dynamic relationships to occur. Before planting them randomly, however, consider their gifts and properties. To determine where in the garden to plant a certain herb, consider first what its growing needs are. Full sun? Dappled shade? Light fluffy soil? A little bit of alkalinity? You can figure this out by reading seed packs or plant tags, or by looking them up online or in a plant book. Many herbs grown for culinary purposes prefer full sun, slight acidity, and a loose soil. This can be obtained by mixing gravel, crushed granite, or even a little sand into your soil and adding compost. Then you need a sunny spot—at the front of a hedge, on a southern facing hill, or along the side of the house where heat accumulates.

Other herbs can handle a little shade. These include chamomile, arugula, basil, chives, mint, and parsley, to name a few. These can be nestled in your dynamic garden of relationship under other plants. In permaculture we talk about a *plant guild*, or planting of different species that interrelate and benefit each other. If your guild is built around a taller food producing tree, like an apple or nut tree, this is a place to utilize the herbs that can handle shade. They will, in turn, repel insects (garlic and chives are good examples) and deter grass, which steals water and nutrients from the tree.

Seamlessly we move from how the plant prefers to be grown to what it can offer. This is the beauty of permaculture: that by listening to the needs and wisdom of the plant we create dynamic harmonies in the garden.

Structural Ideas

Someone who really likes herbs can draw on two interesting permaculture design ideas in addition to the plant guild. The first is the herb spiral, and the second is the keyhole bed.

Herb spirals utilize not only horizontal planting space, but also vertical. The spiral is planted with the center at the highest point, then spiraling downward toward the ground. The spiral is maintained by creating solid walls out of bricks, stones, or wood. It is a simple spiral with only one lower level so that you can still reach the top of the spiral to harvest herbs easily. This design creates multiple niches in a small space. The top of the spiral is dryer and the bottom more wet. The southern exposure is hotter, and on the north side you get some shade (in the Northern Hemisphere). Near the top of your spiral, plant sun-loving plants like lavender, thyme, and rosemary (a creeping rosemary can also drape nicely over the edge). Sage, basil, and cilantro go in the middle, for they prefer more moisture. Mints and parsley, thirsty herbs that can handle a little shade, go near the bottom. On the shady side you might nestle in some moss or shady flowers, or plant cool-season vegetables like lettuces.

Keyhole beds are a raised, round garden plot with a hole in the middle and a little path leading to the hole. In other words, you have a way to enter the round bed along the path and stand in the "hole" part of the keyhole to harvest veggies and herbs. In this way you not only create beds with pleasant, curved lines, but you increase the surface area you can grow in while still being able to reach the plants from all sides. Usually this bed is used to grow food, but as we discussed earlier, in the permaculture garden we seek dynamic relationships. In the veggie bed we include herbs. Many herbs repel insects while providing beauty, food, and medicine. They benefit the dynamic vegetable garden.

When you delve into the dynamic relationships to be cultivated in a permaculture garden you learn even more what many plant enthusiasts already know: that plants are powerful beings with many gifts to offer. By listening to these gifts and planting a garden of relationships, we cultivate an even more powerful purpose; what might be considered the highest harmonic of the garden. We contribute to the healing of the land itself by inviting the powerful exchanges among complex relationships. The garden serves us. It serves the plants, animals, bacteria, and fungi that grow there. And finally it serves the earth, a vast permaculture garden itself that thrives on complex dynamics of interrelated exchange. Gardening becomes more than a hobby or a way to grow food. It becomes a powerful act of healing for the earth itself.

Clea Danaan *writes and gardens from eastern Colorado where she grows plants, chickens, and a couple of homeschooled children. She has a background in outdoor education, energy healing, and massage. She is the author of* Sacred Land: Intuitive Gardening for Personal, Political, & Environmental Change *(Llewellyn, 2007),* Voices of the Earth: The Path of Green Spirituality *(Llewellyn, 2009),* The Way of the Hen: Zen and the Art of Raising Chickens *(Lyons, 2011), and* Living Earth Devotional: 365 Green Practices for Sacred Connection *(Llewellyn, 2013). Visit her at CleaDanaan.com.*

Fenugreek

⪻ By Estha McNevin ⪼

A ll plants use biochemistry to communicate, but some, like our delicious kitchen herbs, use aromatic lactones to entice noninvasive and beneficial pollinators as their roots explore for nutrients beneath the surface of the soil. The consequent fragrance of a few choice herbs is alluring to bees and butterflies, while also scenting the air and soil with antimicrobial chemical compounds. Aromatic herbs produce neyrl acetate, camphor, and geranial citrate among others, thus making them a repugnant deterrent to blight, mold, and parasitic insects. This olfactory feature yields high acidity essential oils, which are bacteria resistant and often pleasant-smelling, branding herb companions

an especially satisfying advantage over pests. For this reason they are strategically planted in the garden.

Manifest Sweet Success

Take for example, the unassuming seed of fenugreek (*Trigonella foenum-graecum*). South Asian gardeners call it *methi* in Hindi, meaning "sweet leaf." This is because it smells saccharine, and helps its neighbors in the garden by supporting other healthful microbiotic life forms and improving soil condition. While the antimicrobial compounds and vigorous pollen cycles of this plant deter wasps, moths, ants, and beetles from its more succulent neighbors, fenugreek's biochemistry also passes rich nutrients like potassium, calcium, and phosphorous into the soil, along with fixed nitrogen. These nutrients are released slowly while the legume is living and are permeated out into the soil in a flourish of rebirth once the plants are harvested. When grown with other vegetables methi improves flavor, helps sugars to mature, and increases the yield of berries, gourds, melons, and potatoes.

Cultivated, especially alongside ground crawling crops, this common kitchen herb will heal and stabilize soil pH by neutralizing acidity on the microbial level and loosening and conditioning the soil. Planting this workhorse as part of a routine crop rotation model can help to establish a more hospitable environment for next season's rambling zucchini, cucumbers, or winter waxgourd.

Fenugreek, when left to seed, will even self-sow remarkably well if it is grouped with beneficial and thirsty companions who are more prone to absorb sweetness from the methi. This herb also helps fruit-producing nitrogen aficionados by holding nutrient rich moisture in the soil for longer periods of time. This improves the texture and water content of potatoes, corn, strawberries, summer savory, bush beans, chowder peas, and buckwheat.

Fenugreek is a crop that repairs the nutrient depletion that occurs after growing large fruiting vegetables. By using nitrogen-fixing bacteria, legumes have evolved to attract the fungi and micronutrients that they rely on. Rhizobium is a soil bacterium that is closely linked with the germination and life cycle of all legumes. This type of bacteria grows with all beans and peas, forming a symbiosis allowing the pair to fix nitrogen in the soil and to store excess nutrients in the tender mithril root networks of the rhizobium for use later.

Once the host Fabaceae is harvested, the stored nitrogen is released back into the soil through the decomposition process. The rhizobium's root nodules enrich any plants left growing around it with a fertile boost of fresh nutrients. They also can ready a garden bed for the next growing season when covered in mulch and simply left to slumber over the winter. This essential bacterium loves compost tea and the rich juices of decomposing leaves, fruits, fish emulsion, and succulent vegetables.

Description and Classification

Fenugreek is an annual seed spice, leafy herb, and edible vegetable related to the pea and bean family, Fabaceae or Leguminosae. Cultivated especially for its sweet and bitter sprouts, fenugreek greens are harvested early and are dried or used fresh. Plants grow to a mature size of four to five feet and give off a mouth-watering maple scent on warm days.

The flowers of fenugreek are small, a half-inch in length, and are pearl white with a soft, hairy calyx evocative of the sweet pea. The rosid flowers appear at the leaf axils in pairs.

Like many other eudicots, they give way to a pair of seedpods conjoined in a pran mudra manner. These hairy seedpods grow up to three inches and contain anywhere from ten to twenty smooth seeds. They are dried or cured to achieve a color relative to flavor, intended use, and region.

Cultivation

Fenugreek prefers rich, well-drained soil and is hardy to zone 6 as long as it gets full sun or partial afternoon shade. It will not tolerate extreme heat without frequent watering, nor will it survive frost or night temperatures below 50°F, even if insulated. This determined warm climate sprouter will, however, cultivate very well indoors and will take off when properly pampered with fish emulsion fertilizer.

Like many other spices, fenugreek thrives in warm window terrariums, or under T5 lights set to a 4-week, 12/12 grow cycle of equal light and dark. The tender greens can become susceptible to root rot if overwatered or grown in compacted soil. For this reason, a rich (yet light) combination of locally sourced sand and organic compost mulch are often favored, along with organic potting soil. Growing fenugreek in a seed flat or long herb box makes harvesting microgreens more efficient, providing that any containers used are well fitted with drainage holes and formfitting drip trays to safeguard success.

It is easy to sow the seeds in any prepared soil. Sprinkle an even layer of seeds, then cover them with a light dusting of sand. Water and allow three to five days for germination. Transplant fenugreek greens after four weeks by gently pulling them apart in clumps and relocating them into prepared containers or garden herb beds.

When left to the rhythm of the seasons, this spice can be

sprouted in any healthy soil as a wholesome green crop. Sweet green leaves are cultivated in resowing rounds every three to four weeks from April until July. Fenugreek can be easily harvested, and new seeds planted along with other fast maturing tabletop greens like radishes, watercress, lettuce, and spinach. At the season's crucial point a final round is planted or is left in pots to flower abundantly in midsummer temperatures. Any full rows are thinned to a distance of two feet on all sides. Each plant is then mounded with fresh soil before being given mulch and compost tea.

When left outside in the arid heat, the seedpods will begin to dry on the stalk, sweetening them for a late harvest from the last of the "dog days" of summer until mid-autumn. Fenugreek is always carefully gathered just before the fattened pods burst, volunteering themselves for another season. This promotes higher levels of mucosal antibodies and sotolon flavor compounds, and will impart a sweeter, smoky flavor profile in the seeds when they are used as a spice.

Harvesting, Storage, and Uses

Sprouts can be harvested every five to ten days. They have a crisp, bitter flavor that leaves a sweet aftertaste and are ideal in mixed salads, leavened breads, and stir-fry. Such micronutrient rich sprouts contain large amounts of protein, minerals, calcium, phosphorus, amino acids, and iron. This makes fenugreek a favorite crisp garnish for garden salads and elaborately roasted meat dishes. It is also ideal for proteinaceous juice blends and fresh curries, considered by many to be an essential daily curative and anticarcinogenic food.

The leaves are best when pulled on warm days, anywhere between four to eight weeks, when they still have a slightly astringent and sweet maple flavor profile. This wonderful aroma is due to the lactone flavor compound sotolon, which is also found in maple syrup. Mature leaves at this stage are especially fragrant and are used in a wide range of household foods as a flavoring agent common in table syrups, flavored teas, and soda pop.

The stalks and roots of fenugreek taste similar to sweet celery and improve the flavor of slow-cooked foods, but they must be used while fresh. The stalks have a texture similar to rhubarb shoots and are especially maple-sweet when caramelized at low temperatures with butter, wilted greens, and fresh beans. The leaves, while also dried for tea, are more commonly used as a flavor enhancer in soups, poultry stocks, and stews where bitter flavors break down gradually and lend a sweet, curative flavor, evocative of so many of our homemade foods. Fresh and dried leaves temper milk-based dishes the world over—cream of leek soup most famously.

The bitter and savory roots of fenugreek have a strong, sour complexity that matures into a sweet caramel or maple aftertaste. They are used to accent rich fruits or complex cheese flavors in mixed salads and, when ground to a paste, fenugreek roots are used in spiced relish, pickles, and chutneys to accent the profile of other spices, namely anise, clove, cardamom, cumin, and fennel.

Garden Gastronomy

The flowers are fragrant and reminiscent of caramel when harvested one or two days after they blossom, 110 to 120 days after planting. Waiting until the flowers fully open will ensure pollination and the development of essential oils in the flower base. Careful plucking makes them ideal for flavoring aged oils, yogurt, cheeses, and delicate teas where they add a subtle sweet and nutty complexity.

Fenugreek seeds take a full 150 to 160 days to mature and are harvested when the pods begin to dry and cleave. Seeds must be dried thoroughly before being packaged or processed. The seeds are pan-roasted or slow cooked vigilantly in a wide range of low-temperature lentil soups and clay-pot stews. This is because, interestingly enough, the same lactone that acts as a digestive aid in some dishes will become a bitter purgative acid when it is overcooked or undercooked; thus, all dishes that contain this spice are made with great precision and care.

Seeds taste best when they are harvested a day or two before the pods become brittle and are dried in the sun for six to eight hours or in a drying room for one to three weeks until all signs of moisture are gone. One way to check if your seeds are dry enough is to collect a few from your warm drying tray and place them in a cold plastic bag. If any signs of vapor or condensation appear inside the bag by the next morning, then the seeds are not dry enough for long-term storage.

Stranger Danger

Like all legumes, fenugreek is prone to waterborne bacteria in seed form, and can carry deadly *E. coli* and other hazards whenever they are improperly processed or stored. Hygienic drying practices are essential to our health and success when growing herbs in the garden for reseeding or kitchen use. Place a small muslin bag filled with large grain rock salt in the bottom of a dry storage container and fill with recently dried seeds. This salt bag will help eliminate environmental moisture from your carefully cultivated crop. If seeds are stored well, after a few seasons the full benefit of growing fenugreek will fill both the home and garden with a renewed sense of health and vigor. Enjoy!

For More Information

For more information, visit the Biodynamic Association at www.biodynamics.com or the Permaculture Institute at www.permaculture.org.

Resources

"Fenugreek." Wikipedia. Wikimedia Foundation, October, 2014.

Kowalchik, Claire, William H. Hylton, and Anna Carr. *Rodale's Illustrated Encyclopedia of Herbs*. Emmaus, PA: Rodale, 1987.

Montagné, Prosper, and Joël Robuchon. *Larousse Gastronomique*. France: Larousse, 1996.

Seymour, John. *The New Self-sufficient Gardener*. New York: DK Pub., 2008.

Estha McNevin (*Missoula, MT*) *is the cofounding Priestess and ceremonial oracle of the non-profit Pagan Temple Haus, Opus Aima Obscuræ. She has served the pagan community for fourteen years as an Eastern Hellenistic Priestess, freelance lecturer, author, artist, and poet. Estha studies and teaches courses on ancient and modern pagan history, multi-cultural metaphysical theory, ritual technique, international cuisine, organic gardening, herbal craft, alchemy, and occult symbolism. In addition to hosting public rituals for the Sabbats, Estha organizes annual philanthropic fundraisers, Full Moon spell crafting ceremonies, and women's divination rituals for each Dark Moon. To learn more, please explore: www.facebook.com/opusaimaobscurae*

Misunderstood Mint

≈ By Charlie Rainbow Wolf ≈

Mention growing mint in the garden and many gardeners will recoil in horror. Mint has long been feared as a problematic and invasive plant that is best just avoided. I've had years of experience with mint—some of those experiences more positive than others—and I firmly believe that with just a bit of care and understanding, mint can be a very valuable asset to the garden.

For a start, there are now dozens of different types of mint, each with their own subtle nuance. Of course, the most commonly known mints are probably spearmint (*Mentha spicata*) and peppermint (*M. balsamea willd*), which is a cross between spearmint and *Mentha aquatica*, or water mint).

mint

Mints are herbaceous and perennial, growing from rhizomes that are fleshy and spreading. It is the growth habit of the rhizomes that make gardeners quake when asked about planting mint.

Those rhizomes do have their uses, though. We live in an area that is heavily infested with deer who like to snack on the young shoots and the mature fruits in our orchard. I threw mint out there. It was actually quite by accident. I put some spearmint next to the wild raspberries to try to keep the deer away from them, and it spread. At first, we felt rather overwhelmed at the prospect of the mint taking over the area between the trees. However, the next year we noticed that the deer were forsaking that area of the orchard for other areas. Now I purposefully plant all kinds of interesting mints out there and just let it rip. We take the mint down with the lawnmower or the weed-eater every now and then, and that just makes it come back thicker and quicker. We don't have as bad of a deer issue, and the orchard smells wonderful when walking through it.

Mint is also useful for large areas where ground cover is desired. When we first moved to our property some nine years ago, there was crown vetch trying to grow on the banks that sloped down to the road, but the weeds were overtaking it. I put some spearmint out there to see what would happen, and over time the mint is crowding out both the crown vetch and the weeds. I have to admit, it is absolutely delightful to go out there when the dew is still on the leaves and bring in sprigs of mint for my morning tea.

Of course, there are those who don't want to encourage the spreading habit of mint. This can be easily controlled by planting it in container gardens. For adding mint to an herb garden, plant it in a large pot first—I have friends who are very fond of the five-gallon plastic laundry tubs that are available from most superstores or farm shops—then sink the pot into the ground. Remember to keep the lip of the pot about an inch above the soil level. This seems to contain the rhizomes from creeping so that the mints can be enjoyed where the other herbs are growing.

What Mint Is Best?

Determining where you want to grow your mint is just part of the story. Next comes the fun in choosing what kind of mint you want to grow. Here at "the old homestead" we have many different mints growing in a variety of places: orange mint is with the jostaberries, apple mint with the gooseberries, chocolate mint with the quince, lime mint with the currants, catmint by the crabapple trees, banana mint by the nectarines, and lemon balm (balm mint) near the strawberries. I lost my anise mint and ginger mint in a recent harsh winter, but they are being replaced. We have the mint in the main garden bordered in four-foot beds, and anything that grows outside of the bed is dealt with by the lawnmower.

I think that there is an advantage for experimenting with the different types of mint. For example, the chocolate mint that I have is particularly cocoa tasting, and it is awesome added to fresh raspberry sorbet. My friend raids my lime mint for her mojitos. I add lemon balm to freshly made lemonade on hot summer evenings, and catmint to my evening tea at the end of busy autumn days. The different varieties of mint are now gaining in popularity, and it's getting easier to find different starts at farm shops and garden centers in the spring. My favorites are mentioned above, but of course, the list is far from complete.

Mints and How to Use Them

When incorporating mints into herbal preparations, teas, potpourris, or other creations, it is the leaves that are used. Pick them when they are young and tender, before the parent plant has started to flower. The best time of day is in the early- to mid-morning. The dew needs to be off the leaves—unless they are going to be used immediately in a tea, infusion, or decoction—but you don't want the heat of the sun on them as this can weaken the scent and flavor.

Anise mint (*Agastache foeniculum*—sometimes called licorice mint or anise hyssop) is one of my all-time favorites. It is in the same family as mint (Lamiaceae), but they're not intimately related. Anise mint is native to the American Great Plains and is drought and deer resistant—the latter being why I plant it! It can grow up to four feet in height and a foot wide, and has dainty purple blooms when mature. In the kitchen I like it as a hot tea, or an addition to iced tea, as well as using it as an edible garnish for main courses or desserts.

Apple mint (*Mentha suaveolens*) has a fuzzy leaf and is a particularly vigorous grower, spreading easily, and reaching over two feet tall when mature. Planting it next to broccoli, cabbage, peas, and tomatoes is said to improve their flavor. In the kitchen it can be used as a tea, incorporated into desserts, or added to salad dressings and garnishes.

Banana mint (*Mentha arvensis* "Banana") is a hybrid mint that has glossy leaves, a low-growing habit, and smells wonderfully like the banana candies of my childhood. Although classed as a hardy perennial zones 5 to 11, this is another one that I have lost previously in a harsh winter. It needs mulching at the end of autumn, but it's worth the extra bit of care for that wonderfully pungent banana scent and flavor. In the kitchen it can be added to banana splits, banana breads and puddings, or for interesting herbal teas.

Catmint *(Nepeta)* is also a favorite one that I will always grow. Here in the Midwest it is a herbaceous perennial. It grows quite tall and woody, and the flowers are tubes of lilac and mauve. It's fairly drought-tolerant and the deer don't seem to like it. In the kitchen it makes a calming tea. I've also known people to add it to herbal smoking mixtures. Catmint can also be used in a decoction as an insect repellent.

Chocolate mint (*Mentha x piperita* "Chocolate") is another hybrid that I will always have in the garden. Be fussy when choosing this, though, and if you can, get a start from someone who has a mint with the flavor you like. Some are more minty than chocolatey, and some are the other way around. The leaves are dark and leathery, and the plant is fairly compact. It has the rhizome spreading habit of most mints. This strain is hardy if you care for it, but it does need regular watering and the occasional feeding to stay healthy and strong. I cut mine back in the autumn, and let it be its own mulch over the winter. In the kitchen it is a wonderful addition to sorbets, sweets, and even my husband's home-brewed ale.

Lavender mint (*Mentha piperita* "Lavandula") is on my list for next year. This mint is hardy in zones 3 to 7, and has a scent that is a divine blend of both mint and lavender. It doesn't need much care: full sun to partial shade, and don't let the soil dry out. This mint is a popular addition to dried herbal sachets and potpourris, and can be added to homemade cosmetics. In the kitchen it makes quite a distinguished tea, a garnish for lemonade or juleps, and a curious addition to strawberry desserts.

Lemon balm (*Melissa officinalis*) is also a member of the mint family and a perennial herb. The leaves have a soothing citrus smell, and mature plants bear small white flowers. Lemon balm, like other mints, can be invasive, but in this instance it is the seeds, not the creeping rhizome, that are the culprit. To prevent it from spreading, simply pinch off the flower heads. The sweet and calming aroma makes it a popular ingredient in potpourris and dream pillows. In the kitchen this is a soothing tea, and it can also be used in a decoction as an insect repellent.

Hopefully this has piqued your curiosity to try something different in the herb garden. Mints are not hard to grow, and once they are understood, they are not hard to manage, either. As you get more familiar with your mints, you'll find a multitude of ways that they can be used: in the garden, in the kitchen, in household items, and more. Explore, experiment, but most of all, enjoy!

Charlie Rainbow Wolf *is happiest when she's creating something, especially if it can be made from items that others have cast aside. She is passionate about writing and deeply intrigued by astrology, tarot, runes, and other divination oracles. Knitting and pottery are her favorite hobbies, although she happily confesses that she's easily distracted by all the wonderful things that life has to offer. Charlie is an advocate of organic gardening and cooking, and lives in the Midwest with her husband and her special needs Great Danes. www.charlierainbow.com*

Wildcrafting "Weeds"

❧ By Dallas Jennifer Cobb ❧

Weeds grow everywhere, not just in rural forests and fields, but in overcrowded urban areas, pushing through sidewalk cracks, taking over lawns, even thriving in the dirty ditches lining highways.

Many plants commonly called weeds are herbs in disguise. Unknown, disregarded, and often disrespected, they face many challenges. In urban areas herbs battle air pollution, litter, a lack of water, and the application of herbicides by landowners and highway maintenance crews. Even in rural areas many valuable herbs face extinction due to overharvesting.

While some people try to get rid of these "pesky weeds," and others drive them into extinction because

of greed and unsustainable harvesting practices, wild herbs (weeds) have powerful cosmetic, culinary, and medicinal uses. Imagine having access to these versatile, powerful healing allies for free.

By learning how to wildcraft or "urban harvest," these weeds, you can tap into extensive, affordable resources. By practicing ethical and sustainable wildcrafting, you can ensure they continue to thrive and produce for years to come. I grew up eating wildcrafted greens like sorrel, young dandelion leaves, cress, lambs quarters, and wild leeks. The care and tending of the beds were always part of the trips to harvest from them.

Commonly Found "Weeds"

Bear in mind I live in Canada, but many of the "weeds" found here are widely available throughout the northern United States and Western Europe. Thankfully, our ancestors took seeds of helpful herbs with them when they ventured out into the world.

While there are literally hundreds of wild herbs that warrant wildcrafting, for the sake of brevity I'll focus on a few highly versatile ones. Start with the proper identification of them, learn when to harvest them, and how to prepare them for use and you'll have a couple of staples in your medicine chest. Then, over time, you can add to your knowledge and build your wildcrafting practice.

Common "weeds" that grow wild include catnip (*Nepeta cataria*), raspberry leaf (*Rubus idaeus*), red clover (*Trifolium pratense*), and St. John's wort (*Hypericum perforatum*). In addition to these "common weeds," many very pricey herbs like goldenseal (*Hydrastis canadensis*), echinacea (*Echinacea purpura*), and bloodroot (*Sanguinaria canadensis*) can also be found growing wild.

Note: Wild American ginseng *(Panax quinquefolius)* used to be a favorite of wildcrafters, but the harvesting and exporting of it is now illegal in many states and provinces. Check your local legislation before even thinking about harvesting wild ginseng.

Aboveground Wildcrafting

It is easy to identify common herbs with a good guide. Get one and use it. Never overharvest, trim only what you will use, and make sure not to overwhelm the plant you are trimming from.

Flowers, leaves, and stems need good air circulation and fast drying in order to maintain herb quality and potency, so either hang them or place them on a screen in a shady spot. Slow drying and sun adversely affect herbs, turning them black. Dried herbs can be stored in glass jars and should be used within a year.

St. John's wort is highly versatile and is widely used to remedy muscle spasms; feminine reproductive system complaints such as premenstrual syndrome symptoms and menopausal disturbances; central nervous system complaints such as shingles and sciatica; the symptoms of most common viruses; mental health symptoms like stress, anxiety, insomnia, and mild to moderate depression; and is even used externally in the treatment of abrasions, scrapes, bruises, and burns. This herb is throughout North America along roadsides and in fields. While some herbalists only use the flowers, Susun Weed suggests using the whole upper flowering section of the plant, including stalks, leaves, flower buds, flowers, and seed pods. Remember sustainability—if you cut the top of a plant, be sure to leave some seeds for sustainable reproduction. Chop and soak plant tops in 100 percent vodka, the green and yellow leaves and flowers produce a red tincture.

Red clover is versatile and readily available to urban and rural wildcrafters. It's rich in isoflavones and the nutrients calcium, chromium, magnesium, niacin, phosphorus, potassium, thiamine, and Vitamin C. Isoflavones help increase "good" cholesterol (HDL), and reduce the risk of blood clots because of its blood thinning properties. It is reputed to reduce hot flashes, night sweats, osteopenia, and osteoporosis in perimenopaus and menopausal women because of its estrogen mimicking properties. Isoflavones also suppress and kill off cancer cell growth, and red clover is especially effective for hormone-sensitive cancers. Make an immune system boosting infusion by putting one ounce of dried red clover blossoms in a quart jar, cover with boiling water, and allow to infuse for four hours. Not just for cancer treatment, take this for prevention too.

Catnip is found in urban and rural locales. It eases stomach upset, nausea, digestive disorders, reduces fevers, promotes sweating, releases toxins, calms nerves, soothes colic in babies, eases nervous complaints, and helps treat diarrhea. An extract called nepetalactone is a common ingredient in herbicides and insect repellents—fleas hate it. The blossoms and leaves are best harvested when the plant is full grown, vibrant, and lush. In my area that's in mid-July. Make a tincture from catnip to use as needed.

Raspberry leaves are a common uterine tonic widely used throughout pregnancy to treat morning sickness, leg cramps, and to tone uterine walls. It's also used during labor to shorten the second stage, and after birth to promote placenta expulsion and the flow of breast milk. Gather and dry the leaves to use as tea.

Belowground Wildcrafting

Look for roots in your daily journey. Make note of the location and return later to harvest mature roots. Please don't overharvest anything. Herbs are renewable resources that will be available year after year when afforded the proper respect and care.

Belowground portions of annuals should be harvested just before the plant flowers. For biennial and perennials, the roots are best harvested in the late fall or early spring. The autumn, before really severe and regular frost sets in, is the ideal time.

Goldenseal and bloodroot roots lay an inch or two below the surface. Carefully insert your digging tool next to the root, prying it to bring the whole plant up unscathed. Brush away dirt and carefully examine the plant. Confirm its identity, maturity, and suitability for harvest. If not, replant it and remember the location.

Wash gathered roots in running water to remove all soil, but don't scrub. Most roots can be split into smaller pieces, and laid outdoors on a screen with good air circulation and indirect sunlight. If you're drying indoors, the screen can be near a heat source, but nothing ferocious, just mild heat and good air circulation. Roots take time to dry and should feel dry to the touch.

Goldenseal is a widely used medicinal herb. It is nicknamed "yellow root" because of the vibrant root color. It commonly grows in large patches, or mats, in a maple leaf style, atop a stem of about eight to ten inches. Locate a goldenseal patch and monitor. Harvest only mature roots four to six years in age. Cultivate a sustainable source of this helpful herb. Dig the roots up, separate nodules off of them, and re-plant the nodules to form another plant. This will ensure you have a sustainable patch for many years. While the roots are the most potent and widely used part of the plant, goldenseal leaves and stems are also used.

Bloodroot is easy to identify and find. Its deeply scalloped leaf is shaped like a walnut-half, about four inches in size, and also resembles elephant ears. It has a single white flower that grows out of the leaf mass. Like goldenseal, the most desirable part of bloodroot is the root. It grows in well-drained soil at the edge of roads, along paths, and in clearings. It can be propagated by splitting root nodules and replanting. The roots are distinct in color, and when they're broken, bleed a bright red "blood." When dried, the root takes on a deep yellow color.

Echinacea promotes white blood cell creation aiding the body in fighting bacteria and infection. It is especially useful against vaginal infections, like yeast. A common garden flower, echinacea is also a native species known as "cone flower." It produces gorgeous, big, daisylike flowers that grace many gardens. Harvested primarily for the root, make sure you harvest it responsibly.

Wildcrafting

Be sure to fully identify all herbs before using them for anything. Seek out the wisdom of a chartered herbalist, and consult reputable herbal guides for accurate identification and use information. Learn what herbs masquerade as commonly found weeds, understand their therapeutic value, know how to properly identify them, and then get to work wildcrafting weeds.

While this is just a starter article, read more and check out the amazing information available on YouTube where knowledgeable herbalists have posted thousands of useful videos on identifying, collecting, processing, and using wildcrafted herbs.

Dallas Jennifer Cobb *practices gratitude magic, giving thanks for personal happiness, health, and prosperity; meaningful, rewarding, and flexible work; and a deliciously joyful life. She is accomplishing her deepest desires. She lives in paradise with her daughter in a waterfront village in rural Ontario, where she regularly swims and runs, chanting: "Thank you, thank you, thank you." Contact her at jennifer.cobb@live.com.*

The World Beneath Our Feet: Microorganisms in the Garden

⤜ By JD Hortwort ⤛

The other day while raking at the edge of the yard, I experienced the soft, sweet smell of decaying leaves and wood wafting into the air. The aroma brought back a memory of long ago.

"You young'uns get the bucket out of the well house and go get me some wood dirt."

The voice of my grandma wafted through the decades like the smell of the composting vegetative material rising up from the ground. She used wood dirt to reinvigorate her flower beds and potted plants.

Wood dirt. It's one of those colloquialisms, I suppose. Wood dirt has very little to do with dirt at all. When Grandma asked for wood dirt, she was really asking us to rake and shovel up the crumbling debris from under the trees in the surrounding woods. And woe be to us if we came back with only a bucket of undecayed leaves!

You might think Grandma's intent was to amend the soil with a compost material, and you would be right, in part. I don't think I ever heard Grandma say the word compost in her life. But she was an experienced enough gardener to know that adding decayed material to a planting site—whether aged manure, old sawdust, or wood dirt—improved the health of the plants there.

What Grandma didn't know was that she was also supplementing the ground with a myriad of tiny critters, both micro- and macroorganisms. These organisms, like good compost, do a lot to improve the tilth and texture of a plant bed.

This is especially important when it comes to growing herbs. Most herbs have very specific requirements. Specifically, they don't want to be overfed in humus-y soils with poor drainage.

New gardeners are frequently reminded that, in order to successfully grow culinary or medicinal herbs full of strong essential oils, they need a lean soil. They mistakenly think that means a barren soil.

Herbs don't need a lot of fertilizer or organic material; they do need to access necessary nutrients and minerals to develop properly. Even in the leanest soil, tiny organisms can help them do that.

What are we talking about when we say soil organisms? Some are obvious.

The Critters We See

Most of us have seen earthworms; wriggly little invertebrates that aerate the soil with their burrowing. Thousands of earthworms exist in the world, but they break down into three categories: epigeic, those that live above ground; endogeic, those that live in the first couple inches of the ground layer; and anecic, those that make deep, vertical tunnels.

At different depths of the soil, worms break down organic material. They mix soil layers, taking organic material deep into the ground where plant roots can get to it. Their tunnels move air and water below the earth's surface.

Then there are insects like pill bugs and millipedes. These are the arthropods. They include spiders, beetles, ants, and centipedes. Like earthworms, these critters burrow. Those burrowing trails become space for roots to grow. It may sound a bit disgusting, but insects defecate in their burrows. In the house this is a bad thing, but in the garden or landscape, it's more nutrients for the plant. Some arthropods eat organisms that could cause disease; others munch on organic material, further breaking it down; and still others are predators.

As I pick through my garden, disturbing the protective mulch, I frequently send little spiders scurrying in all directions. Frankly, spiders creep me out. But I swallow my irrational disdain because I know that every one of those little eight-legged creepy-crawlers is eating his or her weight in bugs that might otherwise eat my veggies. That makes them worth their weight in gold.

And the Critters We Don't

Next, we have to get down on the microscopic level to look at bacteria, fungi, and nematodes.

Bacteria

You might recoil at the thought of having bacteria in the soil with your lavender or basil. We don't really know how many bacteria there are in the world. One source estimates the population at approximately 5×10^{30}. Only a fraction of them are truly bad for humans.

Others, like rhizobia, help us by helping plants. Rhizobia attach to the roots of certain plants and can be pretty particular about which ones they develop relationships with. Those plants they do attach to benefit by the bacteria's ability to provide the plant with nitrogen.

As a rule, bacteria helps to break down nutrients to make them available to plants, improve the condition of the soil, and aid in the plant's defense mechanisms when attacked by disease or when the plant is under stress from adverse growing conditions.

Fungi

Here's another category of organisms that have gotten a bad rap, but don't think of nail fungus or the type of fungus that caused the potato famine in Ireland. Think of mushrooms, lichens, and beneficial molds. These work by breaking down organic materials and loosening up the ground so that plant roots can go farther, easier.

Nematodes

It's possible that today's gardeners aren't well aware of nematodes, which are microscopic round worms. However, Grandma's generation was very aware of them. Root-knot nematodes were not a fun topic. Back in the day, tomato growers especially fought a battle to keep these nematodes out of the garden. If you've ever seen a plant tag that read "VFN resistant" you were seeing an advertisement that the plant would not succumb to a known virus, fungus, or nematode.

Nematodes also attacked fruit trees, other veggies in the garden, and even some ornamental plants. Over time growers developed a lot of tomatoes and other plants that were nematode resistant. The fear of nematodes seems to have fallen from general awareness today.

However, nematodes, like bacteria, aren't all bad. The ones that feed on bacteria and fungus help to move those organisms through the soil. Some nematodes are actually predators that devour their root-eating brethren.

Caring for Your Soil

Regardless of their size, the world of organisms below our feet is expansive and valuable. You need these critters in your soil. Gardeners have many ways to increase their beneficial populations.

First, at every opportunity work compost or humus into the soil. This is breakfast, lunch, and dinner for micro-organisms. If you're wondering about the difference, compost is organic material that has entered the first phase of decomposition. Humus is the end result, a long-lasting end product of the decomposition process. Technically, you would want to use humus for all of your soil amendment chores, but compost will get you there eventually. Plus, since the bits and pieces of compost are larger than those in humus, you get the added benefit of loosening up a compacted soil.

Once you have composted, mulch with an organic material. Decorative stones or gravel are lovely, but they don't add anything to the soil. And forget the plastic layer under your mulch. While a plastic barrier will keep weeds at bay, the barrier will also rob the soil underneath of water and air. Without these, microorganisms can't survive.

These first two steps will help with the next step. Keep the soil pH around 6 to 8, in the neutral to sweet range. Gardeners use the term "sweet" to describe an alkaline soil. The pH scale runs from 1 to 14. The range from 1 to 6 is acidity and from 8 to 14 is alkaline. For example, peat bogs have an acidity of 3 to 4. Areas with a lot of limestone tend toward a pH of 8 or higher.

In between is neutral. Most of your plants will be happier in this range. Your herbs will definitely be happier in this range. Only your azaleas, rhododendrons, and a few other acid-loving ornamental plants will complain. That's okay. You can maintain the right growing environment for them by segregating them to their own spot in the landscape.

Take care with the additives to your soil. Some garden centers will sell you packs of soil organisms to add to the landscape. A lot of organic websites advocate making your own organic teas. The jury is still out on the value of these additives. If conditions aren't right in the landscape, buying drenches to water into the soil is a waste of money. Making your own isn't wasting money, but it might be a waste of time.

Adding fertilizers can impact the microorganisms in your soil. Inorganic fertilizers are salts. The elements they provide to the soil are necessary, but only up to a point. It is very easy to oversalt the ground with inorganic fertilizers. This salty environment is toxic to the critters in your landscape. Use such products carefully, judiciously.

Don't be fooled. You can overapply organic fertilizers, too. A general rule of thumb for the average homeowner in organic gardening is to amend the soil every other year with the right amount of organic manure or compost for the area being planted. Another good rule of thumb is to cover the desired area with compost to a depth of two inches and till it into the soil. This is best done in the fall so that the soil can mellow out through the winter.

Take these steps and the critters below ground will be just as happy as the critters you nurture above ground. They will pay you back by nurturing your plants in the next growing season.

JD Hortwort *lives in Piedmont, North Carolina, and is an avid student of gardening and herbalism. She enjoys the companionship of two sweet dogs and one very opinionated cat! JD has written a garden column for over twenty years on every aspect of horticulture from lawns to container plans. She is an award-winning journalist and editor. JD is a co-leader of a local spiritual group. She periodically teaches classes on ancient Celtic history and presents lectures on gardening to local garden clubs.*

Shade Gardens

⇝ By Emyme ⇜

Open fields of sunflowers, poppies, gladiolas, and lavender. Black-eyed Susan, forsythia, azalea, and holly thriving in southern exposure along the side yard or the front porch. Morning glories climbing sun-drenched trellises year after year. Wild flowers along the open highways. Nature's beautiful scenery for all to enjoy, in every part of this great world.

All of the above have one thing in common other than the obvious splendor. They all grow best in full sun. With the proper soil and enough rain and sun, any number of flowers and plants can be cultivated. But what of the spaces with less than the requisite six to eight hours of sun? Ah, this is where nature has not let us down, for she has thoughtfully provided flowers and plants that flourish in shade.

Centuries ago, in some places where we now have cities, forests ruled. Trees of every size and shape, rising to the sun, provided a canopy of shade below. Shade in which other plants adapted. Where forests continue to grow those shade plants continue also. This article will concentrate on the more domestic of perennial shade plants and flowers.

Grades for the amount of sun are: full sun, full to part sun, part sun, part shade, full to part shade, and full shade. While I do know that part sun and part shade sound alike, they vary in time. There remains some difference of opinion as to how many hours measure in each category. Follow the suggestions on the plant tags or ask your local nursery staff.

Getting My Garden Started

My experience with shade gardens began a decade ago with the purchase of a new home. Southern exposure to the front of the house guarantees any number of plants, shrubs, and flowers will grow, along with abundant weeds. Likewise, it guarantees the back of the house and most of the rear property lie in shade. A number of large oak trees scattered around the back add to the filter of direct sun. Enthusiasm, rather than perfection, is my way; I chose to concentrate my gardening efforts on a dim corner with a ninety-degree angle, under a bedroom and great room windows. The inherited landscaping included many large granite rocks that required relocation. Average size? Think large grapefruit- to football-size. Using the rocks as borders, two beds were designed: a half moon on one side and rectangle under the second set of windows. Empty space awaited me. I could plant anything

I wanted in these spaces. My knowledge of gardening was sparse, and my initial attempts either produced nothing or grew more and faster than I wished.

One of the first plants was lamb's ears (*Stachys byzantina*), which prefer partial shade. Soft and fuzzy, a calming blue-gray-green, I discovered they can be rather invasive, even planted in a full shade. Shoots spread underground and pop up every spring. My little 10 x 3-foot garden was fast becoming overwhelmed. Out the lamb's ears came. Years later I am still finding a new growth occasionally. I recommend these for a space you wish to fill and let run wild. Had I thought to plant them in a forlorn, far corner by a fence they would surely look better than the weeds that now occupy that area.

Over the next few summers I discovered two of my very favorite shade plants: astilbe and coral bells (*Heuchera*). These grow well in any section of a garden that receives no direct sunlight. Both come in a wide variety of colors and sizes. My coral bells feature a bronze/burgundy leaf with thin stalks of tiny, pale pink flowers later in the summer. Three types of astilbe grace the darkest section my garden space: tall dark pink, short (dwarf?) pale pink, and medium-height white. The latter appear to glow at dusk.

A few summers ago these plants, which had been thriving for years, began to look shabby and sad. Nutrients in the soil were depleted. It is important to feed even these hardy souls—do not neglect them. Look for plant food with nitrogen, phosphorus, and potassium.

Adding color and height (12 to 18 inches) is the balloon flower (*Platycodon grandiflorus*). For years this plant has held court over the far corner of one bed. Tiny ivory buds give way to purple flowers in the shape of hot air balloons that soon burst open to a star-shaped flower. Dead-heading those past their prime guarantees weeks of new growth.

Here I must admit to an embarrassing lapse. One plant that has inhabited my garden for over six years is unidentified. I have long since lost the name marker. Slender stalks, bright, yellow-green leaves with a small pink flower that blooms in July. It maintains color from May to October and never grows higher than twelve to eighteen inches. Quite the perfect compliment to the coral bells.

Flower Royalty

The "king" and "queen" of my shade garden are actually dwarf plants: a hydrangea and butterfly bush. The hydrangea is located on a corner that receives approximately two hours of direct sun every day through the warm months, about an hour in the morning and again in the afternoon when the sun has made its way all the way 'round the house. In any summer it has never grown more than three feet high.

The same year the astilbe and coral bells failed to thrive, the hydrangea went dormant and produced no flowers. Beautiful green leaves, but not one bud of the blue/purple bunches of petals I so enjoy. I had ignored the advice to cut them way back during the previous winter but have followed that regime ever since. Plant food brought the plant back quite successfully. Hydrangeas are like litmus paper, coloring depends on the soil and diet. More acid produces shades of blue and dark purple, and alkali gives blooms pink to pale lavender. Feed according to your color choice.

Two spaces over, the butterfly bush reigns supreme. The stalks and leaves are a lush light green, approximately the color of praying mantis. I have found that very insect in the bush many times when watering, and the spray causes them to amble along out of the wet. Blooms of the most delicate sort arrive in August. Petite, pale purple clumps cover the bush, which spill over the rock border no matter how often it is pruned. As soon as the blooms appear, so do the bees. From what hives I have no idea, but they find us. (They also enjoy the holly in the sunny side yard, the large butterfly bush by the front door, and the rogue sunflowers I seem to get every summer.)

As I write this no less than a dozen bees are happily climbing the blooms collecting pollen. Every year I yearn for honey from my own butterfly bush. It is nice to know someone somewhere may be enjoying what I can only imagine is the delicate flavor. In addition to the bees, this little wonder also attracts butterflies, of course. Not for this bush the monarchs or swallowtails or large cabbage whites. This bush attracts the *Pieris (Artogeia) rapae*, or dainty small white (that is the name!). Beauty for the eye, and good for the environment. I suggest most heartily at least one butterfly bush for every yard, in sun or shade.

My Favorites

The two most recent additions to my shade gardens are personal favorites of mine. Born in May, my flower is lily of the valley. How pleased was I when I discovered they are a shade-loving plant. In forests and woods they nestle up under trees and proliferate, creating carpets of dainty white bells with the most exquisite fragrance. What began as three plants has now grown to more than three times that. One caution, they can get "leggy" at the base. Keep them well mulched for optimal protection in winter. These plants die down completely, and you may think they are well gone, but patience is required.

Remove the dead leaves after the last snow and by May you will be rewarded. Lily of the valley might well be considered one of two perfect plants for a shade garden, or a spot made shady due to large flowering shrubs, such as rhododendrons. The other is bleeding hearts.

At my childhood home, tucked in a corner created by the chimney, the rows of bright pink and white heart-shaped blooms drooped. Somewhat sad, yet stately, they brought a spot of color to a bland façade. As with most of the plants cited in this article, bleeding hearts are not really a flower to be picked; they are more a treat to the eye from afar. In my garden they provide a bit of spring color between the hydrangea and butterfly bush. After all the blooms have died and the stalks become yellow, cut them way back; never fear, they will reappear the next spring.

Last words on flowers—day lilies. Proliferate, pedestrian? Dozens of these tall, orange blossoms run riot in our yard. Not in my gardens, but along the fences and around the trees. Do not believe it when told they need full sun; they adapt quite well to shade. I enjoy their color, ignore them after their prime, and ruthlessly cut them down to the ground in the fall. They just keep coming back more than ever in the spring. In any section you do not want to mow grass these are a great choice.

How to Start

If you are new to the shade garden I suggest buying plants in bloom. You can see how the colors will look together, and keep the little plastic cards! Create a notebook or draw a map of your garden with names, both common and Latin. Take pictures, print them, and then write the names on that page. Years from now when someone asks what is the name of that lovely flower, you will be able to answer. As with any garden, place the taller plants to the rear. Gradually work down in height to the front edge. For months of varied color, stagger the dates of full bloom. Annuals, such as begonias and impatiens, help fill in any bare spots and round out the color palette. Happily, shade gardens require less weeding. With less sun to encourage the stray and random, you will spend less time on your knees culling invaders. A good layer of mulch also keeps weeds to a minimum.

Speaking of mulch, in the autumn I do not rake the fallen leaves from the gardens. They are left until mid-April as protection from winter elements. A garden in the corner of a building with little or no sun runs the risk of being drowned in snow drifts. A layer of mulch and/or leaves insulates extremely well.

In addition to the gardens, two flowering shrubs and one tree enhance my sheltered back yard. First the tree—a lovely dogwood with medium pink flowers blossoms every spring. Standing alone with at least fifteen feet of lawn all around it, there are times of the day when this tree enjoys full sun, but not for long. It will never grow very large, and we prefer it that way. In the fall the leaves turn a striking, deep wine red. It is quite dramatic.

The two shrubs sit along one fence—a rhododendron and an azalea. Both would likely be far more comfortable in the sun; however, the lack keeps them small and manageable. Every spring the lavender azalea blooms first, and as the weather warms the rhododendron pops a vivid, dark pink. Due to the varied blooming dates of the beds, the bushes, and the tree, I enjoy a spot of color from spring to fall in my gardens. It was quite by accident; however, any good nursery (or the Internet) can help you achieve the same effect based on your growing zone.

A final word—all these recommendations and suggestions are based on living in southern New Jersey. Many, if not all, of these plants happily adapt to other states and countries with similar weather conditions.

Happy gardening!

Additional Information

Andrews, Jonathan. *The Country Diary Book of Creating a Wildflower Garden*. United Kingdom: Publisher's Guild, 1986.

Everett, Thomas (ed). *Reader's Digest Complete Book of the Garden*. New York: Reader's Digest Association, 1966.

Free, Montague. *A Complete Guide to Gardening*. New York: Perma Books, 1960.

Pollan, Michael. *Second Nature: A Gardener's Education*. New York: Grove Press, 1991.

Seymour, E. L. D. (ed). *The New Garden Encyclopedia*. New York: WM. H. Wise & Company, 1941.

Wyman, Donald. *The Saturday Morning Gardener*. New York: Macmillan, 1974.

Emyme, *an eclectic solitary, resides in a multi-generation, multi-cat household in southern New Jersey—concentrating on candle spells, garden spells, and kitchen witchery. In addition to writing poetry and prose about strong women of mythology and fairy tales, Emyme is creating a series of articles on bed & breakfasts from the point of view of the over-fifty-five, single, female, Wiccan traveler. Please send questions or comments to catsmeow24@verizon.net.*

Culinary
Herbs

A Salute to Spuds

By Alice DeVille

According to the fact-finders among food historians, the Spaniards introduced potatoes, a starchy, tuberous vegetable from the nightshade family, to Europeans in the 1500s after returning from their conquests in South America and cultivating the new crops. I wonder if these explorers had any idea how their discovery would result in thousands of tastebud-popping recipes for generations to come. More than 5,000 varieties of nutrient-rich potatoes, one of the world's most important crops, exist in the potato universe. Potatoes rank high as a comfort food with most consumers.

What is your favorite potato and how do you prepare it? Can you easily answer that question? Or do you visualize all the potato favorites you have ever known, making it impossible to choose? Potatoes challenge you to use your creative cooking skills to cultivate a variety of dishes. Take it from me, you can get into all kinds of trouble if you have a five-pound bag of potatoes in your pantry—but it is trouble that tastes so good! Why not use those spuds you have on hand to start a recipe riot that brings raving fans to the dinner table? This article takes you on a culinary journey using some of the available potato varieties while satisfying discriminating palates. I have honored several of the recipes by naming them after family members because they are a frequently requested dish, and it gives me great pleasure to prepare them.

Best Bets on Baked

Baked potatoes come in handy for use in a variety of dishes. The most commonly used for baking include Idaho, russet, and yams. When I fire up the oven I often bake extra potatoes for use in recipes to be enjoyed later in the week. Cut down on bake time by using a convection oven if you have one. Among my preferences are baking medium to large potatoes for serving with beef, pork, fish, or chicken entrees. Lightly grease the unpeeled potatoes, prick them to release steam, and bake for an hour at 400°F for a crusty skin and a fluffy white interior that is ready for butter, sour cream, or your favorite seasonings. Toppings can also include green chives, bacon bits, shredded cheddar cheese, or chopped onion.

If you prepare the potatoes well ahead of the meal, you can use three potatoes to make a twice-baked potato side dish by cutting them in half diagonally after they cool slightly, then scoop out the pulp and mash it in a small bowl with 3 tablespoons of butter, 2 to 3 tablespoons of milk or cream, and salt and pepper to taste. Then add 2 tablespoons of grated cheddar cheese, 2 tablespoons of diced cooked bacon, 1 tablespoon of green onions, and mix together.

Fill the potato skins with the mixture, top with an additional sprinkle of cheddar cheese, green onions, and a bit of paprika for color. Place on a foil-lined baking sheet and dot with butter; cover and refrigerate until ready to bake. Remove from the refrigerator for 30 minutes before baking, and place in a 350°F oven for 30 minutes. Top lightly with chopped parsley before serving. Ingredients are enough for two large or three medium baked potatoes. Watch your guests savor every bite.

Here's a tasty way to take the extra potato you baked to the breakfast table for a hearty and savory start to the day. Many of the steps resemble those for making an omelet except for the way you prepare the eggs. I always serve this dish when my son visits from the West Coast, and he coined the term noting how this dish differs from omelet preparation. Makes 3 generous servings.

Steve's Scramlettes

3–4 tablespoons butter

1 baked potato, skin removed, and diced into ¼-inch pieces

1 teaspoon salt, divided (or to taste)

½ teaspoon pepper, divided (or to taste)

1 cup breakfast sausage, diced; or 1 cup ham, diced (may also use 4 strips cooked bacon, crumbled)

4 large or extra large eggs

½ cup heavy cream or half-and-half (can also use half milk and half cream)

1 small tomato, seeded and diced

½ cup shredded sharp cheddar cheese

¼ cup shredded swiss cheese

1 tablespoon chopped parsley, for garnish

Melt the butter over medium heat in a 12-inch skillet. Add diced potatoes, and season lightly with salt and pepper. When potatoes have turned golden, add the sausage or ham and sauté quickly. Meanwhile, whisk eggs in a medium bowl, add cream, and salt and pepper to taste, and whip until smooth. Add egg mixture to skillet, topping with tomatoes. At this point, if you chose bacon instead of sausage or ham, sprinkle over egg mixture, cooking on medium-low, allowing uncooked eggs to run onto the pan by lifting slightly with a large spatula. When eggs are firm, add cheeses and fold over until cheese melts. Cut into three wedges, sprinkle lightly with parsley, and serve with toast, biscuits, or buttered English muffins.

Nothing takes the chill away from a cold winter day like a creamy bowl of soup, rich with savory chicken stock, milk, oven baked potatoes, and your favorite toppings. While some cooks leave a lot, or a little bit, of skin on the prepared potatoes, I prefer to cut the baked potatoes in half, scoop out the pulp, and set it aside until ready to incorporate into the broth and other ingredients. Makes 4 to 6 servings.

Baked Potato Soup

4 large baking potatoes

1 stick of butter

1 large onion, chopped

⅔ cup all-purpose flour

4 cups whole milk

2 cups chicken stock or chicken broth (may also use all milk in lieu of broth)

¾ teaspoon salt

½ teaspoon black pepper

4 green onions, chopped, and divided

6 bacon slices, cooked, crumbled, and divided

1 ¼ cups shredded cheddar cheese

1 cup of sour cream (optional)

Bake potatoes for 1 hour or until done. Let cool. Cut potatoes in half lengthwise, then scoop out pulp and set aside, mashing lightly. Discard skins.

Melt butter in large saucepan over low heat, add chopped onion and sauté until soft; then add flour, stirring until smooth. Cook for 1 minute, stirring constantly. Gradually add milk, and then broth. Cook over medium heat, stirring constantly, until mixture is thickened and bubbly.

Add potato pulp (I like mine a little lumpy in consistency, but without chunks; if you like a finer consistency, use an immersion blender), salt, pepper, 2 tablespoons of green onion, half the bacon, and 1 cup of cheese. Cook until thoroughly heated, and stir in sour cream if desired. Add additional milk and seasoning for preferred taste and thickness. Ladle into bowls and sprinkle with remaining green onion, bacon, and cheese as desired. Serve with a green salad.

This potato recipe is a lot of work up front, but once it emerges from the oven you have a tasty, creamy side dish that puts a memorable glow on your dinner table.

Allie's Scalloped Potatoes (named after my daughter)

   6 large baking potatoes

   4 tablespoons butter

   1 medium onion, chopped

   4 tablespoons all-purpose flour

   1 ½ teaspoons salt

   ⅓ teaspoon black pepper

   3 cups whole milk

   ½ teaspoon seasoned salt (from Bud's Spuds recipe below)

   2 extra tablespoons butter

   ½ cup heavy cream

   1 tablespoon flat leaf parsley

Heat oven to 350°F. Grease bottom and sides of 3-quart oblong baking dish with shortening.

Wash potatoes and peel. Cut into thin slices to measure at least 5 cups. Melt butter in 3-quart saucepan over medium heat. Cook onion in butter about 2 minutes, stirring occasionally, until tender. Stir in flour, salt, and pepper. Cook, stirring constantly until smooth and bubbly, then remove from heat. Stir in milk, then heat to boiling, stirring constantly. Boil and stir for 1 minute.

Spread the potatoes into prepared baking dish, overlapping slices. Sprinkle the seasoned salt over potatoes. Pour sauce over potatoes. Dot with the 2 tablespoons of butter.

Cover with foil and bake for 30 minutes. Uncover and bake 1 hour to 1 hour and 15 minutes, or until potatoes are tender. Pour heavy cream over potatoes during the last 25 minutes of baking time. When potatoes are done, remove from the oven and sprinkle parsley over top. Let stand at least 10 minutes before serving. For a taste variation, increase milk amount to 5 ½ cups and add ⅔ cup grated cheddar cheese to sauce mixture after it thickens. Makes 8 to 10 servings.

Mouthwatering Mashed Potatoes

Whenever I prepare mashed potatoes I think fondly of my eldest son, Bud, who has often requested that "Mom's mashed potatoes" appear on the menu at holiday meals or other venues, so I always make extra servings for him to take home. I vary ingredients and even preparation time of this recipe (you can make it ahead of time and put it into a casserole dish for easy reheating) depending upon how many other dishes are going on the table. When this dish is going to be served immediately I either omit the cream cheese or use only 3 ounces, ½ cup of half-and-half, and put a pat of butter on top. Yes, this is a rich dish.

Bud's Spuds

> 5 pounds of russet or yukon gold potatoes
>
> 1 cup butter
>
> ⅓–¾ package cream cheese, softened
>
> ½–¾ cups half-and-half

1 teaspoon seasoned salt (your own mixture or a commercial brand)

½ teaspoon black pepper, if your personal mix does not contain it

Peel the potatoes, and cut them in quarters or sixths if they are large. Bring a large pot of water to a simmer and add the potatoes. Bring to a boil and cook for 30 to 35 minutes. Test with a fork to be sure potatoes are cooked through without falling apart. Drain potatoes in large colander, and when they finish draining, return them to the pot and put the pot on the stove. Mash the potatoes over low heat, allowing the steam to escape before adding in other ingredients.

Turn off the stove and add the butter, softened cream cheese, and half-and-half. Mash until all ingredients are incorporated. Next, add seasoned salt and pepper if using a commercial mix. (My seasoned salt recipe has 1 cup of iodized salt, ½ cup of black pepper, ½ cup of garlic powder, and ½ cup of onion powder that I mix together, and fill a shaker container that I store away from heat for easy use in a variety of dishes. The extra keeps well in the refrigerator for several months, if it lasts that long.) Stir potato mixture well and serve.

If making this dish as a do-ahead item one to two days before serving, place in a medium-sized baking dish and store in refrigerator. Before reheating, take the potatoes out of the refrigerator for about 2 hours. Sprinkle cubed butter over the top, and place the dish in a 350°F oven, heating until the butter is melted and potatoes are warmed through, approximately 25 to 30 minutes. Be prepared for requests for this recipe, and very few leftovers if feeding a crowd. Serves 10 to 12 guests.

No article about potatoes would be complete without including a recipe for the creamy summer treat: potato salad. Although I'm using all-purpose potatoes for this dish, I often use russet potatoes that I have baked, removing most of the skin, and then tossing with the ingredients listed below. The addition of grated carrots gives the presentation more color when you mound your salad on a lettuce-lined plate. Serve it to up to 10 guests.

Classic Potato Salad

> 6 medium, all-purpose white potatoes (about 2 pounds)
>
> ½ cup mayonnaise or salad dressing (or more to taste)
>
> 1 teaspoon prepared yellow or Dijon mustard
>
> 1 ½ teaspoons salt
>
> ¼ teaspoon black pepper
>
> ¼ cup carrots, shredded
>
> ⅔ cup celery, finely diced
>
> ½ cup yellow or white onion, chopped
>
> 4 hard-boiled eggs; chop 3 and save 1 to slice as a garnish for your salad
>
> ½ teaspoon paprika
>
> 2–3 small sprigs of parsley

Scrub unpeeled potatoes and place in a large saucepan, covering with water. Cook 40 to 50 minutes, until tender but not mushy. Remove from heat, drain, and let stand until ready to handle. Then peel and cut each into 8 to 10 chunks. Set aside.

Mix mayonnaise, mustard, salt, and pepper in a large glass bowl. Add cooked potatoes, carrots, celery, and onion; stir in eggs when mixed, and toss. Refrigerate for 3 to 4 hours to blend flavors. Then place potatoes on lettuce-lined serving platter, top with sliced hard-boiled egg slices, and sprinkle paprika over dish. Decorate with sprigs of parsley.

When I serve this next dish I think of my daughter-in-law, Marty, who considers this side a "must have" item on the Thanksgiving menu. I make double the recipe so she has extras to take home for additional meals. Few ingredients go into the recipe, yet it is rich and memorable to the palate. Serves 8 to 12 as a side dish.

Marty's Holiday Praline Yams

For the topping:

¼ cup packed brown sugar

3 tablespoons butter, at room temperature

3 tablespoons all-purpose flour

½ cup pecans, finely chopped

For the casserole:

6 medium yams or sweet potatoes (approximately 3 pounds), peeled and cut into ½-inch-thick rounds, and cooked (may also use canned yams—do not cook first)

1 ½ cups heavy cream, heated

In a bowl, work together the brown sugar, butter, and flour until well combined, then work in pecans. Set aside and keep at room temperature up to 8 hours before using. You can prepare this topping up to a day ahead and refrigerate it, bringing it to room temperature an hour before topping the casserole.

For the casserole, bring a large pot of lightly salted water to a boil. Add yams and cook until tender-crisp, about 5 minutes. Do not overcook. Drain and rinse under cold running water.

Preheat oven to 375°F. Lightly butter a 9 x 13-inch baking dish. Arrange yams in overlapping, vertical rows in dish (you can do this up to 8 hours before baking), then cover tightly with plastic wrap, and refrigerate.

Pour heated cream over yams, and bake for 20 minutes. Crumble pecan mixture over yams, and continue baking until yams are tender and topping is browned, 20 to 30 minutes more. Expect to get requests for the recipe if your guests have never before tasted this dish.

Roasted and Robust

Fingerling potatoes come in a variety of shapes and colors. I buy the mixed medley of white, yellow, purple, and red potatoes at my favorite produce store. Generally uniform in size, they require little prep time, and easily roast in the oven; the perfect side partner for grilled or roasted meats, fish, or poultry. You can also place them in a foil pack and roast them on your grill.

Flavorful Fingerlings

   3 pounds of mixed variety fingerling potatoes

   ¼ cup olive oil or more depending on size of potatoes

   Seasoned salt (with pepper) to taste

   ½ teaspoon Italian seasoning

   1 teaspoon rosemary leaves

Preheat oven to 375°F. Line a large baking pan with foil. Scrub potatoes and dry with paper towels. Place on pan and pour olive oil and seasonings over them, mixing with a spoon to coat them until all the potatoes are covered. Roast uncovered for 45 minutes to 1 hour until done. Serve with your main course, a green salad, and crusty bread. Feeds 8 to 10 guests.

Note: If you enjoy oven-baked steak fries, use the same ingredients, sans the rosemary, but substitute fingerlings for 4 large Idaho or russet potatoes, peeled with uneven ends cut off, and slice into more uniform, thick fries. Preheat oven to 400°F, toss with same ingredients as above, and spread on an oversized baking sheet, roasting for 30 to 40 minutes until crisp. Place immediately on a paper towel–lined plate to drain, and then spoon onto a clean platter when ready to serve.

So many recipes call for leaner, lighter ingredients, but this dish isn't one of them. If you are counting calories and watching fat content in your meals, I suggest you eat less fat and butter for a few days before or after you indulge. I serve it only once or twice a year and never have leftovers. A butter substitute simply won't cut it in this rich, palate-pleasing potato side dish. Although I make my version with baking potatoes, you can use white or new potatoes if you prefer. They melt in your mouth. Makes 8 to 10 servings.

Roasted Melting Potatoes

   3 tablespoons unsalted butter, cut into 6 pieces (plus 1 reserved tablespoon stored in the refrigerator)

   3 tablespoons olive oil

   6 large baking potatoes (approximately 3 pounds)

1 teaspoon kosher salt

Freshly ground black pepper

2 cups chicken stock or canned broth

½ teaspoon crushed thyme leaves for garnish

Place oven rack in top third of oven, and preheat to 500°F. Put 3 tablespoons of butter into an 18x12x2-inch roasting pan. Set the pan over medium heat until the butter has barely melted. Remove from heat. Add the olive oil.

Peel the potatoes. Cut in half lengthwise, then cut each in half crosswise. Cut each quarter into 3 wedges. Roll the wedges in the roasting pan until evenly coated with the butter and oil mix. Arrange in the pan so pieces barely touch. Sprinkle with salt and pepper.

Roast for 15 minutes, turn wedges with a pancake turner; roast another 10 minutes, turn again; roast 10 minutes more. Remove pan from oven. Turn wedges again, making sure to turn the white sides of each wedge face-up. Add the stock or broth. Return to oven for a final 15 minutes. The potatoes can be made up to this point, and then held for 4 to 6 hours, while you prepare remaining meal dishes.

When ready for final steps, dot the wedges with small pieces of the reserved tablespoon of butter. If the potatoes have been at room temperature, roast 15 minutes at 400°F; if they are still warm, just roast for 5 more minutes. Remove potatoes to a platter right away, or they will stick to the pan. Sprinkle thyme leaves lightly over potatoes and serve.

Sources

Recipes in this article are from the personal, handwritten notes, my recipe "treasure map," and abundant recipe files in my collection. Inspiration comes from variations of these recipes found in cookbooks, magazines, and food preparation networks.

Alice DeVille *is an internationally known astrologer, writer, and metaphysical consultant specializing in relationships, health, real estate, government affairs, career and change management, and spiritual development. An accomplished cook, Alice prepares food from a variety of cuisines and enjoys creating new recipes, hosting parties, and organizing holiday feasts. One of her goals is to create a cookbook; another is to appear on the Food Network. Aside from cooking, her work on relationships appears in diverse media outlets and websites, including Oprah's, StarIQ.com, Astral Hearts, Meta Arts, Inner Self, ShareItLiveIt, and World Famous Quotes. Alice's Llewellyn material on relationships has been cited by Sarah Ban Breathnach in* Something More, *on Oprah's website, and in* Through God's Eyes *by Phil Bolsta. Alice is available for writing books and articles for publishers, newspapers, or magazines, and conducting workshops, lectures, and radio or TV interviews. Contact Alice at DeVilleAA@aol.com; on Twitter @AstroOnDemand; and visit her website www.astrologyondemand.com.*

Go a-Blackberrying

⤳ By Natalie Zaman ⤝

A berry by any other name...

A thimbleberry sounds like something a fairy might eat—but
don't let the name fool you. *Thimble*
hints at the prickly nature of this
fruit, also called bramble, bramble-
berry, or more commonly, blackberry. Whatever you choose to call
them, humans have been enjoying
this dark, clustery fruit for thousands
of years.

In the United Kingdom the act
of picking, "blackberrying," is an
unofficial national summer pastime.
Starting in late June, folks flock to the
countryside (and nooks and crannies
in urban areas) armed with baskets
and buckets in the hope of scoring
enough fruit for a few pots of jam

and maybe a tart or two. Wild blackberries are and have been, for the most part, plentiful and free, meaning sweet treats for anyone willing to forage. Tradition holds that it's bad luck to pick after September 29, the day the devil commemorates his fall from heaven by returning to earth to spit (or pee!) on any blackberries he can find. Be it superstition or change of season, blackberry crops thin out when autumn sets in.

The Brits don't have a monopoly on the blackberry season, however. Fruiting time is the same in the United States, the largest producer of blackberries in the world. The plants thrive best in temperate climates, but according to the Department of Agriculture, there are species of blackberry in every state just waiting to be harvested. The question is, are you a gatherer or a gardener?

Grow or Gather?

If you choose to go a-blackberrying in the wild, know what you're looking for. Bushes can grow upwards of 8- to 10-feet tall and have thick canes with thorny, purple spines. They prefer partial shade and a thickety environment, which can make it a bit of a challenge to get to the fruit. Cover your legs and arms, and wear gloves, or prepare to go home with scrapes and scratches.

Look for large, soft, dark berries that are just beginning to lose their gloss. These qualities indicate not only ripeness, but nutritional value—the darker the berry, the higher the antioxidant content. The barest tug will separate the fruit from its stalk. Check a field guide with detailed photos to confirm what you're picking. Always err on the side of caution when it comes to identifying plants in the wild. If you have any doubts about the identity of what you've picked, don't eat it.

And of course, wash all your fruit before consuming it.

Unlike their wild brothers, most blackberry bushes sold in nurseries and garden centers have no thorns. My first blackberry plants were single canes, planted on a narrow strip of earth between a fence and a brick pathway. I only had to wait one season before they produced fruit. The bushes grew quickly and any wandering canes that managed to find earth planted themselves again. I cut the canes down to a few feet in length before winter, and I've had consistent growth and plentiful crops five years and counting.

Blackberries may be alpha plants, but they're not completely invincible. They're susceptible to rust, a fungal infection that can be seen as coating of orange powder on the leaves. There is no cure for this blight, and many sources say that the best thing to do is to remove the whole infected plant as quickly as possible so that the fungus does not spread.

Treats...

Blackberries are loaded with antioxidants and Vitamins C and K, and they can aid with indigestion and improve memory retention. As with most fruits and vegetables, eat your blackberries raw and unprocessed (but washed!) to get the best nutritional value from them.

If you don't want to whip up treats right away, freeze your harvest. Spread your berries out in a single layer on a cookie sheet before putting them into the freezer. Wait until they are frozen hard before moving them into storage containers. This will make the fruit easy to separate when you're ready to use them. Your berries should be good for ten to twelve months—plenty of time to try out some tasty (and colorful!) recipes.

Blackberry Smoothie

I use no measurements when making smoothies. I just keep throwing things into the blender until I like the taste and consistency. All quantities are approximate.

1 cup of Greek yogurt

½ cup of cold water

½ cup of ice

1–2 teaspoons of agave nectar

¼–½ cup of fresh blackberries

1–2 teaspoons of flax or chia seeds

Put all the ingredients in a blender and pulse until smooth.

Blackberry Jam

One of my favorite snacks is a cup of tea and a few slices of toast slathered with organic butter and blackberry jam. To make your own jam (it's easy!) you'll need:

A pot large enough to accommodate your
  berries and sugar

Equal weights of berries and sugar (the traditional
  ratio is 1 to 1, but for sweeter jam use 1 part fruit
  to 2 parts sugar)

1 cooking apple, peeled and cut up (optional)

Recycled jars and lids

Wax paper

Wash your berries and crush them before putting them into the pot. Blackberries are high in pectin (the element that causes jams and jellies to "gel"), but to be safe you can cook the berries with a cut-up apple to raise the amount of pectin and ensure a more gelatinous jam.

Bring the crushed fruit to a slow simmer and cook it until all is soft, then add the sugar. Simmer the mixture gently until the sugar is dissolved and incorporated completely. To see if your jam is ready to be jarred, drip a little bit of it on a plate and pop it in the freezer for a minute or two to check consistency.

Boil your jars and lids to sterilize them, or put them through a cycle by themselves in the dishwasher, and leave them there until you're ready to fill them. When your jam is set, pour it into the jars, and place a sheet of wax paper over each jar mouth before capping it. Leave the jars on the counter to cool; the caps should indent, sealing them (you shouldn't be able to snap the cap when you press it). Jam can be stored in a cupboard, but I always work with small batches and keep mine in the fridge just to be safe.

If you find that your jam is more liquid than gel, it's still very usable. Swirl it into a trifle, or drizzle it over ice cream or baked treats.

Blackberry Crumble

Blackberrying is a British tradition, so it's fitting to incorporate some of your harvest into a time-honored English dessert: the crumble. There are many recipes for the "perfect crumble," but most agree on the basic elements. Refer to your favorite cookbook to determine the amounts of each standard ingredient and any extras to include.

For the compote:

Blackberries

Sugar (to taste)

For the crumble:

Flour and butter in equal measure

Sugar that is half the measure of the flour and butter
(i.e., 1 pound each of flour and butter would require a
half-pound of sugar)

Wash and partially crush the berries, then combine them with sugar. Place this mixture into a large shallow dish.

To make the crumble, combine the sugar, flour, and butter until the mixture is pebbly. Sprinkle the crumble on top of the fruit, then bake it in a 400°F oven for about 30 minutes, or until the top is brown and the juices of the berries bubble between the crumbly bits. Let it cool and set. Serve warm with vanilla ice cream, or better still, warm custard.

Natural Dye

If you've ever splattered blackberry juice on your clothes, you know it has staying power! Dye made from the berries is a good use for overripe fruit that is inedible. You will need:

1 large pot

Blackberries

8 cups of water

½ cup of salt (this acts as a fixative)

Crush the berries and place them in the pot with the water and salt. Put the pot on the stove and heat it up, stirring the ingredients to combine them. Bring the mixture to a very gentle simmer for about 30 minutes, then turn off the heat (if the mixture gets too hot, the tannin in the blackberries can make the dye turn brown).

Strain the liquid to remove any pulp and seeds, and leave it to cool overnight. The dye works best with natural materials such as cotton and silk, or even paper and hard-boiled eggs. Resulting colors will be various hues of bluish-purple depending on the quantity of berries used.

...and Tricks!

While the fat, glossy fruit is certainly the blackberry's main attraction, the whole plant is useful. The canes were used by Native Americans for making rope. According to Elizabethan master herbalist Nicholas Culpeper, the leaves make an excellent hair dye—although I can't say that I've tried that myself. Tea made from the leaves tastes bitter but can soothe inflammation in the gums and throat, and because of their astringent properties, the leaves can also be brewed into a mouthwash and gargled.

Before you use any plant for medicinal purposes, check with your health care provider to make sure that it's the right remedy for you.

Resources

Brill, Steve. "Foraging for Blackberries." *Early American Life Magazine*. August 2006. www.wildmanstevebrill.com /Clippings.folder/ForagingForBlackberries.html.

Cloak, Felicity. "How to make the perfect crumble." *The Guardian*. October 14, 2010. www.theguardian.com /lifeandstyle/wordofmouth/2010/oct/14/how-to-make-perfect-crumble.

Connely, Andy. "The science and magic of jam making." *The Guardian*. October 3, 2013. www.theguardian.com /science/blog/2013/oct/03/science-magic-jam-making.

FP Julia. "Wednes-DIY: Making Natural Dyes." *Free People Blog.* August 31, 2011. http://blog.freepeople .com/2011/08/diy-natural-dyes/.

Haran, Maeve. "Juice stained lips. Cardies snagged on brambles. The last sweet taste of summer. It's blackberrying time again." *Daily Mail.* August 26, 2011. www.dailymail .co.uk/femail/article-2030286/Juice-stained-lips-Cardies-snagged-brambles-The-sweet-taste-summer-Its-blackber-rying-time-again.html.

Moore, Shelley. "What Are The Benefits Of Blackberry Leaves?" *Livestrong.* January 13, 2014. www.livestrong .com/article/257328-what-are-the-benefits-of-blackber-ry-leaves/.

Old Farmers Almanac. "Blackberries." www.almanac.com /plant/blackberries

Simms, Dileen. "Blackberry Facts: 10 Things You May Not Know About The Fruit." *Huffington Post Canada.* March 14, 2013. www.huffingtonpost.ca/2013/01/31/blackber-ry-facts_n_2581622.html.

Natalie Zaman *is the co-author of the* Graven Images Oracle deck *(Galde Press), and the YA novels* Sirenz, Sirenz Back in Fashion *(both from Flux), and* Blonde Ops. *Her work has appeared in* FATE, SageWoman, *and* newWitch *magazines, and she writes the feature "Wandering Witch" for* Witches and Pagans. *For more, visit http://nataliezaman.com or http://broomstix.blogspot.com, a collection of crafts, stories, ritual, and art for Pagan families.*

Tarragon Is More Than Just a Name; It's a Flavor

❧ By Anne Sala ❧

If you ever find yourself at a plant nursery holding a pot of tarragon in your hand, contemplating its addition to your home garden, make sure to pinch off a leaf and take a taste. This quick test will reveal more about the plant than the tag stuck into the soil. Are you face-to-face with the sweet herb prized by a world-famous cuisine, or its bitter cousin from the north? If the leaf has a spicy zing, the little plant before you may be a Central American substitution.

Tarragon is known as the "king of herbs" in France, but it may come as a surprise to learn that for such an esteemed herb, it is often mislabeled or propagated from exhausted source plants in the United States. This is a shame since tarragon is an herb that the rest of the world should get to know better. Its thin leaves have a powerful flavor that can elevate a simple meal.

Follow the Flavor

A perennial, leafy herb, tarragon produces tall, tender stems carrying long, lance-shaped leaves. Depending on the variety, the plant may or may not produce flowers. It has a curling rhizomelike root, reminiscent of a serpent or dragon's tail—giving it its French name *estragon*, which means "dragon." This name, in turn, is thought to come from the Persian word *tarkhun*, which also means "dragon."

Tarragon's origins hail from the cold regions of Siberia and its descendent is Russian tarragon (*Artemisia dracunculoides*), a hardy perennial that unfortunately has a faint and bitter taste. Mongolian invaders carried this herb with them as they pushed their way into Europe and South Asia. When introduced to the Romans, they quickly incorporated it into their medicinal arsenal due to its antifungal and anti-diabetic qualities. It also contains the essential oils estragol, an antimicrobial compound, and eugenol, an anesthetic, making it a popular remedy for toothaches.

Russian tarragon (*Artemisia dracunculoides*) can thrive under harsh conditions and is easily raised from seeds produced by its small, yellowish flowers. Its ease of care makes this variety of tarragon popular with landscapers, but it is not recommended for cooking since its flavor is so weak.

French tarragon (*Artemisia dracunculus*) came on to the scene sometime between the thirteenth and fifteenth centuries. The taste of this variety is sweet, peppery, and anise-like with a hint of mint. One taste—even one sneaked in the herb aisle at the plant nursery—is enough to prove its "king of herbs" moniker. As a more cultivated plant, this version of tarragon is not as easy to grow as its northern cousin. It rarely flowers unless in a very warm climate and its seeds are usually sterile. However, it will readily grow new plants from root cuttings.

For such a prized plant, the myth of tarragon's origins is rather humble. No god transformed a lover into it. No one's tears made it spring from the earth. Indeed, folklore claims it came about simply when someone put a flax seed into a radish root and planted it.

Despite this rather plain story, tarragon's genus name makes reference to the Greek goddess Artemis, the goddess of the moon and chastity. This is because tarragon's green leaves have a slight silvery color, as if seen in moonlight. That being said, centuries ago few travelers would have ventured far without it due to the belief that tarragon could heal not only the bite of snakes and mad dogs, but also the bite of a dragon.

The third variety of this herb, winter tarragon (*Tagetes lucida*) or Mexican marigold, is actually related to marigolds and hails from Central America. The Aztecs burned the herb as an incense, and its yellow flowers are used as a dye. Its flavor is aniselike, quite similar to French tarragon, but with a spicy endnote reminiscent of cinnamon. Plus, as French tarragon is not very cold hardy, many gardeners happily plant winter tarragon instead since it can withstand great temperature ranges.

Stir the Pot

As I was doing research for this article, I leafed through my copy of Ginette Mathiot's *Je Sais Cuisiner* (I Know How to Cook), first published in France in 1932, and took note of every sauce recipe that called for tarragon. I found seven. This includes the familiar Bearnaise and tartar sauces, as well as more mysterious sounding ones, like crapaudine (froglike) sauce, which is served with rabbit.

It seems tarragon could easily be added to almost any recipe, but take your cues from the exhaustive research conducted by generations of French chefs. To make the most of the herb's unique qualities, the French usually pair it with chicken, seafood, eggs, tomatoes, fruit, and berries. It is generally incorporated into a sauce or condiment due to its ability to overpower a dish with its licorice flavor.

An even better way to temper the administration and flavor of tarragon is to combine it with other herbs. *Fines herbes* is a mixture containing equal parts tarragon, parsley, chives, and chervil (another delicate, anise-flavored herb). The flavor is at its peak, of course, when made with fresh leaves, but a bottle of this dried in the cupboard is a secret weapon when its contents are sprinkled on a simmering soup.

Nevertheless, the essential oils in French tarragon dissipate relatively quickly once the herb is dried. A much better way to preserve the plant is to store it in vinegar. Mixing the leaves into butter is another popular way to preserve their flavor, but it does not keep for as long. The recipe is included below.

For the sake of this article, I will focus on using just French tarragon in the recipes, however, winter tarragon can certainly be used.

Tarragon Recipes

Tarragon Vinegar
Makes 1 bottle
Storing tarragon in vinegar is an age-old way to extend this

delicate herb's use. One can easily remove a few leaves and use them just like fresh leaves. As a bonus, you also have a bottle of versatile tarragon vinegar that can be used to flavor salad dressings, fried fish, or anything else that calls for an acidic touch.

> 4–6 sprigs fresh tarragon
>
> 2 cups white wine vinegar

Rinse and thoroughly dry the sprigs, then stuff into a clean, scalded jar. Pour in the vinegar, and cap it. Keep in a dark cupboard at least a week before using. The longer you leave the herbs in the vinegar, the more intense the tarragon vinegar flavor. Use a fork or tongs to fish out a sprig when needed. The tarragon leaves can be used as long as they aren't slimy looking.

Seared Chicken Cutlets with Tarragon Butter Sauce
Serves 4–6

This recipe has hundreds of permutations because it is simply so good. The light sauce can be dressed up with cream or made even easier by substituting dried herbs for fresh.

> 3 tablespoons olive oil, divided
>
> 2 pounds skinless boneless chicken breasts, sliced into thin cutlets
>
> 4 tablespoons unsalted butter
>
> 1 small red onion, chopped
>
> 1 clove garlic
>
> ⅓ cup dry white wine
>
> 1 cup chicken broth

¼ cup fresh tarragon sprigs, chopped

1 tablespoon fresh flat-leaf parsley, chopped

2 teaspoons fresh lemon juice or sherry vinegar

Heat half the oil in a sauté pan or skillet over medium-high heat. Add the chicken cutlets and brown them, turning once, until cooked through. Make sure to not crowd the pieces. Sauté in batches, adding more oil if necessary. Transfer the cooked pieces to a plate and loosely cover with foil.

Return the pan to the heat and melt 1 tablespoon butter. When it has finished foaming, add the red onion. Cook until softened, then add the garlic. As soon as you can smell the garlic's aroma, pour in the wine.

Use a wooden spoon to scrape up the browned bits sticking to the pan, and allow the wine to simmer. Once the liquid has reduced by almost half, add the chicken broth. When it begins to simmer, turn the heat to low, and add the remaining butter. Stir until the butter is incorporated, then remove the pan from the heat. Gently stir in tarragon, parsley, and lemon juice or vinegar. Add salt and pepper to taste. Serve with buttered green beans and crusty bread.

"Fine Herbs" Finishing Oil

Makes about ⅔ cup

I'm calling this "Fine Herbs" instead of *fines herbes* because I could not source fresh chervil for this recipe. Even so, this oil is a divine addition to corn chowder or drizzled over toasted French bread. It will keep in the refrigerator for about 2 weeks but will congeal. Allow it to warm on the counter for at least 30 minutes before use. Have a bowl of ice water and clean tea towels at the ready before blanching the herbs.

2 tablespoons salt

¾ cup tarragon leaves

¾ cup parsley leaves

⅛ cup chives

¾ cup extra virgin olive oil

Fill a large pot about two-thirds of the way with water and place over high heat. Add salt and bring to a boil. Drop in the herbs and blanch for about 10 seconds. Use tongs to quickly remove the herbs from the hot water and immerse them in the cold water. Drain the herbs and dry them in tea towels. Try to remove as much moisture as you can.

Place the herbs and olive oil into a food processor or blender. Purée until smooth. Strain through a fine-mesh sieve into a bowl or measuring cup, pressing down on the solids to extract as much oil as possible. Discard the herbs. Pour the oil into a jar with a lid. It is ready to use immediately.

Roast Salmon with I-Should-Have-Planted-More-Tarragon Pesto

Serves 4

The idea for this dish came to me as I was making the "Fine Herbs" finishing oil. It occurred to me that the addition of just a few more ingredients would make it so the greens didn't need to be discarded. And if you find yourself running out of tarragon before your curiosity is satisfied, this is a good way to stretch those tender leaves. The recipe below, however, does not require you to blanch the herbs first.

1 cup tarragon leaves and tender stems

1 cup parsley

½ cup chives

2 garlic cloves

1 tablespoon lemon zest

1 teaspoon salt, plus more to taste

½ cup extra virgin olive oil

2 pounds salmon fillets with skin, cut into 4 pieces

Pepper to taste

Preheat oven to 425°F. Place the herbs, garlic, lemon zest, and salt into a food processor. Pulse four or five times until the herbs begin to collapse. Pour in the olive oil and blend until the mixture is smooth.

Line a baking sheet with foil, and place the 4 pieces of salmon on top, skin side down. Use a rubber spatula to spread the tarragon pesto on top of each piece, leaving a quarter-inch border of flesh exposed around the edges.

Roast for about 15 minutes or until cooked through. Use a spatula to separate the meat from the skin, which usually sticks to the foil, and discard the skin. Transfer the fillets to plates. Serve with orzo pasta and new peas.

Mashed Peas with Tarragon Cream
Serves 4

⅓ cup heavy cream

1 tablespoon cold unsalted butter

½ teaspoon salt

1 teaspoon dried tarragon

1 cup water

3 cups frozen peas

Salt and pepper to taste

Warm the cream, butter, salt, and tarragon in a small sauce-pan over medium-low. Heat until the butter has melted, but do not let it boil. Cover the pan, turn off the heat, and allow the mixture to steep while you prepare the peas.

Place the water in a medium-size saucepan over high heat and bring to a rapid boil. Add the peas, cover the pan, and bring the contents back up to a boil. Then, lower the heat and simmer the peas for 3 to 5 minutes. Drain.

Pour the cream through a fine mesh colander, and into the pot of peas. Discard the tarragon. Mash the peas with a potato masher until they reach your preferred consistency. Season with salt and pepper. Serve immediately.

Roasted Strawberry Tarragon Mousse
Serves 4

You can roast the strawberries ahead of time. They will keep in the refrigerator for a few days.

1 pint hulled strawberries, patted dry, plus 4 whole
   strawberries for garnish

8 sprigs fresh tarragon, divided

½ cup sugar

1 ½ tablespoons fresh lemon juice

1 scant tablespoon (1 packet) unflavored gelatin

6 tablespoons hot water

1 ⅓ cups whipping cream

1 teaspoon vanilla extract

1 cup (about 12) shortbread cookies, crushed

Preheat oven to 350°F. Place hulled strawberries and 4 tarra-gon sprigs in a glass baking dish. Sprinkle with sugar and lemon juice, and toss to coat. Roast for about 30 minutes, stirring occasionally, until strawberries soften and give up their juice. Set aside to cool.

Remove and discard the tarragon sprigs. Use a spoon or spatula to break up the strawberries into smaller pieces. To speed up the cooling process, you can scrape the strawberries and juices into a nonreactive bowl and set inside another bowl filled with ice water or chill in the refrigerator.

Place the gelatin in a small bowl and add the hot water. Stir until it dissolves, then add to the bowl containing the strawberries. Stir frequently until the gelatin starts to set, coating the spoon in a thin layer. This should take about 10 minutes.

Beat whipping cream and vanilla in chilled bowl with an electric mixer until it holds peaks. Fold three-fourths of the whipped cream into the strawberries until the mixture is tinged pink.

Assemble the dessert by alternating layers of mousse, cookie crumbs, and plain whipped cream into tall glasses. Garnish each with a whole strawberry and sprig of tarragon.

Blackberry and Tarragon Popsicles
Makes 6–8

The tarragon shines through in this simple summertime treat. You will need either a popsicle mold with sticks or an ice cube tray with toothpicks. If there is any leftover after filling the popsicle molds, freeze in an ice cube tray and add to cocktails or lemonade. The sugar is first incorporated into a simple syrup before mixing with the blackberries, so it can be made ahead and stored in the refrigerator for about three months. Feel free to reduce the amount of simple syrup used in the popsicles. It is also possible to replace a portion of the syrup with gin or vodka.

1 cup sugar

½ cup water

1 ½ pints blackberries

⅛ cup fresh tarragon leaves

¼ cup fresh lemon juice

To make the simple syrup, bring the sugar and water to a boil in a small saucepan over high heat, stirring frequently. Cover, reduce the heat, and simmer for 5 minutes. Remove from the heat and allow to cool completely. At this point the syrup can be stored in the refrigerator for up to three months.

Place the blackberries, tarragon, lemon juice, and 1 cup of simple syrup into a blender. Purée until smooth. Strain the mixture into a bowl through a fine sieve. Use a spatula to stir the sieve's contents when the seeds begin to block the holes. Divide the bowl's contents into popsicle molds, insert sticks, and freeze overnight.

For Further Reading

Gilbert, Linda. "Tarragon." *Sally's Place.* www.sallybernstein .com/food/columns/gilbert/tarragon.htm.

Hemphill, John and Rosemary. *What Herb Is That?: How to Grow and Use the Culinary Herbs.* Mechanicsburg, PA: Stackpole Books, 1997.

Hollis, Sarah. *The Country Diary Herbal.* New York: Henry Holt & Company, 1990.

Mathiot, Ginette. *I Know How to Cook.* New York: Phaidon Press, 2009.

McVicar, Jekka. *Jekka's Herb Cookbook.* Buffalo, NY: Firefly Books, Ltd., 2012.

Murray, Michael T., Joseph Pizzorno, and Lara Pizzorno. *The Encyclopedia of Healing Foods*. New York: Atria Books, 2005.

Potterton, David (ed.). *Culpeper's Color Herbal*. New York: Sterling Publishing Co., Inc., 2007.

Witty, Helen. *The Good Stuff Cookbook*. New York: Workman Publishing, 1997.

Anne Sala *is a freelance journalist from Minnesota. This summer, her herbs did not thrive due to unseasonably cold weather. Nevertheless, her two children delighted in every plant and happily harvested leaves for hot tea—bringing the aroma and warmth of summer to their bellies if not to their skin.*

Boletes: Friendly Fungi for the Foraging Herbalist

⮞ By Cliff Seruntine ⮜

In a world where the vast majority of people have forgotten that all domestic foods were bred from original wild stock, folk tend to lose sight of the fact that things like lettuce started their existence as plants very closely related to the common dandelion, and potatoes as well as tomatoes began their existence as plants closely related to nightshade.

Having forgotten such things, many people view wild foraging with suspicion. My wife and I live on a sprawling homestead deep in the Canadian North Woods, and usually when I forage wild foods I am off someplace remote, but sometimes, like if I happen to be on a supply run to one of the villages, I might espy something in a park or hedge and snag it. Harvesting wild foods where others can see never fails to garner strange and curious looks of alarm.

Once while in the village, I came across a thicket of wild cherries in a little park beside a river. I pulled over to gather them, and as I was sweeping the little fruit from the branch into a cloth bag I always keep with me, a passerby paused to observe what I was doing. Her face slowly screwed into an image of horror as she realized I meant to eat them later.

"Don't you know those are poisonous?" she said.

I replied, "No, they're just wild cherries." I explained that wild cherries are bitter raw, but when simmered to a pulp and cut with a little tart juice, they made excellent jelly or syrup.

But she held fast to her position. "No! My mother told me they are poison!"

"I'm sorry, but your mother was wrong," I told her. Of course, people rarely ever take being told their mother is wrong very well. The woman studied me as if I were some kind of bug, then turned on her heal and stormed away. But I simply wasn't going to dump my bagful of lovely wild cherries because of her mother's misconceptions.

And if you think harvesting wild plants gets odd looks, if I happen to snag some wild mushrooms growing in one of those little parks, some people have conniptions. Another time in the village I saw some dryad saddles growing on a massive, fallen poplar—enough mushrooms to fill most of my cloth grocery sack. I was sawing away at the third or fourth mushroom stem with my folding knife when a jogger approached.

Without any preamble, he declared, "Dear god! You'll die if you eat that!"

I replied, "Oh, no, it's just a dryad saddle."

"It's tree mold! If it kills trees it'll kill you, too!"

I shrugged and dropped the fungus into my bag. "Well, when you think about it, all fungi are mold; even the agaricus bisporus they sell at the grocery…"

"What the grocer sells is a mushroom. That's totally different!" he interrupted.

"This fungus grows on dead wood," I said. "The store mushroom grows on chicken manure. I'd rather eat this one."

"You have a lot to learn, buddy!" he declared and then jogged away.

I did learn a lot that day. I learned that dryad saddles sliced thin and sauteed in garlic venison gravy are awesome. But the simple fact is that in a world where most of the old, traditional skills of living by the land have been forgotten; contemporary people fear foraging wild foods. In particular, mushrooms really terrify a lot of people. I have a friend who is retired British military and runs a bushcraft school. He's a pretty tough, courageous guy, but he simply won't touch wild mushrooms.

"It's too hard to tell which is which," he declared once to me.

Yet, it really is no harder than learning to tell one plant from another. Just like fruit and herbs, you have to know what to look for. In this article I'm going to introduce you to a class of my favorite edible mushroom, the bolete, and its close cousin, the leccinum. I have chosen this type of mushroom because it is easily distinguished from other mushrooms, and while some members of the class are poisonous, none are deadly. If you eat a bad bolete or leccinum, you're in for a couple days of stomach cramps and flulike symptoms, but unless you have an unusual allergy, that's about it.

Gilled versus Non-Gilled Mushrooms

Mushrooms come in all shapes and sizes. For example, witch's butter is a rubbery fungi that feeds on dead trees. It is a pretty, yellow blob of no particular shape. But for our purposes, we are only going to deal with the mushrooms that people tend to think of as classically shaped, which is to say they have stems and caps.

There are many species of mushrooms that follow this general pattern, and they are divided into gilled and non-gilled types. Gilled mushrooms include amanitas, russulas, agaricus, and others. The mushroom commonly sold on grocery store shelves—agaricus bisporus—is an example of a gilled mushroom. If you turn it over and look under the cap, you will see paper-thin sheets running from the stem to the cap. Any student of mushrooming learns quickly that most of the seriously toxic mushrooms are found among the gilled fungi. Some are absolutely lethal, like the destroying angel, of the Amanita family. Identifying good from bad gilled mushrooms can be tricky, even for an expert. I've been harvesting wild mushrooms for a long time, but I don't consider gilled mushrooms worth the risk. So for my part, I avoid all of them except the honey mushroom, shaggymane, and the oyster mushroom, which I know well.

There are also many varieties of non-gilled mushrooms, including morels, chanterelles, and our subject of interest, boletes. We are going to focus on boletes because this class has many delicious edibles, and while some are poisonous, they are easily distinguished, and none are deadly.

The bolete has a classic form, which is to say it has a stem and cap. However, if you flip over the cap you will clearly see it does not have gills. Rather, the underside (with a few exceptions; there are always exceptions in the mushroom world) appears to be a dense sponge. The spongy side is actually a mass of spore tubes. In some boletes, they are closely packed and the individual tubes are virtually indistinguishable unless you study them through a loupe. Among other boletes, the spore tubes are large enough that they can be distinguished with the naked eye.

Boletes all share the following characteristics:

- Under the cap they are spongy. They *never* have gills. (If in doubt, throw it out!)

- They have a central stem, which is to say the stem joins the cap at the center.

- The spongy area is a tube layer that can (if desired) be peeled away without too much trouble.

- They have soft but firm flesh.

- They grow from the ground, never out of wood, or dung, or other growing medium.

- They almost always grow within a few yards of trees.

Some boletes have straight stems like other mushrooms, but the stems always join the cap at the center. The stems may feel smooth or reticulated (as if a fine webbing has been laid over them). The caps may feel dry (especially after a rain) or a bit sticky, as if they have been glazed with honey. If the cap feels slimy it's a member of the bolete family called suilus, which are not covered in this article, so avoid it for now.

Some boletes have rough or fuzzy stems. These are leccinums. Their stems are covered with a feature called *scabers*:

small protrusions like tiny, soft scales. For identification and cooking, treat leccinums as boletes with one exception (covered below).

Edible versus Inedible Boletes

Most boletes are edible, but a few are poisonous. None are known to be deadly, though there have been a few cases in which people had very strong reactions to the poisonous ones and died. It is astronomically rare that anyone dies from eating a poisonous bolete, though. I tend to think of a death as more like an allergic reaction—more an issue of the mushroomer's constitution. However, toxic boletes are easily identified, making this class of mushrooms one of the safest for the forager.

When harvesting boletes, simply *test for the blues*. Avoid anything that bruises or cuts blue. Some mushroom guides say you only need to avoid boletes with orange, red, or bright yellow undersides that bruise or cut blue. But mushroomers have a saying: "There are old mushroomers and there are bold mushroomers, but there are no old, bold mushroomers." They also say every mushroomer will eventually eat a mildly poisonous mushroom and suffer cramps. I have never gotten sick from mushrooms because I am exceedingly cautious with them. It's up to you, but I recommend you simply avoid any bolete that bruises or cuts blue.

To test for the blues, pinch a corner when you harvest a bolete. If it turns blue in a few seconds, discard it. If it doesn't, bag it and check again at home. When you get home with your harvest, see if the bruise has turned blue. If not, do a cut test. This will expose the bolete's flesh to air, which may cause a color change. Slice the cap and stem in half and set them aside. Pinch one corner of a half and wait four hours. If any blue appears, discard it. If not, it's a keeper.

Regarding leccinums, check for the blues but also discard any leccinums with orange caps (upper or underside). Now, only one or two species of orange capped leccinums are poisonous, and that refers to the upper side, but better to err on the side of caution.

If you make a mistake, you'll experience something like a stomach flu for a day or two. Drink fluids and consult a doctor, but it'll pass. However, it's so easy to sort good from bad boletes and leccinums that you should never have a problem.

Harvesting Boletes

Harvesting boletes is easy. When you spot one just pluck it by the base of the stem from the ground. While in the field carry them in a cloth bag or some kind of airy basket—never keep them in plastic. Mushrooms will begin to spoil almost immediately if kept in plastic.

Boletes do have one big problem: bugs and worms love them! From a bug's perspective it's a giant, tasty packet of nutritious protein. It's tragic, really. Boletes can become huge, and I've harvested a few with caps some nine inches across weighing nearly two pounds. But it's rare to find usable ones so big because, usually by that time, the bugs are well into them.

So, when you harvest, check the bolete for insect damage. If it's heavily infested, leave it. If it's only lightly damaged and passes the blues test, take it home, slice it thin, and remove the odd worm or bug that may be tunnelling through the mushroom's flesh. The bugs don't spoil the mushroom, and once they are gone, you can still use it. If you are fast to the woods after a rain, though, you can often find young- to middle-age boletes free (or nearly so) of insect or worm damage.

Preserving and Preparing Boletes

Boletes are delicious fresh, but their flavor actually improves if they are dried and stored a while. To dry them, simply slice them thin (no thicker than one-fifth of an inch) and dry them outdoors if the air is cooperative. If not, lay them out on a dehydrator. Dry until they are as firm as potato chips. Once dry, I lightly salt them to help them keep, then store them in a jar.

When you are ready to use them, just throw them directly in your pasta sauce or stew. If you want to fry them, rehydrate them in a bowl of water, just barely covering them, until they are again rubbery. Very few wild mushrooms can be digested raw by the human body, so note that you should *always* cook wild mushrooms before eating.

Further Reading

This article is only a start, and I strongly suggest further study before you start mushrooming. Learning to identify edible mushrooms is really no harder than learning to identify edible plants. The skill remains traditional in continental Europe where every spring, summer, and autumn, hoards of mushroomers wander the meadows and woods in quest of delectable fungi. In the United Kingdom and North America the skill has largely been forgotten, and wild fungi are viewed with grave suspicion. But the truth is that very few wild mushrooms are deadly. Learn to identify a few safe ones common to your area and you can enjoy a whole new kingdom of the natural world.

Boletes grow most everywhere, are fairly common, and are a very safe place for a new mushroomer to start. As you advance, you can learn to make healing poultices, styptics, and wondrous teas from other mushrooms as well. One of my favorite resources for the beginner is *100 Edible Mushrooms* by Michael Kuo. I also highly recommend joining a mushrooming club in your area because working with an expert can quickly instill new levels of confidence.

Good luck and happy hunting!

Cliff Seruntine *is a naturalist, a practicing shaman, a writer, a fiddler, and has a psychotherapist private practice. Since 2007, he has lived with his family on their semi-remote homestead where they teach classes on buschcraft and homesteading. Visit his blog at Cliff-Seruntine.wordpress.com.*

Pickling for Beginners

⤌ By Deborah Castellano ⤍

It took me a long time to get brave enough to make my own pickles. My more experienced friends assured me that traditional canning isn't that hard, but every time I would look at the procedures, all I would see are words like pressure cooker, botulism, and vacuum seal, and it sounded like an incredible amount of work to me; especially since I was just starting out.

My method of pickling is simpler, but there are drawbacks to my method, too. I make refrigerator pickles. Unlike traditionally canned pickles, these need to be kept in the refrigerator (not on the shelf) and they will only be good to eat for a week or two since they are not vacuum sealed.

However, using refrigerator-style pickling means that you have spent a lot less time and effort on your pickles. This is important because your first few batches may not turn out that great. It may take a few batches for you to figure out how crisp you like your vegetables, how you like your vegetables to be cut, what kind of vinegar you prefer, how much vinegar you like in your brine, and how much pickling spice you like in your batch. Refrigerator pickles are also more economical in terms of start-up costs verses traditional canning methods. A dozen Mason jars, a gallon of apple cider vinegar, spices, and a few pounds of vegetables only cost about twenty-five dollars. You can make several different kinds of pickles with that initial investment. If you find you're crazy for pickling, you can always look into learning more about canning and purchase canning supplies later.

Certain vegetables, like radishes, are available nearly year-round in the grocery store. Other vegetables, like kirby cucumbers, are only available during certain times of the year. Shopping with seasonality in mind will also help you get the most budget-friendly prices. I personally prefer to shop at my local farmers' market for pickling because it helps support local agriculture, and I know the vegetables available are at the peak of freshness. If you are new to shopping at farmers' markets and tracking seasonality, two websites that can assist you are:

- Vegetable seasonality: www.cuesa.org/eat-seasonally /charts/vegetables

- Local farmers' market finder: www.localharvest.org

Pickling Recipes

Your pickling mix is your first step, and it's an important one. If you're like me and have only previously eaten commercially prepared pickles, a traditional pickle spice mix may taste very strange to you. I tried to acquire a taste for it, but I couldn't. I'm not a delicate flower when it comes to food. My palate has been described by my family as "garbage dumpsterlike." Try as I did, I just couldn't get used to sweet spices being involved in my pickles. If you have a taste for sweet pickles like bread and butter pickles, it may be an easier hurdle for you to become accustomed to having cinnamon and allspice in your mix. Personally, I like my pickles to taste a bit tart. You can always add additional spices later when you get a better feel for your pickling palate.

I tried fresh herbs in some of my earlier batches, and while they did look very pretty in the bottle, I found that dried herbs really packed the most punch in my pickles. High quality herbs also really help make a good spice mix. If you have a local spice shop, the herbs are generally really fresh and they let you buy herbs in small, economical one-ounce bags. If you don't have a spice shop close to you, I recommend buying from SavorySpiceShop.com. Their prices are very good, their spices are very fresh, and they sell in both small and large quantities.

Pickling Spice Mix

> 2 tablespoons whole mustard seeds
>
> 1 tablespoon whole allspice berries
>
> 2 teaspoons whole coriander seeds

2 teaspoons whole peppercorns

2 bay leaves, crushed

Mix the spices together and keep in an airtight jar.

Dill Cucumber Pickles

Pint and a half wide-mouth Mason jar

3 small kirby cucumbers, cut into spears

2 tablespoons ground dill seeds

3 tablespoons pickling spice

1 clove garlic, chopped

1 tablespoon sea salt

1 cup apple cider vinegar

Water

Make sure your Mason jar has been through the dishwasher, or boiled for 15 minutes, right before you begin pickling so you have a reasonably sterile jar. Put everything but the water into a medium-sized pot and simmer for about 15 minutes. Then let your vegetables cool for 10 minutes. Pour into the Mason jar. Fill the Mason jar the rest of the way with water. Put the ring and the lid on the jar, and seal it shut. Label and date your lid. Give your jar a good shake, and put in the refrigerator. Let brine for 3 days, and then it will be ready to eat. Keep for no longer than a week and a half.

Pickled Asparagus

Pint and a half wide-mouth Mason jar

1 cup apple cider vinegar

½ bunch asparagus, trimmed

2 tablespoons ground dill seeds

3 tablespoons pickling spice

1 clove garlic, chopped

1 tablespoon sea salt

½ lemon, sliced

Water

Make sure your Mason jar has been through the dishwasher, or boiled for 15 minutes, right before you begin pickling so you have a reasonably sterile jar. Fill about a third of your Mason jar with apple cider vinegar. Then pour into a medium-sized pot. Put everything but the water into the pot, and simmer on low heat for about 15 minutes. Shut the heat off, and let your vegetables cool for 10 minutes. Put your asparagus into the Mason jar so that the asparagus is standing up. Pour the brine into the Mason jar. Fill the Mason jar the rest of the way with water. Put the ring and the lid on the jar, and seal it shut. Label and date your lid. Give your jar a good shake, and put in the refrigerator. Let brine for 3 days, and then it will be ready to eat. Keep for no longer than a week and a half.

Farm Stand Mixed Pickle

Pint and a half wide-mouth Mason jar

1 cup apple cider vinegar

6 small whole radishes

1 small carrot, sliced

6 mushrooms, sliced in halves

1 shallot, sliced

2 tablespoons ground dill seeds

3 tablespoons pickling spice mix

1 clove garlic, chopped

1 tablespoon sea salt

Water

Make sure your Mason jar has been through the dishwasher, or boiled for 15 minutes, right before you begin pickling so you have a reasonably sterile jar. Fill about a third of your Mason jar with apple cider vinegar. Pour into a medium-sized pot. Put everything but the water into the pot, and simmer on low heat for about 15 minutes. Shut the heat off. Let your vegetables cool for 10 minutes. Pour into the Mason jar. Fill the Mason jar the rest of the way with water. Put the ring and the lid on the jar, and seal it shut. Label and date your lid. Give your jar a good shake, and put in the refrigerator. Let brine for 3 days, and then it will be ready to eat. Keep for no longer than a week and a half.

Dilly Beans

Pint and a half wide-mouth Mason jar

1 cup apple cider vinegar

1 handful string beans, trimmed

3 tablespoons ground dill seeds

2 tablespoons pickling spice mix

1 clove garlic, chopped

1 tablespoon sea salt

Water

Make sure your Mason jar has been through the dishwasher, or boiled for 15 minutes, right before you begin pickling so you have a reasonably sterile jar. Fill about a third of your Mason jar with apple cider vinegar. Pour into a medium-sized pot. Put everything but the water into the pot, and simmer on low heat for about 15 minutes. Shut the heat off. Let your vegetables cool for 10 minutes. Pour into the Mason jar. Fill the Mason jar the rest of the way with water. Put the ring and the lid on the jar, and seal it shut. Label and date your lid. Give your jar a good shake, and put in the refrigerator. Let brine for 3 days, and then it will be ready to eat. Keep for no longer than a week and a half.

Pickled Fennel

   Pint and a half wide-mouth Mason jar

   1 cup apple cider vinegar

   1 small bulb fennel, including the fern fronds, sliced

   1 tablespoon ground dill seeds

   3 tablespoons pickling spice mix

   1 clove garlic, chopped

   ½ lemon, sliced

   1 tablespoon sea salt

   Water

Make sure your Mason jar has been through the dishwasher, or boiled for 15 minutes, right before you begin pickling so you have a reasonably sterile jar. Fill about a third of your Mason jar with apple cider vinegar. Pour into a medium sized pot. Put everything but the water into the pot, and simmer on low heat for about 15 minutes. Shut the heat off. Let your vegetables cool for 10 minutes. Pour into the Mason jar. Fill the Mason jar the rest of the way with water. Put the ring and the lid on the jar, and seal it shut. Label and date your lid. Give your jar a good shake, and put in the refrigerator. Let brine for 3 days, and then it will be ready to eat. Keep for no longer than a week and a half.

Giardiniera

Pint and a half wide-mouth Mason jar

1 cup apple cider vinegar

8 pearl onions, peeled

1 small carrot, cut into strips

2 ribs celery, chopped

1 small zucchini, cut into strips

¼ cup cauliflower, chopped into small florets

1 teaspoon oregano

3 tablespoons pickling spice mix

2 cloves garlic, chopped

1 tablespoon sea salt

Water

Make sure your Mason jar has been through the dishwasher, or boiled for 15 minutes, right before you begin pickling so you have a reasonably sterile jar. Fill about a third of your Mason jar with apple cider vinegar. Pour into a medium-sized pot. Put everything but the water into the pot, and simmer on low heat for about 15 minutes. Shut the heat off. Let your vegetables cool for 10 minutes. Pour into the Mason jar. Fill the Mason jar the rest of the way with water. Put the ring and the lid on the jar, and seal it shut. Label and date your lid. Give your jar a good shake, and put in the refrigerator. Let brine for 3 days, and then it will be ready to eat. Keep for no longer than a week and a half.

Pickled Fiddlehead Ferns and Ramps

Note: Fiddlehead ferns and ramps have a very short season during the spring. Generally, specialty grocery stores will carry both, so check with them when they usually get them in so you can claim some for yourself!

Pint and a half wide-mouth Mason jar

1 cup apple cider vinegar

½ cup fiddlehead ferns, trimmed

1 teaspoon ground dill seeds

3 tablespoons pickling spice mix

1 clove garlic, chopped

½ lemon, sliced

1 tablespoon sea salt

¼ cup ramps, trimmed

Water

Make sure your Mason jar has been through the dishwasher, or boiled for 15 minutes, right before you begin pickling so you have a reasonably sterile jar. Fill about a third of your Mason jar with apple cider vinegar. Pour into a medium-sized pot. Put everything except for the water and ramps into the pot, and simmer on low heat for about 15 minutes. Shut the heat off and add the ramps, while you let your vegetables cool for 10 minutes. Pour into the Mason jar. Fill the Mason jar the rest of the way with water. Put the ring and the lid on the jar, and seal it shut. Label and date your lid. Give your jar a good shake, and put in the refrigerator. Let brine for 3 days, and then it will be ready to eat. Keep for no longer than a week and a half.

Deborah Castellano *enjoys writing about earth-based topics, though she has been known to write romantic fiction as well. Her craft shop, The Mermaid and The Crow, specializes in handspun yarn and other goodies. She resides in New Jersey with her husband, Jow, and two cats. She has a terrible reality television habit she can't shake and likes St. Germain liqueur, record players, and typewriters. Visit her at www.deborahmcastellano.com.*

Herbs for Health and Beauty

What the Bee Knows: The Happy Herbs

❧ By Tiffany Lazic ❧

D epression. Ten percent of individuals in countries like the US, the UK, and Canada will experience it. Characterized by feelings of deep sadness, negative thought patterns, apathy, and disruptive eating and sleeping patterns, depression can interfere with all aspects of life, including the ability to function at work and interpersonal relationships. "Having the blues" can feel more like "having the grays" with all the color, lightness, and joy drained out of life.

There are several types of depression. Although the experience can feel the same, there are different contributing factors. Two main delineations encompass most cases of depression: clinical depression and situational depression.

Situational depression can result out of a reaction to a devastating life event, such as death of a loved one, job loss, or divorce. It occurs as a natural response to a life challenge indicating that we are in the grips of the grieving process.

Clinical depression can be initially triggered by a life event, but continues long after the apparent resolution of the challenge. In the case of job loss, the depression continues even after employment has been retained. If there is no identifiable life event that can be attributed to depression, this can also be an indication of clinical depression. It arises from nothing external and nothing seems to contribute to relief of the symptoms.

Depression is not a modern phenomenon. Melancholia was the ancient term, dating back to the fifth century BCE, to describe symptoms of sadness or dejection of the mind, characterized by fears and despondencies. Before the advent of modern pharmaceuticals the ancients turned to other means to balance the dispirited person. In the natural world there were many options that evidently alleviated the depressive symptoms.

All herbs have many different benefits and can be used to address a variety of issues. Each herb also has its own kind of personality. Working with herbs can become like meeting up with familiar friends. You know who to turn to for exactly what you need in that moment. Following the trail of the pollen gathering bee can lead us to many of these friends who support us in a variety of ways to ease anxiety, provide confidence, and lift the spirit.

Bee Balm *(Monarda didyma and Monarda fistulosa)*

Bee balm, which is also sometimes referred to as wild bergamot, is a pungent herb that blooms red, pink, or purple flowers sprouting from the top of the plant like a wonderful, wild hairdo. Confusingly, there is also a fruit-bearing tree, the bergamot orange, named for the Italian city of Bergamo. Wild bergamot is part of the mint family and not connected with the tree at all.

Bee balm, well-known for attracting bees, butterflies, and hummingbirds, is strongly antiseptic and was used in days of old as a mouthwash. The Blackfoot tribe drank a hot concoction made of bee balm and shared this warming drink with American patriots who were loath to drink British tea after the Boston Tea Party. This became known as oswego tea. As all parts of the above ground herb are edible, it provides a colorful and cheery addition to cooked foods and salads.

As with many herbs, bee balm can be used to alleviate numerous physical symptoms and disorders, from gastrointestinal to menstrual to bronchial. It has, as a healing theme, the sense of soothing that which has flared up and become inflamed. It is gentle, calming, and uplifting, bringing a lightness of energy. There is something so joyful about bee balm. Named very aptly, it is like a balm for the soul. It encourages releasing that which agitates us and reconnects us to that which fosters enjoyment of life. Bee balm is the eternal optimist that helps us see past the challenge to the ease.

Bee Balm Tincture

Fill a Mason jar with fresh leaves and flowers, and cover with either alcohol (80 proof vodka is recommended) or glycerin. For alcohol, shake the jar every day for ten days. For glycerin, allow to steep for four to six weeks, ensuring there are no air pockets. After the required time frame, strain the leaves and flowers from the liquid, and store. The tincture can be used several times daily.

Alcohol-based tinctures last for years, however, glycerites have a shelf life of one to two years.

Borage *(Borago officinalis)*

Borage is an annual herb that grows quickly from seed to plant, offering up beautiful sky blue, star-shaped flowers, giving borage its alternate name, starflower. It also goes by the names bee bread or bee plant. It does well in temperate growing zones, flowering from June to September. Both leaves and flowers can be used medicinally. You want to harvest the leaves when the plant is coming into flower, but handle with care. Prickly hairs cover the leaves and stems, so gloves are recommended when harvesting.

There is some thought that the name borage derives from a corruption of *cor* and *ago*, Latin for "I bring the heart," or from *barrach*, the Gaelic name for the plant, which translates as "man of courage." This association between borage and the fortitude of the heart is reflected in the Scottish saying "I borage bring courage." And the Romans are said to have made an elixir created from borage, which was used to raise confidence.

Borage has a light, cucumber-y taste that is cleansing and refreshing. Its leaves and flowers can be served as a tea, helping with stress and depression. Its sleep-inducing properties alleviate fatigue and exhaustion, and offer adrenal support. Caution must be exercised if using seeds, including borage seed oil, as they contain pyrrolizidine alkaloids, which can cause liver damage.

Borage's personality is like Gimli the Dwarf in *The Lord of the Rings*: strong, determined, and courageous with a sharp sense of humor. It serves to bolster us in trying times and gives us vitality.

Borage Tea

Pour a cup of boiling water over ¼ cup of chopped leaves and flowers. Steep for 10 minutes. Strain and serve.

Heather *(Calluna vulgaris)*

Heather is a small perennial shrub that bears tiny purple or white bell-shaped flowers that flower from July to September. Flowering stems are best collected in the fall. It has been long associated with the Scottish moors, evoking visions of an endless purple expanse. Heather grows well in temperate zones and likes a lot of sunlight, but it has a strong and hardy nature. It grows well in dry soil, and seems able to resist the cold—an important factor for thriving in the Highlands.

Purple heather is said to bring joy and is a traditional housewarming gift to bring blessings to a new household. With a delicate scent and calming effects, it was used in the Highlands to make heather mattresses, laying the flowering tops of the branches toward the head of the bed. Less common than the purple variety, white heather was thought to bring luck and to grow in places where fairies rested.

There is a beautiful delicacy to heather, which belies the strength and hardiness that lies at its core. Heather's healing energy gives a message that one can walk a challenging path with a lightness of step, and it helps us bring to mind that there may be magic around the corner. Heather is the innocent who connects us to the beauty in the world.

Heather Sachet

Simply place several handfuls of dried heather flowers into a small fabric bag with a drawstring and close. Alternately, cut fabric with an uplifting or soothing pattern into a rectangle.

The size is a matter of personal choice. Fold the fabric in half, pattern-side out, and sew up the two sides, leaving the top open. Turn the sachet inside out so that the pattern is now on the outside, and fill with heather flowers. Sew along the top, taking care to fully close your calming sachet.

Lavender *(Lavendula officinalis)*

What heather is to the Highlands, lavender is to France. It is a beautiful, hardy shrub with flowers that range in color from dark to light purple and white, including the shade that it gives its name. The gorgeous image of purple lavender fields in Provence is often enough to prompt the olfactory response of its familiar scent. As with heather, it prefers sunny places and does well in dry soil. It flowers from June to September and is best harvested just before the flowers open.

Lavender has long been known for its calming benefits. The delicate scent from its flowers are used in everything from soaps to perfumes and potpourris. As well as alleviating symptoms of depression, lavender can soothe in times of restlessness or agitation. It is used to relieve migraines, which from a psychosomatic perspective are linked to repressed anger and negative thoughts, both of which contribute to depression.

Lavender's healing energy is like being enfolded in the comforting arms of a beloved grandmother. It offers respite from negativity and hardship. It is the soft sanctuary that restores us to be able to enter into the fray once again.

Lavender Cookies

½ cup butter, at room temperature

1 cup sugar

2 eggs

½ teaspoon vanilla extract

1 teaspoon lavender flowers, certified organic or wild-crafted

1 ½ cups all-purpose flour

2 teaspoons baking powder

Preheat oven to 375°F. Cream together the butter and sugar. Beat eggs, vanilla, and lavender flowers into the mixture. Combine flour and baking powder separately, then stir into mixture until well-blended. Drop teaspoon-sized balls onto ungreased cookie tray, and bake for 8 to 10 minutes or until lightly brown.

Rosemary *(Rosmarimus officinalis)*

Three herbs are said to connect with feminine cycles. At one end of the spectrum there is the youth of thyme that refreshes. At the other end of the spectrum there is the age-less wisdom of sage. Bridging them is rosemary, the herb that centers.

Rosemary is a hardy evergreen that produces blue, pink, or white flowers in the late spring and mild weather. Its long, thin leaves are best known for culinary purposes, used both to flavor meat dishes and as an addition to vegetables and salad dressings. Though it has a sharp, pungent smell, rosemary tends to calm and restore.

Rosemary is a stimulant that can alleviate muscle pain, improve memory, and boost the immune system. Its healing energy is like the encouraging mother, helping us to connect with that which is best in ourselves. Rosemary awakens and invigorates, guiding us to see the light at the end of the tunnel, and letting us know that we have what it takes within ourselves to reach that point.

Rosemary Dressing

> 1 clove minced garlic
>
> 2 tablespoons honey
>
> 3 tablespoons rice vinegar
>
> 2 teaspoons Dijon mustard
>
> 2 teaspoons fresh rosemary leaves, chopped
>
> ½ cup virgin olive oil
>
> Salt and pepper (optional)

Place all ingredients, except for olive oil and salt/pepper, in a bowl, and whisk until blended. Slowly add the olive oil. If you choose, add salt and pepper to taste.

White Sage *(Salvia apiana)*

Entering the world of the sages is like stepping into a vast smorgasbord of possibility, making it virtually impossible to describe briefly. Garden or kitchen sage *(Salvia officinalis)* is a common culinary herb that has been well known and well used for centuries, but there is a seemingly endless variety of sage available, including the clary sages and the chia sages. Not every sage is ingestible. Some, such as Russian sage, are far better suited to use for their beautiful scent.

The Latin *salvia* means "to heal" or "to save." It gives us the words salve and salvation, both of which offer a sense of the sage's power to support health, both in body and in spirit. It is a stimulant known for relieving conditions of a weak digestion, as well as reducing fevers and calming nervous conditions. White sage, in particular, has come to be associated with use in ceremony and for purification. Known as bee sage, it helps to bring a sense of centeredness and sacredness of purpose when burned in a smudge stick.

All sages, as the name would imply, have the personality of the elder who guides us with heart and objectivity. Sage helps us to rise above what may be keeping us stuck to see the big picture, and to know in our hearts that "this too shall pass."

Sage Smudge
Bundle several branches of fresh white sage together with a length of twine. Wrap the twine several times around the base, leaving a short piece of the twine as a tail. Continue to wrap up to the top, and back down again, knotting the remaining twine with the tail to secure the wrapping. Hang your bundle in a cool, shaded location. When it is dry, it is ready to use.

Wild Thyme *(Thymus serpyllum)*

Thyme, like sage, is an herb of tremendous variety, the most familiar of which is the culinary plant, garden thyme *(Thymus vulgaris)*. It is low-lying and shrub-like with flowering tops that should be collected between June and August.

Thyme, with its youthful association, reduces tiredness, bringing courage and strength, particularly if one feels drained after a long illness or challenge. Wild thyme, which is much favored by honeybees, has a wonderfully uplifting lemon scent that dispels the heaviness of depression.

All thymes have the personality of determination and energy often associated with youth. Not the innocence of heather, instead thyme is the seeker who encourages us to continue on, opening us to explore the mysterious, and providing balance to energy stores so we do not feel overwhelmed by our experiences and adventures.

Thyme Bath
Add several springs of thyme to your bath to bring energy levels to a healthy, balanced flow.

A Balance of Options

When dealing with issues of mental and emotional health, it is very important to be discerning about one's options for treatment. The bee knows the many herbs that bring feelings of peace and calm. However, there are many instances where it is also important to consider seeking professional help, particularly if one is dealing with clinical depression. If one is taking prescribed medication, it is also important to check for possible negative interactions between the herbal and pharmaceutical approaches.

Regardless of whether we use herbs for ingesting, as in foods and teas, or whether we are introducing them into our environment as in sachets and baths, the bee leads us to those happy herbs that bring sweetness back into our lives. The bee teaches us to savor the nectar offered by nature, and to see life as an expansive field waiting to be explored with joy and wonder. And the bee knows that it is through our experiences, as we travel up hill and down dale, that we gather all we need to create the stuff of potent healing and nourishment.

For Further Study

Culpeper, Nicholas. *Culpeper's Complete Herbal: A Book of Natural Remedies for Ancient Ills*. London: Wordsworth Editions, 1995.

Grieve, M. A. *Modern Herbal: The Medicinal, Culinary, Cosmetic, and Economic Properties, Cultivation and Folk-lore of Herbs, Grasses, Fungi, Shrubs, & Trees with All Their Modern Scientific Uses*. New York: Dover Publications, 1971.

Hoffman, David. *Holistic Herbal: A Safe and Practical Guide to Making and Using Herbal Remedies*. London: Thorsons, 2002.

Hopman, Ellen Evert. *Scottish Herbs and Fairy Lore*. Los Angeles: Pendraig Publishing, 2011.

Paine, Angela. *The Healing Power of Celtic Plants: Their History, Their Use, and the Scientific Evidence That They Work*. Winchester, UK: O Books, 2006.

Tiffany Lazic *is a Spiritual Psychotherapist with over sixteen years experience in individual, couples, and group therapy. As the owner of The Hive and Grove Centre for Holistic Wellness, she created and teaches two self-development programs, Patterns of Conscious Living Program and Spiritual Language of the Divine Program, as well as teaching in the Transformational Arts College of Spiritual and Holistic Training's Spiritual Directorship and Divine Connections Training Programs. An international presenter and keynote speaker, Tiffany has conducted workshops for many conferences and organizations in Canada and the UK, including the 2013 Energy Psychology Conference. She is a member of the Sisterhood of*

Avalon where she serves on the Board of Trustees and in the Avalo-
nian Thealogical Seminary. She is the local coordinator for Kitch-
ener's Red Tent Temple. Tiffany is the author of The Great Work:
Self-Knowledge and Healing Through the Wheel of the Year
(Llewellyn, 2015).

Quell Your Anxiety with Plant Spirit Energy

⤞ By Stephanie Rose Bird ⤝

L ife in the twenty-first century makes it impossible to be a stranger to anxiety. It is a word you hear exchanged all too frequently wherever you go. It can sound casual, as in "I'm feeling anxious," yet it is also quite a serious disorder, especially when left unchecked. Increasingly, as our world gets more unbalanced and out of its natural order, people are reaching for pharmaceuticals, such as the prescription drug Xanax, to ease the debilitating effects of anxiety disorder.

Even though Xanax and similar medicines are easy to obtain, this type of treatment just doesn't feel right to many of us. Inside, we realize we mustn't forget our deep connection with the earth and her plentiful sources of remedies. Reaching deep into the earth there are safe and effective remedies to re-establish balance in our lives while alleviating anxiety. Earth remedies help us achieve these goals without wreaking havoc on our system. In Mother Nature lie time-tested, gentle curing agents that nurture the whole being, while setting the mind at ease.

Nature's Medicine Cabinet

One of the most effective ways of reconnecting with the earth's healing abilities, which helps reduce and combat anxiety, is utilizing plant energy. Using plants's spirit medicine, through herbalism and aromatherapy, allows us to bring to the fore plants' practical, useful, and gentle abilities to heal. This article will set you on the path to dealing with anxiety by employing the subtle energy of plants. I will share simple ways to utilize herbs and aromas as healing blends, which enable you to deal effectively with anxiety.

There are some time-honored herbs that will definitely reduce your anxiety. These herbs possess the capacity to calm your nerves to the extent where you can relax. To relax you must disengage from common stressors. Even if your concerns surpass the everyday and you are dealing with seriously stressful, life-changing occurrences, certain herbs will still ease your mind, leaving space for you to regenerate and face difficult challenges.

We are varied in many ways, including energy levels, as well as needs and approaches to healing. There are, thankfully, a wide variety of ways of engaging these anxiety-reducing herbs to suit all. Let's start in the morning and make our way through the day, adding in herbalism and aromatherapy designed to ease you out of an anxious state as you go.

Visualizing Mother Nature's medicine cabinet, you'll find as you read that there are many more helpful cures than you've previously thought. Yes, valerian, lavender, and chamomile are at the forefront, but there are others at the ready as well.

I'm going to take you through an imaginary day of healing, sourcing this cabinet that you will slowly build at home in real life. There are ripe times for herbal healing rituals throughout the day, thus they are highlighted.

Hitting the Water

You will probably be taking a shower to start your day. This is a good place to add in healing herbs, in the form of essential oils, to bolster your spirits.

Here is a cheery morning blend. You can imbue your shower with healing aromas that combat anxiety by trying a balancing blend. As I said, anxiety takes root in an unbalanced mind and spirit. This essential oil blend merges ancient and ethereal clary sage with spirit-brightening lime, grounded by the earthiness of fir.

- 1 drop clary sage
- 1 drop lime essential oil
- 1 drop fir

Run a hot shower. Drop one of each of these essential oils into your shower. The mist from the steaming water will rise and you will be enveloped in a balancing blend that will fortify your day. Tap back into the energy derived from this anti-anxiety shower throughout the day.

If you bathe instead of shower, simply add a drop of each of these oils to your bath water and enjoy the benefits.

Just a Dab

This is where you're still damp from cleansing yourself and your head is filled with strength for facing your day from the bolstering essential oil blend. After towel drying, add a dab of scent with staying power to reinforce your shower work using the power of aromatherapy.

- 1 drop palma rosa
- 1 drop rose otto
- 1 drop bergamot
- 1 drop sandalwood
- 1 teaspoon sweet almond oil

Mix these ingredients in a non-reactive bowl, such as a Pyrex dish, using a glass stirring wand. As you mix, breathe your intention of staying calm and balanced all day long into the bowl of oils.

Dab your pulse points gently with the oil before getting dressed and embarking on the rest of your day.

Relax with Herbal Teas

The simple act of making tea redirects your attention away from stimulating, busy activities, wherein you are ruminating on the sources of your anxiety, moving you instead toward a more tranquil state. Making a soulful cup of nurturing tea requires you to slow down and engage in the elements of water, fire, and plants—gifts from Mother Earth. As you make the following blend of antianxiety tea, recall what you know of tea's ancient history and its intimate connection with the elements of fire, water, and earth. Herbs you'll want as the foundation of your herbal tea are chamomile and lavender, with the addition of valerian if you can tolerate it. Lemon balm brings its own lemony charms to the table. Mix them as desired.

Chamomile (*Matricaria recultita*)

Chamomile is an ancient remedy for calming nervous energy. This perky, daisylike plant was used as a panacea in Egypt, Greece, Rome, and particularly in Europe during the Middle Ages. It has many powerful chemical components, including the flavonoid apinegrin and the volatile oil bisibolol. The reason you'll want to include it in your antianxiety tea is that it is sedative, relaxing, and antispasmodic.

Lavender (*Lavandula augustifolia; Lavandula officinalis*)

Lavender is a beautifully balancing and purifying herb, making it perfect to address a spirit that is on edge. It is notable that the name is derived from *lavare* ("to wash") because it cleanses away all sorts of ills. Its two chief chemical constituents are linalool and linalyl acetate. Useful in anxiety are its nervine, sedative, and antispasmodic properties.

Chamomile and lavender make a synergistic blend. They will work beautifully in concert to bring your energy into a calmer state. This is a nice way to engage with the earth by using herbs from your garden or farmer's market.

- 8 ounces water
- 1 tablespoon fresh chamomile flowers (if dried use half the amount)
- 1 tablespoon fresh lavender buds (if dried use half the amount)
- Honey, to taste

Bring water almost to a boil. While heating water, bless your flowers and buds, and then put them in a tea ball or tea bag. Turn off water when it begins to bubble. Let sit for a minute or two, and as it does, concentrate on grounding and centering away from anxiety. Pour water over tea bag or ball in a teacup. Cover. Infuse for 8 minutes. Remove the herbs. Sweeten with honey if desired.

Valerian (*Valeriana officinalis*)

Valerian, also called "all heal," is a very relaxing herb, though a bit stinky. It's not suitable for everyone and that's why I say, if you can tolerate it, use it. This is a very effective anti-anxiety herb with antispasmodic, hypnotic, relaxant, and nervine properties. Using a little will ease anxiety, but using too much will put you to sleep.

- 1 tablespoon valerian root, cut and sifted
- 8 ounces water

Put roots in pot of water. Simmer 15 minutes. Pour through a strainer into a cup. Sweeten as desired. Drink alone as is, or add to lemon balm brew, which follows.

Lemon Balm (*Melissa officinalis*)

This is a fragrant herb in the mint family of Lamiaceae. Well-known for its honeylike sweetness, lemon balm is calming and soothing. It has been used to treat anxiety and stress since the Middle Ages. It has numerous tannins, phytochemicals, and acids. The fresh leaves are aromatic and especially healing. You can mix this brew with the valerian tea previously shared. The two, like chamomile and lavender, work wonderfully together. Pick fresh leaves from the garden in the afternoon, respectfully saluting their energy force as you do so.

- 8 ounces water
- ½ cup fresh lemon balm leaves (¼ cup dried)

Bring water almost to a boil. Remove from heat when water starts to bubble. Set aside. Put leaves in tea bag or tea ball. Pour water over bag or ball in a teacup. Cover. Infuse while asking for assistance from the leaves in terms of healing medicine. Do this focus and infuse for 8 minutes. Remove herbs. Add to valerian or drink on its own.

Diffusing the Issues

Depending on your life/work situation, it may well be possible to use a calming essential oil blend throughout the day to quell anxiety. If you can't do it throughout the day, pick your time and use this lovely healing blend.

- Orange (*Citrus aurantium*) for anxiety
- Sandalwood (*Santalum album*) as a sedative
- Rose (*Rosa damascena*) eases nervous tension

Add a good amount of tap water to your diffuser. As you add the water, ask it to serve as a good receptor for the healing energy of your oils. Add a drop of each of the oils saying *away anxiety; calm me; and vanish nervous tension* with each addition. Swirl gently to mix the water and the three oils. Add a tea light candle to the bottom of the diffuser. Light it with the intention of the fire spreading the unique energy of each of the oils through your space, head, and heart.

Whiffs

In the Victorian times it was more common to see people inhaling healing vapors from their handkerchiefs. They knew that little infusions of scent throughout the day during challenging times fortify the spirit.

In closing, I want to remind you of this older practice and invite you to bring it into your daily calming practice. Here are some oils that calm anxiety, anytime and anywhere. All you need to add is one drop to your handkerchief or tissue and sniff.

- Marjoram (*Origanum majorana*)
- Hops (*Humulus lupulus*)
- Frankincense (*Boswellia carteri*)
- Lavender (*Lavandula augustifolia; L. officinalis*)

Each day that you struggle with anxiety, try any combination of these herbal remedies to help alleviate the strain being ill at ease puts on your mind, body, and spirit.

Stephanie Rose Bird *is a modern eclectic pagan. She practices Hoodoo, Green Witchcraft, and Shamanism. Deeply into painting, meditation, and yoga, she is also a creative visionary. She's had five books published:* Big Book of Soul; A Healing Grove; Light, Bright, Damn Near White; Sticks, Stones, Roots and Bones; *and* Four Seasons of Mojo. *Her soon-to-be published books include* 365 Days of Root Magick: Hoodoo & African-based Spirituality for Contemporary Practitioners *(Llewellyn Worldwide) and two young adult novels focused around magick and folklore.*

Herbal Help for Chronic Diseases and Conditions

❧ By Sally Cragin ❧

In 2013 when I developed lyme disease from a tick bite (I live in the northeast where lyme is highly prevalent), I was devastated. A bump on the knee burgeoned into a large, swollen mass that was painful. Fortunately, an alert doctor suggested a lyme test, which came back positive. I am not someone who rejects all pharmaceuticals—after all, thousands of people who've received top-notch educations are in this field—and a month of antibiotics put this condition into a "sort of" remission.

I say sort of because I found that if I eat too much sugar or get stressed out or over scheduled, symptoms such as joint pain and fatigue return.

Since I am a journalist, I went at this chronic condition with a researcher's mind. I wanted to prevent this from happening again, so what could I eat or ingest to prevent a recurrence?

What's scary is that my body will always test positive for lyme, so if I get bitten again I wouldn't necessarily know it unless I get a physical symptom, such as the swollen knee that occurred last time. So it's in my best interest—and that of my family—that I stay on top of "the dreaded lyme" and avoid situations and conditions that might bring on a relapse.

I wanted to see what it was like to live with lyme for at least a year before writing an article about it, and along the way I found that chronic conditions are scarily frequent among the population. *Chronic* means a condition that is always present and can be controlled but not cured. According to the Centers for Disease Control and Prevention, chronic illnesses are a worldwide problem and are the leading cause of death and disability in the United States.

That "can be controlled" part of the equation is crucial to us all. Managing a chronic illness is about *not* doing something as much as it is about doing something. So if we have problems with our lungs, we shouldn't smoke and we should try to get exercise so that we are keeping our bodies healthy to support our lungs and other organs (all of which are affected by smoking). Sometimes it isn't easy to support health with a chronic condition. Have you tried a gluten-free diet? This takes some planning. Eliminating sugar and sugary ingredients from your eating is also a challenge.

Herbs and other natural substances will not provide a quick fix but can, over time, support a pattern of healthfulness. Here are some chronic conditions and herbal and food based suggestions to help you on a path of health.

Lyme Disease

Try a regimen reducing the sugar and carbs in your diet and including cat's claw, turmeric (capsules or tea), and garlic. This will help make your body inhospitable to the *spirochetes*, which carry the lyme disease and cause fatigue and joint pain. Lyme is a tricky customer, but the upside is that one is forced to have a more mindful diet. Since being diagnosed with lyme I have been careful with what I eat, and according to the doctor's scale (I don't own one; I gauge my health by how well my clothes fit!), I lost fifteen pounds this year, which was fine by me.

Obesity

This chronic condition can lead to a stellium of health concerns, including diabetes, heart disease, and stroke. Chronic obesity can also bring stress and anxiety, which can lead to compulsive eating and an unhealthy cycle that only brings more misery. If you go into any bookstore you'll find shelves of cookbooks relating to diet and endless variants on methods to prevent obesity. However, as I have researched this topic as well as speaking to friends and family members who are struggling with obesity, I've noticed several similarities among people who are successful in losing weight and keeping it off. These include reducing drastically or eliminating sugar from their diet. A good friend has also been attending Overeaters Anonymous and gets her "sugar fix" from walnuts, fruit salad, and blenderizing fruits and making ice pops in the freezer.

Arthritis

Arthritis is truly cruel, and I've known more knitters, crafters, woodsmen, and other artisans who develop this crippling condition of the joints. Arthritis occurs when there is inflammation of one or more joints (where your bones meet, such as in the fingers). Herbal remedies that seem to have a minimal number of possible side effects or reactions include eucalyptus, ginger, and green tea. I work with a massage therapist, Christopher Benoit, based in Fitchburg, Massachusetts, who recommends taking ginger, which you can take in capsules or in a tea.

"It's rich in inflammation fighting compounds such as gingerols, which may reduce the aches of osteoarthritis and soothe sore muscles," Benoit says. Ginger extract can also be taken as an injection.

Eucalyptus is one of my favorite smells and is an ingredient in oral medications. Topical oil extracts and the leaves are used to treat arthritis pain. The leaves contain tannins that can help reduce swelling and pain.

Of course, we all know about green tea, but what makes it so special and why do billions of people worldwide drink it? It's loaded with *flavonoids*, which are phytochemicals present in most plants that have antioxidative and anticarcinogenic properties. Green tea may help reduce symptoms of osteoarthritis and rheumatoid arthritis, whether taken as an extract, tablet, or in your favorite mug.

Asthma

Asthma is a chronic condition that is—chillingly—on the rise among children, particularly those growing up in urban environments or are low income. Supplementing a doctor supervised treatment may include swapping out animal protein for plant-based (and reducing your protein ingestion), eliminating dairy and getting calcium elsewhere, making sure you drink lots of water to hydrate your respiratory system, and experimenting with your diet to see if some foods are further irritating your condition. Try eliminating wheat for six to eight weeks. If there is no improvement, try eliminating sugar and then corn for a similar length of time.

Herbs that help with an anti-inflammatory diet include ginger and turmeric (see end of piece for recipes).

Allergies

Allergies and asthma are partners in crime in that both will affect your breathing and cause discomfort. I don't have allergies so I have not tried these remedies, but these items are frequently mentioned in literature as assisting with the symptoms of allergies (either seasonal or chronic).

There are all kinds of allergies. There's a remedy for pollen allergies made from a plant called *Phleum pratense*—the idea being that you're treating a big problem with pollen with a small amount. Pollen allergies, or hay fever, may also be successfully treated if you consume locally made honey, which will have microscopic pollen in suspension.

Other recommendations include botanicals that may include cowslip, verbena, or gentian root.

Sleeplessness

Of course, if you have a chronic condition chances are you're worrying about it. And too much worry can bring sleeplessness, which can also be a chronic condition. I've had insomnia for most of my life and the most effective cure was having children, because then you never get enough sleep! Of course, that's not a "cure" for everyone, and if you want to try something herbal or natural consider valerian tea, chamomile tea, or melatonin. I eliminated caffeine from coffee in my diet a few years ago and that helped immeasurably with the insomnia (I still will get caffeine in chocolate however—I am not made of stone!).

This is not an herbal recipe, but it could help. If you like to read in bed (which I live for), consider reading something ver-r-ry tedious before bed. Try an instruction manual, math problems, or some writing that taxes your brain in a different way. Try reading a poem and then memorizing it two lines at a time. See whether your brain doesn't cry "uncle!" and then shut down.

Easy Herbal Recipes

Turmeric Anti-inflammatory Drink

    1 teaspoon of turmeric

    ½ or ¼ teaspoon of cinnamon

Blend this with 8 ounces or more almond or rice milk. When you blend spices and herbs, versus shaking in a jar, they disperse more effectively. Add a banana for thickener. I try to drink this every day.

Switchel

Old-style Yankee drink that gives you a little sweetness without sending you over the edge!

    1 tablespoon apple cider vinegar

    1 teaspoon honey (or less)

    8 ounces water

Combine. Drink it hot or drink it cold, it's refreshing.

Kappha Tea

Invigorate your digestion and get energized. This may also be helpful for pursuing a weight loss regimen.

½ teaspoon dry ginger extract

¼ teaspoon each of fenugreek and dill

Mix these together, and pour 8 ounces boiling water over. Strain and drink.

Sources

Benoit, Christopher, LMT.

Centers for Disease Control and Prevention, www.cdc.gov.

Cherney, Kristeen, "9 Herbs to Fight Arthritis Pain." Healthline. October 8, 2013. www.healthline.com/health/osteoarthritis/herbs-arthritis-pain.

Dr. Weil online, www.drweil.com.

WebMD, www.webmd.com.

Sally Cragin *is a longtime astrology writer whose books include* Born on the Cusp, *for people whose birthdays are at the end or beginning of a sun sign, and* The Astrological Elements, *a general-interest book on astrology helpful to beginners and those with a little experience, published by Llewellyn Worldwide. Both books have been sold in numerous countries overseas, including India, Russia, Canada, British Virgin Islands, the Czech Republic, and Estonia. Her column "Moon Signs" was carried in the* Boston Phoenix *newspaper chain for seventeen years. She is also an award-winning arts writer, and before being elected to the Fitchburg School Committee, reviewed plays and wrote about the theater for the* Boston Globe,

Boston Phoenix, St. Louis Riverfront Times, LA Reader, Yankee Magazine, Rolling Stone, Village Voice, *and many other magazines that have become defunct in the post-Internet age. Her short plays have been produced in Provincetown, Fitchburg, MA, Lesley College, and other venues. Reach her at sallycragin@verizon .net or moonsigns.net*

Herbs for Mental Clarity and Peace

≫ By Darcey Blue French ≪

In today's busy world, our brains are expected to be *on* at all times and performing multiple tasks at the same time; and not only that, our minds are constantly stimulated by noise, cell phones, computers, televisions, and high stress environments. It's no surprise, then, that our minds can become overwhelmed, overtired, and begin to lose clarity, focus, and the ability to retain information. On the flip side, our brains are one of the most beautifully functioning miracles of the human body, of which we only tap into a small percentage of its abilities consciously!

Many studies have shown the power of practices like meditation and yoga increase mental focus and peace of mind, and also increase the ability to achieve "super-natural" abilities, including spontaneous healing of the body, telepathy, or clairvoyance. Our mind has far more capability to grow and do miraculous things when it is in balance and peaceful. So how do we bridge our mentally overwhelming culture and the natural peaceful and powerful state of the mind?

Practices and tools such as meditation, breathwork, and yoga are absolutely essential in moving toward mental health, peace, and focus; but for many of us, it's a long road between our current state of mental mayhem to being able to sit in meditation for even fifteen minutes a day. Plant allies offer us a natural and effective way to cultivate mental clarity, focus, peace, and improve memory and mental acuity for our necessary daily mental gymnastics.

I'm going to share with you my favorite herbal allies that can help bring peace and relaxation, improve mental focus and memory, and restore healthy brain function.

Along with our beautiful plant friends, our minds require many nutrients to function well. A balanced diet abundant in antioxidants from brightly colored fruits and vegetables; Omega-3 fatty acids from deep-sea fish, algae, and some nuts and seeds; B vitamins; and adequate proteins help to build neurotransmitters that influence our mental state on a daily basis, and this goes far beyond serotonin and depression.

The study of neurotransmitters and mental health is a topic far beyond our scope here, but we need adequate healthy protein and strong digestion to build neurotransmitters in adequate supply.

Tulsi/holy basil *(Ocimum sanctum)*: In the mint family and related to garden basil, holy basil is revered in its native land of India as a spiritual and physical medicine, and is grown at the door of the house. Tulsi is a medicine for cultivating peace of mind and is called *sattva* in Ayurveda. Tulsi brings us peace, calm, clarity of thought, and is said to enhance meditative states and general mental well-being throughout the day.

I use tulsi specifically to clear out "brain fog" from being overtired, overworked, using too many recreational substances, or for the black fog of depression. Tulsi brings back the sparkle to the mind and is mildly energizing to the body, yet is relaxing to the mind and spirit. It is a perfect balance. It also helps to alleviate stress and reduce stress hormones, like cortisol, it can help manage blood sugar, and support and clear the respiratory system during colds and flu. Tulsi can be sipped as a flavorful tea or used as a potent mind-clearing tincture, and can also be purchased in health food stores in a capsule form.

Wood betony (*Stachys betonica*): One of my very favorite mind allies, wood betony has been beloved as a healing and protective plant in Europe since the Roman empire. There is a proverb from Italy that says, "Sell your coat and buy betony," indicating its high regard for healing! Wood betony has been used for centuries to relieve headaches and tension in the head. It increases circulation to the brain while reducing tension that causes headaches. Wood betony is also very protective and connects you with your intuition that comes from the gut/solar plexus.

I use wood betony when there is a lot of stress and mental agitation, which results in being ungrounded and disconnected from the body in the present moment. This is another plant ally that is helpful to cultivate a peaceful mind for relaxation or meditation, but I also find it helps with insomnia related to mental over-stimulation, stress, tension, and even bad dreams.

When you feel spun out, ungrounded, overthinking something (thoughts going around like a merry-go-round), tense, or headachy, reach for a little wood betony tincture (15–45 drops), or brew up a cup of wood betony tea with honey.

Gotu kola *(Centella asiatica)*: This is a cooling and moisturizing herb that is a wonderful and rejuvenative mind tonic. It improves circulation to the brain tissues, strengthens the venous walls, sharpens neural function, and improves concentration and memory. It is considered an adaptogen, rejuvenative, and nourishing herb for the whole body, as well as the mind. Gotu kola is best used over several months when the mind has been taxed, overworked, or is overtired. But it just as well can be used to keep the mind in good shape *before* it gets overworked. In Asia it has been touted as a longevity tonic, and there is a saying "two leaves a day keeps old age away."

It is generally considered safe and gentle for adults, children, and elders, but too much can cause headaches. I like to use gota kola as a tea, blended with other brain supporting herbs, especially tulsi and wood betony!

Rosemary *(Rosmarinus officinalis)*: "Rosemary, that's for remembrance," recites Ophelia in Shakespeare's *Hamlet*. Aromatic, stimulating, uplifting, and clearing—rosemary energetically fosters a clear mind, the mind of what I like to call "eagle eyes." This is the state of mind where you can see and envision clearly the big picture of your life from way up high, and at the same time have the ability to focus on the tiniest of details, like the tiny mouse in the field below, in great detail, so you can swoop down at just the right moment to pick up what you need, or take action on a project or situation.

Just the fragrance of fresh rosemary or essential oil can stimulate memory and clear focus; it is wonderful for students or those in heavy or intense study or memorization to improve memory and recollection of facts. I like to tuck a fresh sprig of rosemary from the garden behind my ear when I need mental clarity and support during work. Rosemary stimulates circulation to the brain so effectively that some folks will get a headache when they take it in medicinal doses. Most of us are familiar with cooking with fresh or dried rosemary on poultry or in Italian sauces, but rosemary tea, or rosemary tincture, will distinctly stimulate the brain and the memory.

Start with small doses, 4 ounces of tea or 10 drops of tincture, and graduate to larger doses if you can tolerate it. This plant is a wonderful afternoon revitilizer and pick-me-up when you feel sluggish or sleepy after sitting too long. Rather than an over-stimulating cup of coffee, try a zesty cup of rosemary tea with lemon and honey.

Rosemary is also a potent antioxidant and protects the tissues of the brain and the liver from free radical damage, which is important in long-term memory and cognition preservation. And let's not forget that rosemary is a warming and stimulating digestive ally that clears heavy, sad, and dark emotions and thoughts from the mind and spirit. Brushing the skin, face, and forehead with fresh rosemary sprigs, or misting with the essential oil, can help shift the energy when you are stuck in a heavy or sad state of mind. Rosemary is used ceremonially by traditional curanderos in their healing *limpias* ("cleansing ceremony"). Never underestimate the power of this potent little garden ally!

Sage *(Salvia officinalis)*: Sage has been touted by herbalists since medieval ages to improve memory and strengthen the mind, and it has been backed up by modern science showing that it helps to slow the breakdown of neurotransmitters, like acetylcholine, which aid in memory retention. Sage is a plant of wisdom that, like other plants, improves brain circulation, protects vascular and brain cell tissues from damage by free radical oxidation, and protects the longevity of a clear mind. It is also a very good ally for calming anxiety, giving us "strength of mind" and resolve to maintain ourselves in our truth. Despite the temptations or challenges that life hands us, sage helps us maintain alignment with our higher good and spiritual truth, whatever that may be, instead of getting carried away by emotions, momentary pleasure, or distractions from our purpose.

Sage has a way of helping us to focus on the truth that speaks to our soul, and to keep our minds clear and focused on such truth. It can be cooked into food like many other kitchen herbs. It also doubles as a medicinal ally when taken as a tincture or as a tea on a daily basis. Garden sage tea is a strong, aromatic, and slightly bitter tasting tea that can be combined with honey and peppermint for taste. A cup of sage tea every day strengthens the mind, the spirit, and the belly. As the saying goes, "Why should a man die when he has sage in the garden?"

Rhodiola *(Rhodiola rosea)*: When you need powerful, strong, and immediate aid for your mental state, rhodiola can be a good solution. This is one of the more powerful and stimulating plant allies for the brain and has very specific uses. I do not generally use rhodiola on a daily basis for extended periods of time, as large doses seem to have an unwanted effect of causing a similar "crash" to excess caffeine.

If you are sensitive to stimulants like coffee or chocolate, rhodiola may have similar side effects. But it is a remarkable ally for clearing mental fog and depression, energizing the mind and the body, and improving oxygenation of the brain. My favorite and most common reason to recommend rhodiola is for those traveling to high altitudes at risk of *soroche,* or "altitude sickness." Rhodiola dramatically improves mental clarity and circulation of oxygen to the brain, even when oxygen levels are reduced. Usually, rhodiola and gingko work best together for this. Rhodiola may also increase neurotransmitters like serotonin. I find it is best to work with a tincture of rhodiola for most purposes because the dose is so flexible; you can take 1 drop, 10 drops, or 30 drops, finding the dose best for you and your needs.

I also generally recommend using rhodiola as part of a formula rather than by itself. If you are using it for altitude sickness prevention when traveling, you may find capsules are effective and easy to travel with for a limited period of time. Just note that if you feel overstimulated, experience headaches, or feel exhausted after using rhodiola, you may need to reduce the dose.

Ginkgo *(Ginkgo biloba)*: Gingko leaf extract is a modern herbal product derived from the ancient tree. Ginkgo nuts have been used for hundreds of years in traditional Chinese medicine, the leaves have been studied extensively as a brain and memory tonic, and it is a potent antioxidant rich in polyphenols that protects sensitive tissues of the vascular system in the brain and the rest of the body. Ginkgo improves circulation and oxygenation to the brain and increases neurotransmitter synthesis, especially dopamine.

Ginkgo leaf is usually taken as a standardized extract because large amounts of raw leaf have been known to cause digestive upset. It is also a wonderful ally for addressing the symptoms of altitude sickness, along with rhodiola. Gingko can aid with memory, cognition, mental acuity, and protection of the delicate brain tissues as we age.

Sources

Mars, Brigitte. *The Desktop Guide to Herbal Medicine*. Laguna Beach, CA: Basic Health Publications, 2007.

Darcey Blue French *is a shamanic and clinical herbalist and wildcrafter of plant medicines. She calls herself a devotee of all that is sacred on this wild, beautiful earth. She learns from the plants and listens for the quiet, intuitive knowing of a plant communicating to her its love, its medicine, its nature enveloped and rooted in the magic of the natural world—the place where the heart hears what is being said. She is here to dive deep into the wild world and to experience, to sense, to taste, to feel the magic of the plants and the wisdom of spirit within each of us. Darcey lives and works in the southwestern deserts and mountains of Tucson, Arizona, where she maintains her private healing practice and offers an Herbal Medicine CSA, a shamanic herbal apprenticeship, medicinal plant walks, and plant medicine retreats. She was trained in clinical herbalism/ nutrition at the North American Institute for Medical Herbalism. Visit Darcey online at www.shamanaflora.com.*

Cream of the Crop:
Herbal Balms and Salves

⇝ By Elizabeth Barrette ⇜

Herbal body care products come in many forms, including lotion, cream, ointment, salve, and balm. They differ primarily in texture and somewhat in their base ingredients. These factors influence what the compound is good for and how potent it is. More oil-based products, such as ointments and salves, are stronger and less perishable than water-based creams and lotions.

Natural ingredients tend to be soothing and nourishing for the skin, and most of them are gentler than harsh chemicals found in commercial products. Herbal compounds can be designed to address a wide range of complaints such as arthritis, bruises, burns, inflammation, insect bites and stings, gout, muscle aches, rashes, sores, sprains, strains, wounds, and other conditions.

Healing Herbs

Herbs used for body care products should be organic, if possible. You can grow your own or buy them from a reputable supplier. Herbs are often available in dried, essential oil, or tincture form. Some, such as aloe vera, may come as a gel, liquid, or other version. Below are some of the herbs most often used to make body products.

Aloe vera *(Aloe barbadensis)* Succulent leaves yield a thick gel. It is anti-bacterial, anti-inflammatory, anti-viral, healing, moisturizing, and soothing. Primarily used for burns, aloe vera can also aid dry skin conditions such as eczema. It has an adaptogenic effect on the immune system, stimulating it to fight off infection or reducing it to soothe allergies. Adding aloe vera gel to a salve makes it lighter and easier to spread, as well as increasing the curative properties. This is also the preferred base for burn gels.

Arnica *(Arnica montana)* Fresh or dried flower heads are infused into oil. It is analgesic, healing, and soothing. It helps bruises, joint pain, muscle recovery, strains, sprains, and swelling. Avoid contact with damaged skin.

Calendula *(Calendula officinalis)* Bright orange flower petals may be infused in oil, or dried and powdered. It is anti-inflammatory, antiseptic, soothing, nourishing, and mildly scented. It also aids cellular repair. Use it for bruises, burns, cracked or dry skin, diaper rash, eczema, garden hands, sore nipples, and varicose veins. Among the gentlest of herbs, calendula appears in many products for the delicate skin of infants or elders. For infants, a rich cream is helpful. For elders, use a light oil or lotion to avoid a greasy texture. The vivid color of the flower yields a product of golden yellow, peach, or orange. Because calendula is edible, it works well in lip balm.

Chamomile *(Matricaria recutita)* It is anti-allergenic, anti-bacterial, and anti-inflammatory. It rejuvenates tissue encourages cell growth, relieves itching, softens and smoothes skin, and relaxes muscles. It promotes healing with less scar tissue. Chamomile helps with burns, eczema, hemorrhoids, minor wounds, and rashes. It makes an excellent lotion for widespread skin problems such as sunburn. Chamomile is also edible so it's suitable for lip balm.

Elder *(Sambucus nigra)* The flowers are used to infuse oil. It is anti-inflammatory, antiseptic, anti-viral, astringent, and stimulant. As an adaptogen, it cleanses and revitalizes the body, creating balance. It softens skin, soothes allergies, and supports the immune system. It treats arthritis, bleeding, burns, gout, rheumatism, and swelling. Elderflower salve is particularly useful for soothing muscle or joint problems made worse by cold weather.

Eucalyptus *(Eucalyptus globulus)* The leaves and branch tips produce a medicinal oil that may be added to herbal compounds. It is analgesic, anti-bacterial, anti-fungal, anti-viral, and decongestant. Eucalyptus relieves arthritis, boils, colds, congestion, coughs, joint pain, minor wounds, and sore muscles. The smell tends to repel insects, ticks, and other pests.

Ginger *(Zingiber officinale)* Ginger root may be turned into juice, essential oil, or grated fresh into salves. It is anti-bacterial, anti-viral, stimulating, and warming. It aids the respiratory system, breaks up mucus, increases circulation, soothes muscles, and stimulates perspiration. Ginger deals with colds, flu, menstrual cramps, and pelvic inflammation.

Lavender *(Lavandula angustifolia)* The flowers produce essential oil, which can be added to herbal products. Lavender is anti-bacterial, anti-viral, cleansing, purifying, soothing, and uplifting. It helps with acne, candidiasis, eczema, exhaustion, fungal infections, headaches, insomnia, joint aches, minor wounds, pain, sore muscles, and stress. For physical complaints, a salve keeps the medicine in one place; for psychological effects, lotion works well to disperse the scent. It's edible and therefore safe for lip balm.

Marshmallow *(Althaea officinalis)* The leaves, and especially the root, give a thick mucilage. It heals, lubricates, moisturizes, nourishes, numbs, softens, and soothes. It also stimulates the immune system. Marshmallow treats diaper rash, dry, irritated skin, minor wounds, and tattoos. Adding the mucilage to a lotion, cream, or salve will make it more slippery and easy to spread. Its sweet taste makes it popular in lip balm.

Mullein *(Verbascum thapsus)* Mullein flowers are infused into olive oil to treat skin problems, creating an electric yellow oil that lends a softer, buttery color to products made from it. This herb is cleansing, soothing, and very gentle. It treats diaper rash, minor cuts, and scrapes.

Neem *(Azadirachta indica)* Leaf powder is used in lotions, creams, and salves, or it may be added to an aloe base to make a gel. Neem oil can be bought and added to ointments or other compounds. It is anti-biotic, anti-fungal, and anti-viral. It smoothes and moisturizes skin. It helps with dermatitis, dry or itchy skin, eczema, hemorrhoids, lice, minor wounds, and skin diseases.

Plantain *(Plantago major)* Although the leaves are most often used fresh, they may be infused in oil for herbal preparations. Plantain is soothing and detoxifying. It treats insect bites and stings, along with diaper rash.

Rosemary *(Rosmarinus officinalis)* The narrow leaves may be infused into oil. It is analgesic, anti-microbial, anti-oxidant, and uplifting. It treats arthritis, eczema, indigestion, menstrual cramps, and muscle pain. It aids the circulatory and nervous systems, improves concentration and memory, and relieves muscle pains and spasms. The smell also repels mosquitoes and other pests. Adding rosemary oil acts as a preservative in lotions, salves, and other preparations. Because it's edible, rosemary works in lip balm.

Slippery elm *(Ulmus fulva)* The inner bark is powdered, and when reconstituted with water, creates a slick mucilage with a consistency similar to egg white. It is anti-inflammatory, antiseptic, demulcent, diuretic, emollient, expectorant, and nutritive. It soothes boils, burns, and minor wounds. Adding slippery elm to a salve makes it easier to spread and also helps preserve fatty ingredients.

St. John's wort *(Hypericum perforatum)* Fresh flowers and leaves can be infused into oil. St. John's wort is anti-inflammatory, anti-viral, astringent, nervine, and uplifting. It treats bruises, burns, dry or damaged skin, muscle or nerve pain, and trauma. St. John's wort salve keeps best when refrigerated; blend it for a softer consistency to account for thickening due to the cold. It can make skin more vulnerable to sunlight, so it is best used for spot application via salve, rather than lotion spread over large areas. Treated areas should be covered with cloth before exposure to sunlight.

Tea tree (*Melaleuca alternifolia*) The leaves make an oil infusion that is most often added to creams or ointments. It is analgesic, anti-inflammatory, antimicrobial, anti-parasitic, astringent, decongestant, immune stimulant, and insecticide. It treats acne, athlete's foot, boils, burns, cuts, dandruff, insect bites, itching, and skin fungus. Tea tree is not for internal use.

Wintergreen (*Gaultheria procumbens*) Essential oil is produced by fermenting the leaves. It is anodyne, antiseptic, aromatic, astringent, soothing, stimulant, tonic, and warming. It treats joint aches, lumbago, rheumatism, sciatica, and sore muscles. In cold weather wintergreen salve helps protect from frostbite. Do not put a heating pad over areas treated with wintergreen because the warming effect will amplify it too much. A very small amount of the oil goes a long way.

Yarrow (*Achillea millefolium*) Leaves and flowers may be used to infuse oil, or the dry, powdered herb can be added directly to medicinal compounds. Yarrow is analgesic, anti-inflammatory, and anti-microbial. It promotes relaxation and healing, and stops bleeding from minor wounds. It helps with boils, broken skin, bruises, cramps, hemorrhoids, itching, mosquito bites, pimples, rashes, sprains, and swelling.

- To stop itching: neem, tea tree, yarrow

- To heal damaged skin: calendula, chamomile, mullein, neem, slippery elm, yarrow

- To soften dry or irritated skin: aloe vera, calendula, marshmallow, slippery elm

- To soothe sore muscles: arnica, calendula, chamomile, eucalyptus, ginger, lavender, rosemary, St. John's wort, wintergreen

• For all-purpose healing compounds: arnica, calendula, elder flower, marshmallow, plantain, slippery elm, yarrow

Other Ingredients

Additional ingredients for healing compounds include carriers, thickeners, and preservatives. Carriers may be liquid or semisolid, including water and a variety of oils. Thickeners include waxes and fats that are semisolid or solid at room temperature. Preservatives may be chemical or natural. These materials combine to make the base of an herbal compound to which various active ingredients may be added for the desired effect.

Vegetable shortening is a sticky fat that is solid, yet malleable, at room temperature and softens readily at body temperature. It avoids the disadvantages of petroleum or animal products making it a good base for ointments.

Almond oil is light, almost colorless and odorless, affordable, and readily available. It resists going rancid and makes an excellent carrier.

Jojoba oil is actually a wax, but performs like an oil. It absorbs easily into the skin and gives excellent texture in salves or creams. It's more expensive, though.

Olive oil has a light to medium color and consistency with some odor. It nourishes the skin and goes rancid slowly. It is affordable and widely available. However, it can make the texture of salves less consistent due to temperature shifts.

Beeswax is a natural thickener that melts at low temperature. It allows the skin to breathe and has a pleasant, honey-like fragrance. It offers protective, soothing, emollient, nourishing, and healing properties. It's affordable and easy to find.

Cocoa butter melts very easily and offers a rich, creamy texture. It has a nice nutty fragrance. A drawback is that it's more expensive.

Shea butter heals dry or damaged skin. It has a pronounced smoky, nutty smell that some people like, but others dislike.

Citric acid comes as a powder with antioxidant and antibacterial qualities. It stabilizes the compound and is readily metabolized in the body. Because it is acidic, it can help balance an alkaline product. It is among the gentler preservatives.

Benzoin is an herb with antioxidant and antibacterial qualities available as essential oil, tincture, or dried. It can be irritating, though.

Grapefruit seed extract slows the growth of molds, yeasts, fungi, and some bacteria. It's broad-spectrum, but irritating, so use in small amounts.

The above ingredients are just a sample of the more popular ones. Animal fats, petroleum jelly, and paraffin wax have all been used for making ointments and salves, but these ingredients have largely fallen out of favor. Animal fat is prone to going rancid and many people don't like using animal products. Petroleum jelly and paraffin wax clog the pores and most folks prefer to avoid such unsustainable products. Chemical preservatives may be used in any body care product, but people who make their own herbal compounds usually don't want those.

Types of Herbal Preparations

There is no universal definition for the names of body care products. People often use different terms as synonyms. This may come from the fact that many of them incorporate the same ingredients, just in different proportions. However, it's possible to sort them out into a spectrum based on texture and use.

Lotion usually consists of oil mixed with water, although it may contain alcohol to speed drying or an emulsifier for binding. It is liquid at room temperature. It is thin enough to use in a flip-top or pump-action bottle. It is the easiest to spread over the whole body, but it can run if too much is applied at once. Lotion evaporates or absorbs quickly without leaving a sticky residue. It tends to be emollient. It is suitable for hairy places and oily skin prone to acne. Its effects don't last very long, though.

Cream is an emulsion of oil and water in approximately equal proportions. It is semiliquid at room temperature. It is too thick for a bottle with a narrow closure, but too liquid for a tube, and maintains its shape somewhat when removed from its container. Thinner oil-in-water creams may come in a bottle with a wide mouth. Heavier water-in-oil creams are usually packaged in a tin that may be dipped into. Cream is easy to spread over medium to large areas, does not run, and usually absorbs without leaving much residue. It is safe for injured or irritated skin where a thicker product might be uncomfortable. Use a light cream with more water and cooling, astringent herbs for a red and itchy, or weeping and hot condition. Use a rich cream with more oil and warming, soothing herbs for dry and flaky, or cold and chapped skin in need of protection. The more oil, the longer the effects last.

Ointment is a homogenous, viscous preparation that is made from a thick oil or fat, sometimes with a small amount of water. It is semisolid at room temperature with a distinct greasy texture. It often comes in a squeezable tube, although it can be packaged in a tin. It is soft enough to spread readily over damaged areas, but it leaves a gooey coating on the skin and it stays exactly where it is put. Ointment tends to be very emollient and protective with an occlusive effect that enhances penetration. It is good for dry skin. Because it is sticky and holds in body fluids, it is not suitable for weepy skin conditions, hairy places, skin prone to acne, or hot weather. However, it lasts longer than water-based compounds.

Salve is typically a mixture of oils thickened with wax, but can use a denser fat as a base without needing the wax. It is semi-solid at room temperature with a more waxy texture. It typically comes in a tin. It can be spread, but does not go as far as softer compounds, and stays put very well. Thicker salve may be uncomfortable to spread over damaged areas. It does not soak into skin much and leaves a protective, waxy coating. Salve lasts longer than water-based compounds.

Balm is a mixture of wax and herbal infused oil or essential oil. It is a soft solid at room temperature. Balm holds its shape well enough to use in a push-up tube, as lip balm is often packaged. It can be difficult to spread, especially over injured or sensitive skin, so it is used on small areas. It does not soak into skin and it leaves a waxy coating that lasts a long time.

Recipes

While body care products differ in consistency and purpose, the preparation is similar. It usually involves heating the base materials and blending them together. Always use a double-boiler or water bath to heat fats and waxes, never direct heat, because they are flammable. Sometimes active ingredients will already be incorporated into the base, as with herb infused oils; other times they are added later, as with essential oils blended in after the mixture begins to cool.

Herbal Infused Oil

    1 part dried herb

    5 parts oil

    1 tablespoon white vinegar

Combine all ingredients in a clean, glass jar, and cover tightly. Place in a warm, sunny window, and shake once a day for 2 weeks. Then strain out the solids, and discard them. Store the infused oil in a clean, dark jar.

Anti-Itch Lotion

    6 ounces distilled water

    1 ounce almond oil, infused with yarrow

    ½ ounce shea butter

    ½ ounce beeswax, grated

    1 pinch fine slippery elm powder

    ⅛ teaspoon citric acid

    ¼ teaspoon Vitamin E oil

    6 drops tea tree essential oil

In one container heat the water. In another container, heat the almond oil, shea butter, and beeswax until fully combined. Add a pinch of slippery elm powder to the water and whisk. Slowly, add the oil mixture to the water until the desired thickness is reached, then add the citric acid. Whisk thoroughly until smooth. Allow the lotion to cool, whisking every 15 minutes. When it is cool, add the Vitamin E oil and the tea tree essential oil. Store in a bottle.

Moisturizing Cream

> 1 ½ teaspoons powdered marshmallow root
>
> 9 ounces cold, distilled water
>
> 6 ounces jojoba oil, infused with mullein
>
> 3 ounces cocoa butter
>
> 1 ounce beeswax, grated
>
> ¼ teaspoon citric acid
>
> 3 drops grapefruit seed extract

First, put the marshmallow root in a jar, add the cold water, and leave it to infuse overnight. This should produce a relatively smooth, thin mucilage. If there are lumps of dried root left, you may need to squeeze it through cheesecloth to strain out those bits.

Next, heat the jojoba oil. Add the cocoa butter and stir until combined. Add the beeswax and stir until fully melted. Remove from the heat, and let it cool until comfortable to touch.

Warm the marshmallow infusion to body temperature. Put it in a blender with the citric acid and grapefruit seed extract. Turn the blender on high, and slowly add the oil mixture. Blend until you have a smooth, thick cream. Pour the cream into tins and allow it to set.

Sore Muscle Ointment

> 1 cup vegetable shortening
>
> ¼ cup olive oil, infused with arnica

¼ teaspoon tincture of benzoin

2 drops wintergreen essential oil

Slowly heat the vegetable shortening over low heat until fully melted. Stir in the olive oil. When combined, remove from heat. Add the tincture of benzoin, and stir. Finally, add the wintergreen essential oil and stir. Pour into tins, and allow the ointment to cool and solidify. Keep it in a cool, dry place.

Healing Salve

6 ounces olive oil, infused with calendula

2 ounces almond oil, infused with elder flower

1 ounce jojoba oil, infused with plantain

2 ounces beeswax, grated

Warm the olive oil, almond oil, and jojoba oil over low heat. Add the beeswax and stir until fully melted. Pour into tins and allow the salve to solidify.

Soothing Lip Balm

⅓ cup almond oil, infused with chamomile

⅓ cup cocoa butter

⅓ cup beeswax, grated

3 drops lavender essential oil

Set up the empty tubes or tins to be filled. Warm the almond oil over low heat. Add the cocoa butter, and stir until it melts. Add the grated beeswax and stir until it melts. Stir in the lavender essential oil. Quickly pour the mixture into the waiting containers; it tends to cool and solidify very quickly.

Elizabeth Barrette *has been involved with the Pagan community for more than twenty-five years. She served as Managing Editor of* PanGaia *for eight years and Dean of Studies at the Grey School of Wizardry for four years. She has written columns on beginning and intermediate Pagan practice, Pagan culture, and Pagan leadership. Her book* Composing Magic: How to Create Magical Spells, Rituals, Blessings, Chants, and Prayers *explains how to combine writing and spirituality. She lives in central Illinois, where she has done much networking with Pagans in her area, such as coffeehouse meetings and open sabbats. Her other public activities feature Pagan picnics and science fiction conventions. She enjoys magical crafts, historic religions, and gardening for wildlife. Her other writing fields include speculative fiction, gender studies, and social and environmental issues. Visit her blog* The Wordsmith's Forge, *http://ysabetwordsmith.livejournal.com, or her website* PenUltimate Productions, *http://penultimateproductions.weebly.com. Her coven site with extensive Pagan materials is* Greenhaven Tradition, http://greenhaventradition.weebly.com.

Herb Crafts

Herbal Perfumes

⪼ By Suzanne Ress ⪻

I think the most impressive quality of aromatic herbs is their scent. The odors of fennel, parsley, and fenugreek remind me of my grandmother; bay leaf and mint of my father; horehound of my grandfather; and lavender and lemon verbena of the summer I was eleven years old. The reason for these associations is not always clear. Perhaps there was a derivative of one of these herbs in a perfume or cosmetic, or even a household cleaner, associated with a person, time, or place that I was barely aware of at the time.

The part of our brains that receives and interprets the odors of airborne volatiles is called the olfactory bulb. Information about odors is stored in long-term memory, the same area of the brain that stores emotional memory, so it comes as no surprise that odors frequently trigger strong memories and can have an effect on one's emotions.

When my oldest child was just over a year old, she would toddle into my side-yard herb garden to pick basil leaves. Inhaling their fragrance brought a smile to both our faces. I still think of this whenever I smell basil.

Since antiquity people have been enticed by various and complex aromas. For this and other reasons, herbal plants, with their pleasantly strong and distinctive aromas, were held with reverence and considered sacred by ancient people. Herbs were used in religious ceremonies, burned as incense, presented as gifts, and treasured for their power of spiritual transport.

In ancient Egypt dried aromatic herbs and spices were burned as incense, or fresh aromatic herbs and flowers were macerated in oils until their own essential oils mingled with the carrier oil to create precious, scented oils.

Distillation of plant aromas was first done about a thousand years ago. Persian alchemists invented the alembic steam distiller system. The Arabian physician Avicenna used this system to create rose water. One hundred and fifty years after that, in 1150, the water-cooled condenser was discovered. This was followed shortly by alcohol distillation, which also made it possible to more easily and effectively distill almost any herbal aroma into an essential oil.

Perfume making spread to Italy, and then to France and Spain, and into the rest of Europe; its use became quite widespread in the 1600s when people used it to conceal offensive body odors. Grand perfumeries were started at that time, especially in Grasse, France, known for its mild climate and vast lavender fields. Many of these perfumeries are still producing today.

In 1824 Friedrich Wohler first synthesized a carbon-based substance, oxalic acid, previously believed only to be found in nature. In 1882 the first synthetic material was used in perfumery. It was the chemical compound coumarin, which smells like newly mown hay. In the years that followed, vanillin, linalool, and more materials were synthesized in a laboratory for use in perfumery. These synthetically produced aromas were blended with natural ones to form previously impossible fragrances.

With time, more and more aromas have been synthetically produced, so that now most mass-produced fragrances contain at least some synthetics.

The Chemistry of Scent

I find it fascinating that by combining certain molecules, called terpenes, one can create a scent, and that the scent of any herb can be broken down into a list of identified terpene molecules. We know, for example, that the chemical components that create the scent of basil are eugenol, myrcene, pinene, orimene, linalool, cineole, terpineol, and more. A single one of these terpenes has its own odor. Take eugenol, for example: this molecule is also found in cloves, nutmeg, bay laurel, cinnamon, and, in smaller amounts in dill, lemon balm, celery, and vanilla. Eugenol is extracted and separated from fresh basil plants and used widely in perfumes, antiseptics, and more. Try reading the ingredients list on the labels of all your household, yard, and personal care products one day. Many of those ingredients that sound like dangerous chemicals come from herbs!

Another of basil's terpenes, linalool, is also present in many of the mints, bay laurel, coriander, lavender, hops, and mugwort. This one is widely used in perfumery, cleaning products, insecticides, and is cheaper and easier to synthesize in a laboratory than to extract from plants.

Basil grows well in hot, humid climates, and is grown for its organic linalool content in Brazil as a replacement for rosewood, which has become endangered. About ten tons of basil per acre are harvested every three months, four times a year. The basil plants are cut down very close to their bases. They do not die, but grow up again, fuller and bigger than before. In the Brazilian climate, the same basil plants continue this intensive production for two or three years before they are replaced. Basil essential oil, later refined to separate the linalool, is extracted right in the field. This oil then fetches a price of about one hundred dollars per pound.

Although linalool can be easily synthesized, and is one of the most common fragrances added to just about anything scented, the more expensive, natural linalool produced by plants is preferred for perfume making.

Cineole, also known as eucalyptol, is another component of basil and is found in sage, ginger, and bay laurel. It is sometimes called eucalyptol because the eucalyptus plant contains up to 90 percent of this terpene. Synthetic cineole is widely used in mouthwash, insect repellents, candy, sweets, beverages, cigarettes, and cosmetics.

Plants are still the largest source of fragrance compounds used in perfumery. Besides an herb's leaves, compounds are extracted from its flowers, blossoms, fruit, seeds, and in some cases, from its bark (cinnamon, birch), twigs, resins, roots, and rhizomes.

There are some human-made synthetic aromas that do not even exist in nature. One of these is the terpene calone, first synthesized in 1966. It is widely used in perfumes and other perfumed products to create a sea breeze, marine-like smell.

Fragrance Families

Fragrances used in perfumery are divided, like flavors in cooking, into families. The classification system is not yet standardized, but all have a citrus family and a floral family. Into the citrus family one could put the scents of herbs such as lemon balm, lemon verbena, and lemongrass. Herbs with floral scents usually are better known as flowers than as herbs—rose and violet, for example.

Personally, I would create an herbal scent category called sharp or balsamic green that would contain the scents of rosemary, costmary, southernwood, sage, and wormwood; a category called fresh green that might contain basil, mint, chervil, and tarragon; perhaps a warm, spicy category for fennel, fenugreek, and curry plant; and a fruity green that would contain pineapple sage, apple mint, and maybe chamomile. There would still remain herbal aromas that don't seem to fit into any category, like hyssop and horehound, which both contain the diterpene marubiin.

Fragrance blending is much like flavor blending. It's best to start out simple and work your way along to more complex recipes. A handy rule for beginners is the rule of three. Number one is the top note of the blend, which will be the first odor you perceive—the lightest—and the one that will evaporate most quickly. This could be a lemony scented herb or a mint. Number two is the middle note, the one you perceive after the top note blows past. A flowery or fresh green smell, like basil or rose, could work here. Number three is the base note, which is the one holding the blend together and usually the heaviest smell. Something balsamic or spicy, such as fennel or costmary, would fit the bill.

Fresh Herb Recipes

When making your own herbal fragrance blends feel free to add non-herbal ingredients, too. These perk up a fragrance and add interest. You might add orange peel, vanilla bean, ginger root, peppercorns, licorice root, birch bark, or anything else you find appealing. Anyone with an herb garden, even a small one, can formulate their own unique aromatic blends for personal use and gift giving, and most of what is needed will likely be found on hand.

Freshly picked or dried herbs from your garden will generally make a light scent that does not last as long as homemade fragrances made from herbal essential oils.

Herb Oil

You will need an unscented carrier oil with a long shelf life, like jojoba.

- Pour 2 ounces into a wide, shallow container, such as an emptied and thoroughly washed and dried hand cream jar.

- Gather up a large handful of the herbs you wish to use. Nice combinations are lavender and bay, or rosemary and lemon balm, but use your own judgment and imagination.

- Tear the herbs into smaller pieces so they will release their essential oils, then press them into the jojoba oil so they are all covered. Put the lid on, and leave in a cool dark place for three or four days.

- Then strain the oil through a tea strainer into a small glass. Press the herbs to get all the oil out, and discard the herbs. Put the oil back into the original jar, and re-peat the entire process two or three more times.

Smooth a little bit of this oil over the palms of your hands before giving a massage. Or, using a dropper, put a few drops into your warm bath once it is drawn for a skin softening ex-perience that will leave you lightly scented.

Herbal Cologne

You will need ethyl alcohol, a few large handfuls of your se-lected herbs, and a 6- or 8-ounce glass jar with a lid.

- Stuff all of the herbs into the glass jar, crushing them a little as you do so. Pack them in tightly.

- Pour ethyl alcohol over all, screw on the lid, and leave on a sunny windowsill for one week.

- Then open, and strain using a wire kitchen strainer and a small funnel, into a brown, green, or blue glass jar. Cork it or screw on the lid, and store in a cool, dark place.

This refreshing cologne can be splashed on for a light scent any time.

Using Essential Oils

When I first became interested in making herbal perfumes I thought of buying a small alembic steam distiller to make my own essential oils from herbs. Then I discovered that the yield of essential oil from fresh herbs is only 0.7 percent!

For one-tenth of an ounce of essential oil, you need one pound of fresh herbs! Herbs are very light in weight, and a pound is probably more than most people have of any one herb growing in a household garden. For longer lasting, stronger-scented, unique herbal fragrance, your best bet is to use purchased vials of pure, natural essential oils from a whole foods market or herbalist's shop.

To start, you need to formulate a blend that pleases you. Experiment with various combinations over the course of a few days, trying them out by vaporizing them together in an aromatherapy diffuser, or mixing some drops together into your bath water. Here are two that I like:

"Old Money"

    5 parts basil essential oil

    5 parts ginger essential oil

    1 part mint essential oil

"Sassy Clean"

    3 parts lavender essential oil

    2 parts lemongrass essential oil

    1 part myrtle essential oil

Massage, Body, and Bath Oil

To make a rich and nourishing body oil, drop your essential oils, starting with the minimum amount, into a glass jar. A little goes a long way, so don't be tempted to overdo it at first. Then add unscented jojoba oil. Cover the jar and gently swirl to blend, then uncover and sniff. If it seems right, dip your fingertip in and massage a drop of the oil into your hands. If the fragrance is not as strong as you'd like, add another round of essential oils, remembering to stick to the proportions, and to carefully blend the essential oils into the carrier oil before smelling it. Sometimes you have to wear it around for a few hours to realize how strong it is.

When it is to your liking, cover the jar and keep it in a cool dark place. It can be used as a signature massage or bath oil. You can also use a few drops in place of body creams and lotions, to soothe dry, sunburned, or itchy skin.

Perfumed Body Powder

Mix up your selected essential oils in a tiny jar, such as an empty and cleaned sampler honey or jam jar, with a lid.

- In a 16-ounce jar with a lid, pour unscented talcum or cornstarch in to fill it three-quarters of the way.

- Now, get one cotton ball, and put it into the tiny jar with the essential oil, roll it around to soak up all of the essential oils, and then drop it into the larger jar with the powder. Cover the jar, and shake well.

- Keep the powder jar in a cool, dark place, and shake it well, twice a day for three days. After that you can transfer this marvelously scented body powder to a fancy ceramic powder jar or box with a powder puff and lid. Dust your dried body all over after a shower for a light and refreshing scent.

Cologne

Use a base of 2 ounces of ethyl alcohol. Put it into a small glass jar with a lid, and carefully add your essential oils, drop by drop. Gently agitate. This can be used immediately. It should be kept closed tightly, in a cool, dark place.

Solid Perfume

5 grams (about ⅕ of an ounce) beeswax

15 grams (½ an ounce) jojoba oil

Fragrance essential oil blend

Melt the beeswax in a very small Pyrex bowl over simmering water. Pour the jojoba oil into a small glass, and add your fragrance blend oils, drop by drop. Add the melted wax to the oil blend, then pour into a container with a lid; a tiny sample jam or honey jar will work well. Dab a little bit on your pulse points for a subtle fragrance effect.

Perfumed Soap

Buy a chunk of unscented glycerin soap at a hobby or crafts store. You'll need soap molds, too, which you can also buy at the craft store. Alternatively, use something you already have, such as ice cube trays, empty and clean hand cream containers, or even plastic egg cartons. Gather together anything you'd like to add to your soap for interest or a scrubbing effect, such as fennel or caraway seeds, dried crumbled herb leaves, or dried herb flower petals.

Cut off a piece of glycerin and melt it in a double boiler or in a Pyrex bowl in the microwave. While still hot, stir in your essential oil blend. Mix in your dried herbs and seeds.

Spray your molds with rubbing alcohol. Then quickly pour the glycerin mixture into the molds. Spray a little more alcohol on top of the soaps as they begin to cool. When they are completely cool, remove them from the molds. Store in an airtight container.

Have fun!

Suzanne Ress *recently published her first novel,* The Trial of Goody Gilbert. *When she is not writing, Suzanne enjoys herb gardening, beekeeping, creating mosaic artworks, silver and coppersmithing, horse riding, and long-distance running. She lives in the foothills of the Italian Alps with her husband, daughter, and many animals.*

Deep Sleep Using Nature's Medicine Cabinet

✺ By Stephanie Rose Bird ✺

The inability to fall asleep and stay asleep for at least six hours straight is called insomnia. Chances are, you or someone you know are one of the millions of people who have restless nights because of the inability to relax into a deep sleep. While there are many pharmaceuticals available to treat insomnia, Ambien being chief among them, this article's focus is on natural ways to alleviate sleep disruptions, with a specific focus on herbs and ritual. These ways of dealing with insomnia are derived from ancient wisdom regarding sleep, which is still applicable today.

There is a confluence of factors playing a role in insomnia. Many

different cures are being offered in the marketplace, ranging from pharmaceuticals such as the Ambien type of medicine to manufactured melatonin. Many of us are aware that there is another source for curing what ails us, including difficulty sleeping: earth wisdom, spirituality, and plant medicines. If we combine these gifts and aim them toward healing, a nurturing, deep, and replenishing sleep is easily obtainable.

Insomnia in America by the Numbers

Before we can heal, first let's examine the problem close up. It's sobering, but somewhat comforting, to know you're far from alone if you suffer with sleep issues. Let's take a look at how sleep disturbances affect Americans.

According to the National Sleep Foundation:

- 50–70 million American adults battle general sleep disorders
- 48% have occasional insomnia
- 22% suffer from regular insomnia

According to the Centers for Disease Control and Prevention:

- 35–45% of Americans fall asleep or nap unintentionally because they have not been able to fully rest
- A whopping 9 million people take sleeping pills for insomnia

Problematic Aspects of Sleeping Pills

What's the problem with nine million people taking sleeping pills? Well, there are many. Some folks never wake up due to adverse physical reactions to the pills. Others wake up drowsy and are unable to fully function for several hours upon waking. People with dependency issues find themselves becoming addicted to various pharmaceutical sleep aids. Moreover, many prescriptions help you fall asleep, but during the night you wake up and are restless anyway.

Stepping away from the medicine cabinet and pharmacy has many benefits regarding a good night's sleep. In the process, you open the door to age-old wisdom, while also engaging in nature by reaching for natural remedies as sleep aids. Let's explore some gentle, yet effective, sleep inducing rituals that combine nature, spirituality, and herbs.

Engaging Hygeia

These days there's a great deal of talk concerning sleep hygiene. You may be wondering exactly what that means. Let's look at it from a historical and spiritual perspective. The word *hygiene* is derived from the Greek goddess Hygeia. She is a moon goddess who inspires health through cleanliness. To her mind, disease and illness can be prevented by cleanliness, particularly of the household and personal types. I'm going to lead you through several ways to combine Hygeia's wisdom with herbalism to ensure a good night's sleep.

Since we're thinking back to Greek times by engaging the Greek goddess of hygiene, we can go back even further to the time when our ancestors lived in caves and slept in dens. Try visualizing this type of space; hear the sounds and think about how you could simulate that lifestyle in your home every night.

Clearing mental and physical clutter from your bedroom, returning to simpler times when we all lived closer to nature, brings many rewards, including peacefulness that leads to better sleep. In order to transform your bedroom to a primal den, you need to remove or neutralize your modern conveniences.

Unplug and silence devices, and make sure your room is as pitch black and quiet as possible. If you live on a busy street or near a train, try playing natural sounds of rain, birds, or crashing waves at sea to bring you closer to Mother Nature as you head off to dreamland.

Natural Embellishments

Hygeia utilizes herbs and natural remedies to purify and heal. Taking a tip from her, prepare your bed nicely. Activate its nurturing spirit with a gentle kiss of herbs, as this would be a good way to follow her lead. I have found a few tricks that help me get to sleep, and stay asleep, using some favorites from the herbal kingdom.

Lavender-Kissed Bedclothes

People have been stuffing pillows with lavender and strewing the herb in rooms for hundreds of years. Today we can use our clothes dryer to bring relaxing lavender into our lives in a contemporary way.

Add a few drops of lavender essential oil to an unscented dryer sheet; dry bedclothes, and enjoy the scent of lavender as you nestle into a soft, clean, sleep-inducing bed.

Stuff muslin pouches with dried lavender buds. Seal well. Add to dryer along with bedclothes. Dry your sheets and blankets this way to enjoy the aromatherapeutic benefits lavender provides. You're employing lavender's abilities of soothing your nerves and easing daily tensions as you go to sleep.

Sweet Dream Pillows

One of my all-time favorite ways of incorporating herbs in a good night's sleep is in dream pillows. The herbs I've found to have the best ability to work well together, while inducing deep relaxation that is long-term during the night, are:

- Lavender
- Chamomile
- Catmint
- Hops

Crumble a couple tablespoons of each in your hands, rubbing quite firmly to release the essential oils. Do this over a bowl while concentrating on your intention to sleep well.

Thinking of pleasant imagery, such as the softness of sheep's wool or holding a pebble found on the beach, drop 2 drops each of hops, lavender, chamomile, and lemon balm on the herbs.

Stuff this herbal blend into the pillows. These sweet dream pillows can then be stuffed into your larger bed pillows, put on nearby bookshelves, or the night stand.

Aromatic Room Spritz

You can add further to this cozy den atmosphere with an aromatic room spray. Each of these herbs is known historically to aid sleep and create a comforting environment.

2 ounces water

1 ounce grain alcohol or vodka

8 drops lavender essential oil

7 drops German chamomile essential oil

5 drops clary sage essential oil

Add these ingredients to a Pyrex measuring cup. Pour into a spray bottle. Use as an aromatic spray just before bedtime in the bedroom to help you fall asleep.

Soothing Soak

A couple of hours before bedtime, try an herbal foot soak to get your mind and body ready for sleep. I especially enjoy this one because it brings in various elements of nature, including herbs.

½ cup powdered milk

1 drop lavender

1 drop marjoram

1 drop Roman chamomile

½ pound pea gravel (small smooth pebbles)

Pour milk in a glass or stainless steel bowl. Drop in essential oils. Make rough paste. Add to very hot water in a basin, whisking to remove any lumps. Add pebbles. Soak feet for 30 minutes to 1 hour, meditating to bring peacefulness or collecting thoughts while listening to nature sounds.

Relaxing Shower

Rose is a gorgeous flower with connotations of love, well wishes, and the heart. Sandalwood gives off a soothing aroma and cultivates an environment of healing. Bring the two together in the shower as you prepare for bed by dropping one drop of each essential oil on the bottom of the bathtub as you begin to shower.

Herbal Nightcaps

After adding lavender aroma to your bedclothes, and herbal blend to your bedroom, and having showered or soaked, it's time to head off to dreamland—after a comforting drink. Hygeia always had a bowl of healing elixir, and you can cap off this healthy sleep regimen with one as well.

Try a cold glass of tart cherry juice. This will help you restore mind, body, and spiritual balance. It is healthy and also encourages your body to release melatonin naturally. Melatonin helps regulate your sleep patterns.

Cardamom and milk work beautifully together to encourage sleep because, when warmed together, both relax your nerves and release natural sleep chemicals in your brain, such as melatonin and tryptophan. Add 2 to 3 crushed cardamom pods to a cup of your favorite type of milk. Warm this blend up in a saucepan. Strain to remove cardamom. Enjoy this warm with a dash of nutmeg.

DIY sleepy tea will surely help you sleep. Have a tablespoon and a half of herbs as a tea. Effective sleep herbs include hops, lemon balm, chamomile, and lavender or passion flower. Mix bits of each for a tasty blend or choose your favorite, and enjoy a strong brew with honey just before bedtime.

Stephanie Rose Bird *is a modern eclectic pagan. She practices Hoodoo, Green Witchcraft, and Shamanism. Deeply into painting, meditation, and yoga, she is also a creative visionary. She's had five books published:* Big Book of Soul; A Healing Grove; Light, Bright, Damn Near White; Sticks, Stones, Roots and Bones; *and* Four Seasons of Mojo. *Her soon-to-be published books include* 365 Days of Root Magick: Hoodoo & African-based Spirituality for Contemporary Practitioners *(Llewellyn Worldwide) and two young adult novels focused around magick and folklore.*

Natural Insect Repellents Made from Essential Oils

❧ By Peg Aloi ❧

If you like to spend time outdoors, and don't enjoy getting eaten alive by mosquitos or deerflies, then chances are you tend to use some kind of insect repellent. Citronella candles are nice at night, but we can't always be right next to them. Yet, most commercial insect repellents used on the skin are not all natural like those citronella candles. In fact, some commercial formulas are downright chock-full of nasty chemicals. They tend to smell really awful, too, in my experience. Some formulas even contain the ingredient known as DEET, which is not a repellent, but an actual insecticide meant to kill insects! You definitely do not want this ingredient in any product you're going to put on your skin.

It's possible to make your own natural insect repellents using natural essential oils; they will effectively keep mosquitos and other biting insects away and will smell great! You can add any essential oils you want to your blend, making it into a signature fragrance blend if you want.

Most insect repellent blends contain citronella, which is a plant that naturally repels mosquitos. You can make yours without citronella, but I do recommend it. One essential oil that can be substituted for it is geranium, which is a related plant and smells similar, though is slightly more flowery and pleasant than citronella. In addition to creating natural insect repellents in a water base, you can also add essential oils to unscented candles. Be careful though, because essential oils can be flammable! Just put a few drops of essential oil on the top of an unlit candle, away from the wick area. Light it carefully, and when the candle wax melts the essential oil will warm up and disperse into the air creating a natural insect repelling aura of fragrance.

It is worth noting that natural insect repellents are not generally very effective against the types of mosquitos that spread dangerous diseases in tropical regions, according to scientific studies. So, if you are traveling in such regions and want to avoid mosquito-borne transmission of dengue fever, etc., you will want to look into more potent formulas. But for the average North American or European camper or gardener, natural formulas can, and do, work very well if applied frequently.

Making Your Own

You will need a glass bottle with atomizer attachment (look for these online or at your local health food store). Amber or other colored glass is best as sunlight can degrade essential oils's effectiveness over time. It's important to use glass because essential oils can eat into plastic as well.

You also need a small amount of clear alcohol as a dispersant—clear vodka works fine. You can also use gin, which will gain a slight juniper berry fragrance. You also need distilled water.

You'll probably want to make at least a 4-ounce bottle of insect repellent. You can always make more if you need it. Store in a cool, dark place (not on the seat of your car in summer!) and it should last you an entire season. You can store it indoors over the winter, but may need to refresh it with some additional essential oil again in spring.

Natural insect repellents have a gentler action than commercial formulas and so must be applied more often. This is a small price to pay for being able to avoid the harsh and toxic chemicals in the store-bought brands. Spray lightly onto your exposed skin—close your eyes when spraying your face. The light misting action of the atomizer will provide a good layer of protection. Be sure to shake the bottle gently before use, as some of the essential oil molecules need to be broken up a bit to blend together after sitting for a while. The smaller the molecules the easier it is to spray them, so if you see balls of oil floating in your bottle, shake gently until they are dispersed and dissolved again.

The main essential oils used that are most effective are: citronella, cedarwood, lavender, lemongrass, peppermint, geranium, and patchouli. You can use any or all of these, but again, using some citronella is the best mosquito preventive. These essential oils are all fairly inexpensive and can be purchased from your health food store or online. It is not necessary to use organic or wildcrafted essential oils for insect repellent.

You will also want to add some essential oils to help create a pleasing fragrance The following are recommended to help create woodsy, green fragrance blends with the essential oils already listed: lemon, lime, sweet orange, clary sage, frankincense, black pepper, palmarosa, petitgrain, fir, and sweet basil. These are also moderately priced.

You may want to avoid some of the sweeter, more cloying essential oils (such as ylang ylang, peru balsam, jasmine, etc.) because these may actually attract insects! Also, be sure you are using 100 percent essential oils, not fragrance oils or other scented products.

Creating a Fragrant Blend

Fill your 4-ounce glass bottle about eight-tenths full of distilled water. Add a teaspoon of the vodka or gin. Then you will begin to add drops of essential oils. Start with a simple blend, perhaps citronella, cedarwood, lavender, and lemongrass. I like the peppermint in a blend because it has a slight cooling effect on a hot day. Speaking of peppermint, if you are making these blends for children to use, they are perfectly safe, but peppermint can have a somewhat stimulating effect on kids before naptime or bedtime.

Gently blend the mixture by putting the atomizer top firmly on the bottle and gently roll the bottle between your palms. This is a more effective method of blending than shaking the bottle. Then spray onto your skin. The scent should be gentle, but not too faint and not too strong, either. You can add as much essential oil as you like, but usually somewhere between twenty to thirty drops is enough. If your essential oils don't come with dropper tops you can purchase a dropper to use.

If you want to spruce up the fragrance, slowly add additional oils until the blend comes together. You can leave it overnight, roll gently, and try again to see how it's coming together fragrance-wise. It is possible to create a really pleasing, woodsy fragrance enjoyed by men and women alike. Patchouli can be very overpowering, but a small amount helps to harmonize other scents. Cedarwood is likewise strong and can overpower the blend, so don't use too much of it. Basil and clary sage are both nice green scents, and also go well with black pepper and lemon or orange, along with some citronella, lavender, and cedarwood. Continue to experiment until you get the blend you want.

Some Recipes to Try

These recipes will provide very nice blends for your natural insect repellent. Don't worry if you don't get the droplet count exactly right—there can be fun in experimenting!

To your distilled water and alcohol base, add:

Recipe #1:

  10 drops citronella

  4 drops lavender

  2 drops peppermint

  2 drops patchouli

  3 drops sweet orange

  3 drops lemon

Recipe #2:

  8 drops citronella

  3 drops cedarwood

3 drops lavender

2 drops basil

2 drops black pepper

3 drops lemon

3 drops patchouli

2 drops clary sage

Recipe #3:

8 drops citronella

3 drops lemongrass

3 drops lavender

3 drops geranium

3 drops clary sage

3 drops sweet orange

3 drops black pepper

Peg Aloi *is a freelance writer and media studies scholar. She has written on diverse subjects ranging from color symbolism in film to aromatherapy to women's sexual health. Her blog* The Witching Hour *(at Patheos) explores popular media related to witchcraft, paganism, and the occult.*

What Dreams Are Made Of: Your Very Own Dream Garden

⤛ By Monica Crosson ⤜

When I was a little girl, during the hottest months of July and August, I would cross the field behind our barn and crawl over the fence that separated my parents' property from my grandparents'. Once on my grandparents' farm, I would spend lazy afternoons behind my grandmother's greenhouse, where the mint and lemon balm were allowed to grow wild and tiger swallowtail butterflies fluttered above swaying leaves.

I would bring my dolls, and tuck down beneath the foliage and play until the intoxicating fragrance would lull me to sleep, only to be awakened by my grandmother. Her earth-stained hands would gently caress my cheek.

"Wake up, sleepyhead," she would say. "Your mama's wondering where you are." Then I would scurry back home, to be met by my mother, who would greet me with her hands on her hips.

"Where have you been? I have been calling for you," she would scold.

"I'm sorry." I would say. "I fell asleep in Grandma's garden. But it's okay, she woke me up!"

As I grew older, dolls were exchanged for novels, journals, and sketchbooks. It was my private nest—a place of relaxation and contemplation. A hiding place from my little sisters and the stress of academics. A place to dream.

A Place for Dreaming

Imagine an outdoor space dedicated to sleep and dreaming a place where the scent of lemon balm and lavender beckons you to a hammock or comfortable lounge chair. As you relax with a hot cup of chamomile tea, the scent of peppermint compels you to close your eyes and drift into a heavenly sleep. Jasmine invades your sleeping senses and induces prophetic dreams. A new lover perhaps? Is this a form of guided meditation? No, it's your very own dream garden. The idea of a garden as a resting place goes back to the beginning of gardening. Pliny the Younger wrote of a resting place in his own garden—an alcove with a couch—in amongst the springing fountains.

Many modern gardens lack a simple place to unwind. And considering our modern life pressures, such a place seems to have more relevance than ever before. A dream garden is meant to gently settle and soothe the senses into submission.

You can tuck your garden in a section of your backyard, deck, or balcony. Add elements that are sensory treats. Consider creeping thyme between soft shale stones or a brick path. Add a water fountain or birdbath for the soothing sound of trickling water or the soft splashing of bathing birds. Fill the garden with statuary or mementos from your childhood or from a special vacation. My own dream garden is dedicated to a Celtic goddess of dreams, Caer Ibormeith, so I added a cement cast swan alongside a small stone altar tucked beneath cottage roses. Remember, this is your sacred place, so add plants and elements with color, texture, scent, and form that are pleasing to you.

The Perfect Location

Before we begin, you must ask yourself what you need. This is your dream garden—your personal place to rest. So what constitutes relaxation for you? It could be a hammock and a good book tucked in a shady nook. How about a reclining lawn chair surrounded by fragrant potted herbs on a balcony? Or just a place to lie and watch the clouds drift by. What about location? Do you want to be tucked away where no one can bother you or within direct reach of the house?

If you have a large yard or acreage, explore your property for the best location. You'd be surprised at how many microclimates your garden offers. Watch your garden. Record the number of hours of light any one spot receives during the day. Even the smallest gardens have sun traps, cool shady spots, and places blown by wind. Your dream garden demands only the most luxurious climate your garden offers. So find the spot in your garden with the maximum number of comfortable hours.

The next consideration is distractions. If you live in an urban area you will want to shield yourself from the noise of traffic or passersby. This is easily done with a cleverly located arbor, a trellising plant, or by placing a water feature, such as a fountain (even a tabletop one), in your garden. Wind chimes are a nice, inexpensive solution as well. Adding gentle, soothing sounds can help relieve outside noises.

Digging In

Now that you have found the perfect location for your dream garden, it's time for the fun part—picking out the perfect plants. Remember to play with sensory qualities like color and scent. Some colors that are known for their restful qualities include green, which calms the nerves; blue-green, which brings about a passive, dreamy state; pink, associated with tranquility; and violet for introspection and peace.

Aromatherapy comes into play, too. A number of scents are reputed to have a calming effect, which you may like to include in your garden. Rose, lavender, lemon balm, chamomile, jasmine, and tangerine are all known for their calming effects.

You could also add plants that stir pleasant memories. Use those memories as a springboard for dreamy possibilities. Did you spend summers at your grandparents' farm? You could add old-fashioned favorites such as lilac, hollyhock, and foxglove to your dream garden. Maybe it was vacations at the beach. Think about fountain grass, sea thrift, or yarrow.

I have included a plant list to get you started, and remember, if you're a city or apartment dweller, all the plants listed can be planted in containers and hanging baskets around a comfortable lounge chair or portable hammock.

Lavender (*Lavandula angustifolia*): A semi-woody perennial that typically grows to twelve to eighteen inches tall and wide. Lavender's blue flowers appear in terminal spikes from late spring well into summer and have a wonderful fragrance.

Lemon balm (*Melissa officinalis*): The green leaves of lemon balm have the scent of lemon with a hint of mint. Lemon balm can grow twenty-four to thirty-six inches tall, and makes a nice green clump of medium-textured leaves among the other herbs and flowers in your garden.

German chamomile (*Matricaria recutita*): An annual, growing twelve inches tall and wide. It is in flower from June to July, and the seeds ripen from July to August. The young sprigs are used as a seasoning, and the dried flowers are used to make herbal teas.

Valerian (*Valeriana officinalis*): Known for its sedative properties, it is a perennial growing to five feet tall. It is hardy to zone 5 and is not frost tender. It is in flower from June to August and has a vanilla musklike fragrance.

Catnip (*Nepeta cataria*): Typically grows in a spreading clump to two to three feet tall. Erect, branched, square stems clad with aromatic, opposite, coarsely toothed, triangular to ovate leaves. Small, white flowers bloom in spikelike terminal clusters at the stem ends from late spring well into summer.

Passionflower (*Passiflora incarnate*): A rapid-growing, tendril-climbing vine. Features showy, two-and-a-half-inch fringed flowers having white petals and sepals, and a central crown of pinkish-purple filaments. Flowers bloom in summer and are fragrant. Prefers a warm climate.

Rosemary (*Rosmarinus officinalis*): A native to the Mediterranean, a woody, perennial herb with fragrant, evergreen, needlelike leaves. These plants thrive in warm, humid environments. Colder climates should consider growing rosemary in containers.

Polyantha rose (The Fairy): Blooms nonstop from June until frost, with double, rosette-shaped blossoms of light pink. It grows two to three feet high and wide.

Peppermint (*Mentha piperita*): Square stems tend to run rampant. In small garden spaces it's best to tuck peppermint into a container. This plant thrives alongside water gardens or in damp spots in the yard, but will also survive in drier soil.

Jasmine (*Jasminum officinale*): It is a sprawling, somewhat twining, deciduous shrub, usually pruned heavily to keep its size contained. The foliage is slightly downy with pinnate leaves, having five to nine leaflets. The flowers are white or very pale pink and fragrant from early summer to autumn. Winter hardy to zones 7 to 10, may be planted as an annual in colder climates or planted in a container.

Creeping thyme (*Thymus serpyllum*): Creeping thyme is a very easy plant to grow. It likes well-drained soil, grows about two to four inches high, and can spread up to two or more feet in width. The leaves are very small, but dense, and cover the low growing plants.

Anise hyssop (*Agastache foeniculum*): Grows up to four feet high and one foot wide in a clumplike, upright shape with flowers appearing in showy false whorls, and occasionally branching. The leaves have an oval and toothed shape. Anise blooms from June to September with bright lavender flowers.

The Garden Bed

The most important feature in your dream garden isn't the plants, but the garden furniture. Maybe your idea of a dream garden is a place where ideas bloom. In that case, you may want to include a chaise lounge and a decorative side table to place journals or sketch pads on. If sharing a pot of tea with a friend or loved one is part of your idea of rest and relaxation, maybe add a small bistro set under a tree.

But if your idea of rest and dreaming is more literal, I have the perfect garden project for you—a garden bed.

The first thing you will need is a head and footboard from an old bed. An antique iron headboard is ideal. You can still find them in antique and junk shops. I bought mine at an estate sale for twenty dollars. But really, any head- and foot-board will do. If it's wood, you will need to coat it with either a varnish or a coat of paint to protect it from the elements.

Next, depending on the size of the headboard, you will need to fit it to a raised garden bed. I have included instructions for a raised bed that will fit a twin-sized head- and foot-board.

For this 2' x 3' x 6' raised bed you will need:

- One 4' x 4' x 8' post for corners
- Two 2' x 12' x 12' boards
- Two 2' x 12' x 8' boards
- One 1-pound box of 16d (3½ in.) galvanized nails

To make the corner posts, measure and cut the 8-foot 4 x 4 into four 24-inch lengths. To make the long sides of the bed, cut the 2 x 2 x 12 boards in half, and nail boards one at a time to two corner posts. Repeat this step to form the second long side. Cut the remaining 2 x 12 x 8 boards in half so you have four 4-foot 2 x 12 boards for the ends. Trim each board to measure 3 feet.

Stand the two lengths with posts up, parallel to each other, approximately 3 feet apart. Nail the 2 x 12 end pieces to the corner posts. They should be aligned flush with the posts. The raised bed form is complete.

Fill with approximately 15 cubic feet of a good soil mix. A good rule of thumb is 60 percent topsoil, 30 percent compost, and 10 percent soilless growing mix that contains peat moss, perlite, and/or vermiculite. Now attach your head- and footboards to the ends, and you have a garden bed!

As for the planting, it's up to you. If you plan on using your bed for the occasional afternoon catnap, I would suggest planting it with creeping thyme, Irish moss, or blue star creeper—something that doesn't mind a little abuse.

If you're using it to just add a touch of whimsy to your dream garden, create a patchwork of your favorite annuals or trailing plants. Your plants may include petunias, alyssum, or pansies. Complete your bed by growing trellising plants at the head and footboard. How about sweet peas or moonflowers, perhaps?

To Ensure Pleasant Dreams

You have planted your garden and created your bed. Why not make a dream pillow? These simple, aromatic pillows have been used for centuries to induce peaceful sleep, enhance dreams, and encourage dream memory.

To make your own pillow, simply cut two squares, rectangles, or whatever shape pleases you from scrap material (try using cotton or another natural fiber). With the right sides together, stitch along the edges, leaving a ¼-inch seam allowance, and make sure to leave an open space along one side. Flip the pillow through the open space and fill with your herbal blend. Finish the pillow by stitching the open area shut.

Take it out to your garden hideaway and let the herbal blend induce wonderful dreams. Or better yet, make a blend from the herbs growing in your own dream garden to induce pleasant dreams all night long.

Whether you want to enhance your dreams or dispel nightmares, blend any of the following:

Lavender: Helps to promote a soothing, relaxing state.

Mugwort: Enhances vivid, lucid, and prophetic dreams. Helps with remembering dreams.

Anise: With its licoricelike fragrance, this plant is used in dream pillows to keep nightmares away.

Clove: Brings warmth and an exotic feel to dreams.

Sage: Leaves can be used to bring more peacefulness and healing to your dreams. Helps to make dreams come true.

Mullein: Used to help ward off nightmares and have pleasant dreams.

Jasmine: Known to enhance erotic and romantic dreams.

Lemongrass: This plant can boost your boring dreams by adding color and exotic elements.

Rose petals: Add a few rose petals to bring a loving sense of warmth to dreams.

Clary sage: Ready for a nocturnal adventure? This herb's super-fragrant scent can provide you with some vivid and strange dreams.

Yarrow: Induces prophetic dreams.

Dreamy Me

My grandmother died over a decade ago, and though her property remains in the family, her greenhouse and gardens are gone. But it's okay—I made my own dream garden and planted lots of lemon balm in her honor. It's just a tiny nook for me to go and lie in the grass surrounded by the lush and lovely sights and sounds of nature. It's where I take my journals and write my stories.

And yes, sometimes under a dreamy sun, when the bees are humming and the wind chimes sing, I have been known to drift off into quiet slumber. Once, a few years ago, I dreamt my grandmother was talking to me.

"Wake up, sleepyhead," she said, "before your family starts to worry about you."

As I groggily made way back to my house, my son, Josh, approached me, hands on his hips. "Where were you? I've been calling for you," he scolded.

"I'm sorry, honey," I replied. "I fell asleep in the garden." I smiled. "But it's okay. Grandma woke me up." Josh was very confused.

Sources

Myers-Cooke, Brodee. *Gardens for Pleasure*, Angus & Robertson, 1996.

Monica Crosson *is a master gardener who lives in the beautiful Pacific Northwest, happily digging in the dirt and tending her raspberries with her husband, three kids, two goats, two dogs, three cats, a dozen chickens, and Rosetta the donkey. She is the author of* Summer Sage, *a novel for tweens. Visit her at www.monicacrosson.com.*

The Herb Cupboard: Taking an Inventory

❧ By Doreen Shababy ❧

Every so often you have to clean your cupboards, and the herb cupboard is no exception. As I begin writing this, I realize that I'm really talking about two different cupboards. Originally, I thought of what, here at home, I call the medicine hutch. Several years ago my husband, the "wood wizard," built a beautiful pine and cedar hutch that I use for storing our herbal concoctions, all the ingredients, tinctures, salves, dark amber bottles, small dropper bottles, jars of green ointment, golden calendula oil, and so on. The other herb cupboard, well, I guess a lot of people would call that the spice rack, but again, I tend to have a spice rack, a spice shelf, a rolling spice cart, what have you ... let's

just say, I'm a bit of a fanatic! The herb cupboard we will discuss here is the first kind: the cupboard of lotions and potions.

Best Used by …

I try to be diligent about rotating my "inventory," which is a very important concept, but *c'est la vie*, sometimes things do get overlooked or go stale. I keep the bottles labeled and dated, and when I see something is getting near the end of fresh, I try to use it up in a good way. If it's a bunch of dried mint or thyme, for example, I might use them as bath herbs. Aromatic seeds and spices are easy to use up as a real simmering pot-pourri; you can also sprinkle a tiny bit onto your woodstove to send the fumes wafting. I've even been known to sprinkle the seeds along the borders of the garden for an edible weed effect—go figure!

If you come across homemade salve that's over a year old, it's time to start giving it away. Tinctures, which will keep practically forever, can also run into overstock if you never use them. Share them with others—that's what they're for. You can harvest and make more this coming summer. I have discovered over the years that when you share the herbal remedies you make (or anything else from your loving hands), you are gifted in return in ways you might never imagine.

And yes, sometimes old, dried herbs do go by way of the compost heap. There's nothing wrong with that, either. It's a learning experience.

Decisions, Decisions

In any event, how do you know what kind of homemade herbal products you need? And how much?

First, take a look at your family or housemates. For instance, if you have school-aged children—the little petri dishes that they are—you will first and foremost want kid-safe remedies for colds and flu. This could include elderberry syrup for sore throats; dried lemon balm for easing aches and pains, and helping break a fever (use as tea or in the bath); and fragrant and penetrating cottonwood salve as a chest rub and for chapped noses. You will also want gentle calendula ointment for any type of ouchie. Most households won't have any problem using homemade insect repellents, especially during picnic season.

If you do a lot of physical work for a living, including gardening, you might want cottonwood salve to soothe achy muscles, lots of dried spearmint for refreshing, hydrating teas, and white willow bark tincture for easing inflammation.

What's in Your Medicine Hutch?

I used to want to make tinctures of all the herbs I could pick, and then I realized I only need to pick what I actually use. In my own herb cupboard, I mostly keep remedies made from what I have picked in the wild or grown in my garden, such as Grandma's Magic Healing Salve (a general, all-purpose herbal green salve); cottonwood bud oil and tincture; St. John's wort tincture and oil; calendula petals for oil or salve; dandelion tincture (whole plant); and lomatium root tincture for treating infections and lung congestion. I purchase herbs such as slippery elm bark for soothing the intestines. Then there are the base ingredients such as olive oil, beeswax, and pure-grain alcohol for making the remedies. I keep those on hand as well.

Do I expect everyone to keep an actual apothecary in their kitchen like me? Certainly not.

I once read a criticism about my book noting all the equipment and supplies needed, but what did you expect, really?

Most items called for are common, and I can tell you, it keeps things interesting on the kitchen table, looking at lotions and potions brewing away like in some primitive chemistry lab. And consider this, if you keep over-the-counter drugstore "remedies," why not keep ones you know won't have negative side-effects when used accordingly, especially for children? When you know for certain what is going into your remedies, you can dispense them with confidence and a feeling of satisfaction at having a hand in their creation.

Plan Your Work, Work Your Plan

If you are new to making herbal home remedies, I recommend not making too big a batch of anything. Early on in my herbal creation enthusiasm, I would make a gallon of salve at a time. Have you ever tried to strain a gallon of hot, slippery oil filled with wilted leaves and flowers? Saying you have to be very careful is a bit of an understatement. Unless you are selling your herbal remedies, a quart at a time is plenty for most households. If you want to make extra to make as gifts (as in the case of homemade herbal salve), I suggest making it in two batches, for safety's sake as well as convenience. The same goes for tinctures; a fifth at a time or less will generally last for years, depending on what it is. I have yarrow tincture that is over ten years old. So you see, you might not use what you make if you make too much.

I can see the medicine hutch right here from where I'm typing, and I see a purchased bottle of Lebanese orange flower water in there, a bottle of glycerin, herbal chest rub that my friend Jackie made (smells great), three or four paper bags with tincture jars steeping (to keep them from the sunlight), a big glass jar full of bay leaves (I don't care if they're in the light, they're also out for decoration), cottonwood bud oil, a bag of empty gelatin capsules, and a couple stacks of books and magazines (there's no place in my house where you can't see books). These are just what I can see without opening the drawer or doors! Also, these are the things I use in my household for myself, my husband, and for my friends and family who need them. What kind of remedies do you think your household would use? If you identify your actual needs then you can figure out what herbs you might want to use to make your creations.

Storing Your Stuff

If you think of the herb cupboard as a combined and expanded first aid kit and medicine cabinet, you are getting the idea. I also keep Ace bandages, rolls of clean cotton for wrapping, scissors, a sterile eye cup, a hot water bottle, and so on in the drawer of the hutch—things that might ordinarily be in a bathroom, but we have limited space in that room, so the hutch is where it's at. If storage is an issue in your home too, look for a new or used cabinet-type storage unit you can anchor up on the wall for handy dispensing. The trick is to narrow down what you think you'll really need for herbal first aid, the supplies you'll need to make them, and then find a nice cool, dry, and dark place to store your herbal concoctions.

To tell the truth, you really can't have too much Grandma's Magic Healing Salve.

Calendula Lip Balm
Calendula (*Calendula officinalis*) petals are often used for delicate skin and in formulas for babies and children. So clean out your cupboard and baby your lips at the same time!

1 cup sweet almond oil

1 cup dried calendula petals (not the whole flower head), rose petals, or both

1 ounce cocoa butter (purchase at pharmacy, specialty baking, or natural food stores)

1 ounce beeswax, grated or beads (approximately)

Steep the oil and petals over very low heat for two to three hours, until the oil is golden from the petals. Do not over-heat! Add the cocoa butter, stir until melted. Carefully strain this warm oil over a heatproof bowl, removing the petals. Pour the strained oil back into the pan, add the beeswax, and stir until melted. To test for hardness, take a teaspoon of the blend, place it on a small plate, and refrigerate for a few minutes to see how it sets up, like for testing jelly. Adjust the amount of wax to lip balm hardness, then carefully ladle into small containers, appropriate for dipping your pinky finger. Let cool before covering. Makes about 10 ounces.

Optional: For additional flavor add ½ teaspoon of vanilla or strawberry flavoring (not extract) before you add the wax. Mmmm!

Elderberry Syrup

This is a simple but effective remedy styled after a basic herbal syrup. You can use honey (preferred) or cane sugar in the preparation. Use elderberry syrup to ease coughs from a cold or flu. Elderberry has been shown to ease inflammation and increase perspiration, helping break a fever. Do not eat fresh elderberries in any quantity as they are purgative until cooked or dried!

In a small pan place 1 quart water with 2 ounces dried (or 4 ounces fresh) elderberries, and bring to a boil. Lower heat, and allow to simmer uncovered until reduced by half (that is 1 pint or 2 cups), about twenty minutes. Strain, and then add ½ cup honey, stirring until blended. If using cane sugar, use 1 cup sugar, and be sure it is fully dissolved by briefly reheating the brew. Carefully pour the hot syrup into sterilized bottles, label, and date. Refrigerate the elderberry syrup for up to three months. Makes about 2 ½ cups.

Sources

Chevallier, Andrew. *The Encyclopedia of Medicinal Plants*. New York: Dorling Kindersley Publishing, 1996.

Duke, James A., PhD. *The Green Pharmacy*. Emmaus, PA: Rodale Press, 1998.

Shababy, Doreen. *The Wild & Weedy Apothecary*. St. Paul, MN: Llewellyn Publications, 2010.

Doreen Shababy *is the author of* The Wild & Weedy Apothecary, *and co-owner of her business by the same name. She has been using, growing, and teaching others about herbs for decades, and she is also involved with energy work. Please visit her blog at www. thewildnweedykitchen.blogspot.com.*

Herb History,
Myth, and Lore

Georgia O'Keeffe's Garden

⤳ By Thea Fiore-Bloom ⤶

In the early 1960s Folgers was try-ing to convince American women they had a choice: buy Folgers instant coffee or risk losing their husband. Georgia O'Keeffe opted for "none of the above." In the early 1960s Miss O'Keeffe, instead, chose to walk the New Mexican hills with her two dogs, grow an unruly paradise of a garden, and create some of the best American art of the twentieth century.

O'Keeffe kept on ignoring Madi-son Avenue's plans for her through-out the rest of her long life. She just kept on painting. She also kept on grinding her own flour, baking her own bread, making her own yogurt from local sheep's milk, and living in her unique, independent, fiercely feisty way until just shy of her ninety-ninth birthday.

One of the most nurturing and enduring inspirations I have ever come across has been the day-to-day life of Georgia O'Keeffe. Reading various O'Keeffe biographies, perusing her letters to friends, watching video interviews of her, or viewing photos of her throughout her life never ceases to inspire me. I see O'Keeffe as having been a grounded sage of sorts, who had turned her share of personal suffering into wisdom, and whose steadying anchor in the stormy sea of life was the land.

For O'Keeffe was a natural gardener. Much of her contentment, outside of art-making, stemmed from observing nature and growing and preparing food from her own bit of earth in New Mexico. Come with me on a short walk through the garden and kitchen of one of America's favorite painters.

The Surprise to Be Found at O'Keeffe's Home and Studio

A few years back I took a pilgrimage to O'Keeffe's home and studio in Abiquiú, New Mexico. It was not surprising that her sparsely furnished, clay-walled home had the same stark look that her paintings have. What was surprising was the whimsy and lush beauty of O'Keeffe's garden. Black, branchy tree shadows draped over coral-beige enclosing adobe walls. Buzzing bees navigated through the plum, apple, and apricot trees. Sagebrush, Russian olive, and greasewood trees graced the eastern rooms of the house where O'Keeffe's sister, Claudia, often stayed (Lynes/Lopez, 216).

I felt enchanted by the property's many whispering tamarisks. I imagined how the place would feel after a rainstorm with all the irrigation channels open to create paths of gurgling waterways. The most memorable sound for me was the billowy rustle and percussive pop of clean, white sheets still set out to dry on O'Keeffe's windy clothesline just west of the north garden. This lucky clothesline was nestled between sweeping willow trees and fragrant lilacs. In the north garden itself, O'Keeffe's inky green junipers curved round in bonsai waves against the turquoise sky.

At this point in my walk through the property it dawned on me that O'Keeffe did not just make a garden here; she created what the ancient Greeks referred to as a *temenos*. A temenos is a sanctuary, a bit of land spared from urban use. Swiss psychologist Carl Jung later defined a temenos as a purposefully created, bounded place where one's most important work is encouraged to come to fruition. O'Keeffe made a clay-walled temenos at Abiquiú, a place where she grew and refined her thought process in the midst of her wondrous garden. Maybe we can all do this. We all have our own unique brand of genius. Perhaps all our gardens are the seeds with which we each can begin our own temenos. And we can start with an herb garden.

O'Keeffe Loved Herbs

O'Keeffe adored herbs. She enjoyed the unique flavor herbs imparted to her meals. The artist also honored herbs for their sensual appeal. She appreciated the beauty of their physical forms, their tactile allure, and their varying enticing aromas.

Margaret Wood, one of O'Keeffe's live-in cooks/assistants in her later years, describes the introduction she got from O'Keeffe to the herbal kingdom, "Miss O'Keeffe acquainted me with wiry tarragon, feathery dill, stalky lovage, bushy green and purple basil, and other herbs" (Wood, 1). O'Keeffe's unruly herb garden also gave forth sorrel, summer savory, chives, tarragon, parsley, marjoram, and many mints (Wood, xiv). But O'Keeffe's herbs were not grown just for pleasure. Like everyone and everything connected to her home, they had their work to do.

O'Keeffe was well aware of the restorative properties of herbs and their abilities to make a significant contribution to overall wellness. She was a health nut, and she was amazingly strong, radiant, and active. She was still rafting the Colorado River and camping in the wilderness in her late seventies. The artist was an early adopter of the teachings of exercise and bodywork pioneer Ida Rolf. O'Keeffe was also personal friends with the rebellious biochemist, nutritionist, and author Adele Davis. Nutrition had a lot to do with O'Keeffe's vim and vigor. Salad was on the menu daily for lunch, and though O'Keeffe's cooks often prepared meals, Georgia herself usually made the daily lunch salads with freshly picked lettuce, herbs, and vegetables (Wood, 1).

O'Keeffe Was a Foodie, a Slow Foodie

Like most successful artists, O'Keeffe had a fierce and fast work ethic. But when she was not working, she understood the pleasure and meditative importance of life in the slow lane. One of her favorite books was the 1906 classic *The Book of Tea* by Okakura Kakuzo, which lyrically describes the Japanese tea ceremony, the merits of simplicity, and the philosophy underpinning tea (Udall, 220). O'Keeffe enjoyed taking tea daily, often favoring a spearmint tisane plucked fresh from the garden and slowly served from her modest, yet comely, Japanese teapot.

Inside O'Keeffe's Kitchen

O'Keeffe's recipes, like her teapot, were not meant to impress; they were no-nonsense and good for you. However, that did not mean food from her kitchen was bland or put together in a slapdash fashion. Celebrity chef and author Deborah Madison has been quoted as saying the following about O'Keeffe's ostensibly overly simple recipes, "It looks as if there's nothing special going on with the recipes, but read between the lines and everything that promises deep goodness is there, mainly the fruits of the garden translated with a sure hand into, say, a salad of torn herbs or a soup scented with lovage"(Wood, ix). Why not peruse one of O'Keeffe's personal recipes written by Margaret Wood and decide for yourself?

O'Keeffe's Herb Salad Dressing

From *A Painter's Kitchen: Recipes from the Kitchen of Georgia O'Keeffe*, courtesy of The Museum of New Mexico Press, 2009© by Margaret Wood.

- 2 teaspoons herbs: lovage, tarragon, dill, basil, parsley

- 2 tablespoons olive oil

- 2 tablespoons safflower oil or other high quality vegetable oil

- 1 teaspoon lemon juice, or more to taste

- ¼ teaspoon whole seed mustard

- 2 garlic cloves

- Herb salt, to taste

- Freshly ground pepper, to taste

- Pinch of sugar (optional)

- Chives, as garnish

Wash the herbs and pat them dry. Then chop all herbs medium fine, except the chives. Blend the olive oil and safflower oils with a fork, add the lemon juice and mustard. Squeeze one medium garlic clove through a garlic press and add it to the liquid. Then add the chopped herbs to the dressing. Add herb salt and freshly ground pepper to taste. Add a pinch of sugar if the mixture is too sour. Allow this dressing to stand for an hour, if possible, so that the herb and garlic flavors can permeate the dressing. This quantity will dress a salad for 4 to 6 people.

Before serving the salad, rub a wooden bowl with a garlic clove split in half. Add the lettuce to the bowl. Pour the dressing over the lettuce and toss the salad. Chop the chives into ¼-inch pieces and sprinkle them on top.

Note: There are quite a number of herbs included in this dressing. For practicality, use the herbs available or preferred. Sliced or quartered sweet cherry tomatoes, thinly sliced small radishes, or chopped and seeded cucumbers are possible additions to this salad. In the salad dressing, a variation for the lemon juice is balsamic vinegar; the vinegar lends a rich, slightly sweet taste to the dressing.

People get weirdly enthusiastic about salad when it has a homemade herbal dressing like this on it. Maybe it's the unique taste imparted by unusual ingredients like lovage. Why does lovage keep cropping up in an American kitchen in the southwest?

Lovage: O'Keeffe's Favorite Herb

The answer is because O'Keeffe loved lovage; it was her favorite herb. She had this in common with the medieval emperor

Charlemagne. He was so enamored with the look and taste of lovage that he commanded all his estate gardens overflow with it. However, lovage was not just a favorite with the royals. Lovage was a staple in the healing gardens of monks and very popular amongst the common folk, as it was a vital ingredient in love potions. In fact, lovage used to be commonly known as "love root."

Etymologically, lovage was derived from two words: love and ache (ache being a medieval word for parsley). So technically, lovage is the parsley of love. For the last few centuries, though, lovage's popularity has wilted, and with occasional exceptions, it has languished on the sidelines of herbal history. O'Keeffe paid popular sentiment no mind and enjoyed lovage anyway. And so should you. Here are six ways to delight in that certain je-ne-sais-quoi nuance lovage can offer.

Six Sumptuous Ways to Love Lovage in Your Kitchen

Roast It in a Chicken

Gail Monaghan of the *Wall Street Journal* recommends that cooks "Tuck a sprig or two inside a whole chicken or fish before roasting, and you'll be rewarded with intriguing, je-ne-sais-quoi nuances; guests will be racking their brains to decipher the delicious enigma." (Monaghan)

Candy It

You can candy thick lovage stems to decorate a cake top or enhance homemade biscotti. Use them in a dish as you would use candied fruit pieces or the candied stems of angelica (lovage's botanical cousin).

Pretend It's Bok Choy

Lovage stems can be simply steamed and eaten with a splash of balsamic vinegar. Personally, I prefer to douse my steamed greens with soy sauce or a bit of Braggs Liquid Aminos™… delicious and healthy.

Make Soup

As we saw earlier, O'Keeffe added lovage to salad dressing and used it for salad greens, but the craftiest way she deployed lovage was in her soups. Lovage was actually the star ingredient that could make ordinary tomato soup, in O'Keeffe's words, into something, "quite special." (Wood, 20).

Pretend It's Fennel

Lovage's root can be chopped, grated, or shaved like fennel. Include it as one of a few ingredients in an easy but daring salad combination. For example, you could put it in a version of a blood orange salad served in Sicily, a country whose dishes benefit from an exotic North African influence. Grate or chop lovage root over navel and blood orange sections, add a bit of mint, some very thin slivers of red onion, and serve with a tangy, hot paprika vinaigrette.

Lovage: The Cocktail

Or better yet, use mature lovage stems as savory Bloody Mary straws. O'Keeffe didn't imbibe much, but that shouldn't prevent you from occasionally partaking in a refreshing herbal cocktail.

Lovage in Your Garden

Lovage is a member of the tasty Umbelliferae family, along with the likes of dill, celery, carrot, fennel, coriander, and parsley. If given the right conditions, this perennial will reach six feet tall and resemble parsley on steroids. If you want to experience lovage, you may have to order the seed online and grow it from seed. I have yet to find it at Southern California farmer's markets or local grocery stores. And poor Charlemagne might be horrified to hear that many United States nurseries do not carry lovage seedlings, though some sell lovage seeds. You may meet with more success in your own area. (For improving your lovage's odds of thriving, see the Underhill and Nakjavani link in endnotes). If you give ho-hum, ordinary lovage a chance, the reward may be extraordinary.

The Extraordinary Ordinary

Celebrating the extraordinary within the ordinary was a big, silky theme that threaded itself through O'Keeffe's life and art. She wanted people to see the magnificence she saw in the simplest of natural things. O'Keeffe is famous for her huge, arresting paintings of flowers, but it is her renderings of bones on canvas that personally send me to the moon. The artist also did a heck of a job on rocks and shells. An entire O'Keeffe canvas like *Inside Clam Shell* (1930) could be devoted to showing the miniature, watery universe contained within a humble shell—a universe that a viewer of her work may have been too busy to notice. To physically feel the wallop that even a wee 7" x 9" O'Keeffe shell painting can pack, nothing beats viewing one in person. Or better yet, see a few in a row.

Make Your Own Pilgrimage
to O'Keeffe Country

Why not visit her museum? The Georgia O'Keeffe Museum in downtown Santa Fe holds the largest collection of her work in the world with over a thousand of her pieces. While you are in the area, fast becoming known as "O'Keeffe Country," don't miss touring her home/studio and garden. Travel writer and pilgrimage scholar Phil Cousineau has declared the visiting of O'Keeffe's home and museum a modern pilgrimage, one especially important for American women. Any important journey can bring you face to face with some of your own fears. O'Keeffe, like all of us, constantly encountered her own fears. As she used to say, "I've been absolutely terrified every moment of my life—and I've never let it keep me from doing a single thing I wanted to do."

If you are at all inspired by Georgia O'Keeffe's life or her paintings, I urge you to leave the comforts of your own home and journey to her home. This journey could help you to continue to uncover your own unique brand of genius. And besides, it beats staying home and worrying if you are making someone else the right brand of instant coffee.

Further Info

A little advance planning and a rental car will make it possible for you to easily tour the O'Keeffe Museum, and Georgia O'Keeffe's home and studio in Abiquiú on the same day. Be on the safe side: book a tour reservation a few months ahead of time. Tour groups are small and conducted sparingly from March to November. Private tours can be scheduled off-season. Visit www.okeeffemuseum.org/abiquiu-home--studio.html.

Travel Tip

You may find some of O'Keeffe's quotes as inspiring as her paintings, her life, and her garden. Pack the best selling *Por-*

trait of an Artist: A Biography of Georgia O'Keeffe by Laurie Lisle as a companion on your voyage.

Endnotes

Lisle, Laurie. *Portrait of an Artist: A Biography of Georgia O'Keeffe*. New York: Simon & Schuster, 1980.

Lynes, Barbara Buhler, and Agapita Lopez. *Georgia O'Keeffe and Her Houses: Ghost Ranch and Abiquiu*. New York: Abrams, 2012.

Monaghan, Gail. "Lovage Recipes for Summer." *Wall Street Journal*. June 17, 2013. www.wsj.com/news/articles/SB1 0001424127887324866904578515731301003910.

Udall, Sharyn Rohlfsen. *Carr, O'Keeffe, Kahlo: Places of Their Own*. New Haven, CT: Yale University Press, 2000.

Underhill, Linda L., and Jeanne Nakjavani. "Plant Profile: Lovage Herb." *Mother Earth Living*. October/November 1992. www.motherearthliving.com/gardening/herb-gardening/lovage-herb-zmaz92onzgoe.aspx.

Wood, Margaret. *A Painter's Kitchen: Recipes from the Kitchen of Georgia O'Keeffe*. Santa Fe, NM: Museum of New Mexico Press, 2009

Thea Fiore-Bloom, PhD *is a California-based writer, artist, and gardener. She teaches writing, creativity, and art history to children and graduate school students.*

Stalking the Wild Oregano

⫷ By Jill Henderson ⫸

Fall in my neck of the woods is a treasure trove of wild edible and medicinal plants. It is a veritable fantasyland for wild foragers and herbalists. Some of the best fare include wild mushrooms, hickory nuts, black walnuts, and the ugly but ever so sweet American persimmon. Even a short walk through field and forest will fill the attentive forager's basket overflowing. One of my favorite fall activities is stalking the wild oregano, otherwise known as American dittany (*Cunila origanoides*). This incredible edible is often overlooked by foragers and herbalists because of its small size and sparse growth habit. But don't let appearances fool you. Wild oregano

is an exceptional culinary seasoning and a powerful medicinal herb as well.

Identification in the Wild

Wild oregano is a herbaceous perennial that is very closely related to garden oregano (*Origanum vulgare*), as well as other cultivated herbs belonging to the mint family such as marjoram (*Origanum marjorana*), dittany of Crete (*Origanum dictamnus*), thyme (*Thymus vulgaris*), winter and summer savory (*Satureja spp.*), and bee balm (*Monarda spp.*).

Although wild oregano resembles and smells very much like true oregano, it has a much more intense aroma and taste, and a very different growth habit than its cultivated cousins. Unlike culinary oregano, which has slightly fuzzy leaves and a sprawling, creeping nature, wild oregano grows upright to slightly prostrate, has smooth, bright green, teardrop-shaped leaves, and seldom grows more than ten to twelve inches tall. In fact, wild oregano is often so small and unassuming that it is completely overlooked by almost all who encounter it. Yet wild oregano can be found growing in dry, rocky woods and clearings from the far reaches of the Northeast all the way to southern Florida and the western portions of Texas, Oklahoma, and the northern Midwest—basically the entire eastern half of North America.

Because of its diminutive size and sparsely spaced leaves, wild oregano is often difficult to spot against a backdrop of forest leaf litter. A good time to look for wild oregano is in early spring when the newly emerging leaves are temporarily deep-purple in color, or in late summer when it bears a number of soft, round inflorescences of impossibly small, clear-purple flowers born at the leaf axils. One sure-fire way to identify this pungent herb is by its spicy, oregano-like aroma, which many foragers smell long before they get a glimpse of the actual plant. In fact, there is no other native North American plant that smells and tastes as strongly of true oregano, than wild oregano. So if you smell oregano, slow down and look for a very unassuming herb hugging the ground.

Good and Good for You

Much like its herbaceous cousin oregano, the summer leaves of dittany are wonderfully fragrant and spicy, and can be used fresh or dried as a seasoning for food and as a delicate hot tea on cold winter nights.

Because of its close family ties to numerous medicinal and culinary herbs, wild oregano is a naturally powerful healer containing phytochemicals such as thymol, limonine, and carvacrol. These scientifically proven medicinal compounds have traditionally been used to inhibit or destroy food-borne pathogens such as giardia, E. coli, K. pneumoniae, salmonella, and staphylococcus.

Like most mint family members, wild oregano also has the ability to soothe the effects of poor digestion, including gas, bloating, upset stomach, abdominal cramps, and heartburn. A simple tea taken by the cupful as needed will do wonders to ease digestive upset. Like true oregano, the essential oil of this native herb has the potential to ease rheumatic and muscular pain when applied topically.

Wild oregano is also a strong infection fighter that can be used to treat respiratory and sinus congestion and other related infections. The healing properties found in the "oreganos" have long been employed to treat coughs, tonsillitis, bronchitis, asthma, and even emphysema.

Like true oregano, wild oregano also has strong antifungal properties that are well-suited for eliminating fungal infections such as athlete's foot, jock itch, and nail fungus. Wild oregano can also be used externally to speed the healing and prevention of infection in minor wounds, and to soothe the pain and reduce the itching of bites, stings, and rashes. One warning to those who would use this herb for medicinal purposes: wild oregano and all of its culinary relatives contain phytoprogesterones. In medicinal doses, these plant hormones might induce menstruation (or labor), and should not be used by those who are or who may become pregnant.

A Wild Beauty in the Garden

Because of its delicate beauty and usefulness, wild oregano is more than a welcome addition to any perennial garden. It can be transplanted from the wild (but only from private lands where the plant is abundant) or started by seed sown in the fall. When given full sun to partial shade and average, well-drained soil, wild oregano will easily grow into a very attractive sub-shrub with a rounded or mounding habit that is perfect for any perennial flower border.

If all that goodness doesn't tempt you into stalking the wild oregano, you might be very intrigued to learn that this one little herb is among a mere handful of plants in the entire world that produces one of nature's most elusive and ephemeral winter blossoms.

Wild regano is also known as a frost flower because it blooms most spectacularly in the winter. Many a frost flower fan admit to discovering their very first frost flower quite by accident—often while walking the dog, feeding livestock, or fetching the mail early on a cold winter morning. Usually, their eye is caught by a brilliantly white and luminescent object amidst an otherwise drab landscape. When they move in for a closer look they find an improbably delicate sculpture made of long, thin, striated ribbons of curled and contorted ice of extraordinary complexity and fragility. And when touched even lightly, they quickly find out that the fragile flower simply crumbles to bits.

While researchers are still studying the exact mechanics of the formation of frost flowers, the basic premise is quite simple. Very cold temperatures cause water within the main stem or under the bark to freeze. It starts when water within the stem becomes super-cold, and slowly ice crystals begin to form. As the icy slush expands, the stem becomes fractured. As the slush leaves the stem through these fractures and hits the freezing air, the slush freezes solid. In this slow and methodical way, layer upon layer of translucent, striated, and contorted ribbons of ice are created. Some frost flowers are very small—less than an inch in diameter. But many, and especially the first ones of the season, can be five or six inches in diameter. And like a snowflake, no two frost flowers are ever the same.

It is not yet known exactly how many plants in the world have the ability to generate frost flowers, but at present the list is very small. In North America we are blessed with three: wild oregano/American dittany (*Cunila origanoides*), white crownbeard (*Verbesina virginica*), and frostweed or rock rose (*Helianthemum canadense*).

The occurrence of frost flowers is hard to time with any precision. However, when the weather suddenly turns to freezing and there has been a relatively good amount of moisture preceding the temperature change, chances are good for spotting one of these rare beauties. Early morning hikes in open woodland or woodland edges and clearings are best for hunting elusive frost flowers. Set out early, for the moment the sun glances off their icy surface these fleeting flowers return to the earth from where they came. Such transitory and rare beauty is what I love about living so closely with nature.

As a gardener, herbalist, wild forager, and lover of good food it is no wonder that wild oregano tops my list of favorite native herbs. And even though I have my own little patch growing just outside my back door, I never tire of stalking the wild oregano in the out of the way places it calls home.

Happy foraging!

Jill Henderson *is an artist, author, and world traveler with a penchant for wild edible and medicinal plants, culinary herbs, and nature ecology. She has written three books:* The Healing Power of Kitchen Herbs: Growing and Using Nature's Remedies, A Journey of Seasons: A Year in the Ozarks High Country, *and* The Garden Seed Saving Guide: Seed Saving for Everyone.

A lifelong organic gardener and seed saver with a passion for sustainable agriculture and local food production, Jill presents workshops to teach gardeners about the detrimental impacts of bio-engineered food crops and how to grow and save open-pollinated and heirloom seeds. Jill also writes and edits Show Me Oz *(ShowMeOz.wordpress .com), a weekly blog filled with gardening and seed-saving tips, homesteading wisdom, edible and medicinal plants, nature, and more. She is a regular contributor to* Llewellyn's Herbal Almanac, Acres USA, *and the* Permaculture Activist.

In her spare time, Jill is a professional artist specializing in custom pet portraits and wildlife art. You can view some of her work at ForeverPetPortraits.wordpress.com. Jill and her husband, Dean, live and work in the heart of the rugged Ozark Mountains.

Roots of Gold: Turmeric

❧ By Diana Rajchel ❧

People often confuse turmeric with curry. Both, in powdered form, have a distinct yellow color. Both also appear in spice packets for the dishes called curries. Both also end up confused with each other and with other spices that appear in those packet mixes.

Once you isolate turmeric from its fellow curry-packet spices, its unique qualities become clear. It has a bright yellow color when dried and a deep bitter flavor. Like myrrh in fragrances, turmeric mediates and blends conflicting flavors. It moderates the heat in curry, amplifies the sweetness in chili powder, and calms the challenging flavor of cumin. Its effect is subtle enough that some cooks think it only serves as food coloring.

Placing a piece of turmeric directly on the tongue destroys illusions of subtlety and insignificance.

Cooking Tips

To get the most from curry, try adding it to routine Western dishes. Its flavors work especially well with coriander, garlic, onion, and basil. It adds a delightful quality to salmon, tilapia, and chicken. For vegetarians, turmeric can enliven rice and beans, especially if accompanied with lemon juice and raisins.

History and Folklore

To touch this reticent, yellow powder is to touch ancient history. Turmeric root has deep symbolism in Indian culture. It serves as a medicine, as a symbol of women's lives, and in folklore, as a magical amulet. A translation of a popular Indian folk song praises the root:

> "The goddess of turmeric brings color in life.
> It is the ornament of married women.
> Any woman who puts turmeric in her purse,
> Her purse will never be empty."

The herb figures into Indian spirituality from birth to death. In ancient India, family members rubbed newborn children in turmeric powder to protect them from evil spirits, women received an elixir of milk and turmeric after childbirth, and brides used turmeric as one of the paints they applied to their bodies. In some regions of India, a groom received a turmeric rubdown from the women in his family on the night before his wedding to make the feeling of his skin pleasant to his bride. Healers also used it to treat jaundice and many other liver ailments. Hindus prepare dead bodies with turmeric before cremation.

Word spread about turmeric to other parts of the world. Marco Polo wrote of the herb, "There is also a vegetable that has all the properties of true saffron...but is not saffron." Given the expense required to produce even a small amount of saffron, discovering all of its desirable qualities in an easy-to-grow root must have delighted Polo's customers.

Modern Hinduism retains a sacred role for the yellow root. Indian folklore tells tales of saints and gods providing heroes with turmeric as a magical charm, and homeowners burn it as an incense to keep ghosts at bay. Some people, acting on a folk superstition, carry turmeric in a pocket or wear it on a yellow ribbon around their neck as an amulet for health and safety. During the holiday Shital Shasthi (a marriage ritual of a god and goddess), priests coat statues of Shiva and Parvati in turmeric before bathing the figures in water. In the ceremony of Durga puja, turmeric represents nine devas.

Turmeric in the Modern World

Nicknamed "Indian saffron," turmeric *(Curcuma longa)* is a member of the ginger family. Manufacturers produce the spice by drying and powdering the rhizome. While used mostly in Indian and Thai cuisine for flavor and color, it also has industrial applications as a fabric dye and food colorant.

Called *haldi* by Ayurvedic practitioners, poultices of turmeric treat pink eye and related swelling infections. It also serves as an antiseptic and antifungal. Historically women received a treatment of turmeric, milk, and honey for post-partum care. Practitioners still praise the plant for its capacity to detoxify the liver. Some Ayurveda practitioners believe that it can prevent gallstones (unsubstantiated for now), and that it prevents heavy metals from embedding in the liver (also unsubstantiated).

Doctors in ancient India prescribed turmeric as an herb specific to women at all points in their life cycles. A woman's puberty ritual required bathing in turmeric, and in one tribe, married women wore a string smeared in turmeric. Widows could not use the root because of its sacred associations with life. All worship of the gods required the presence of the turmeric. To bless a garment, someone smeared a small bit of turmeric paste on a corner of the hem. Many women also used it as a cosmetic.

If, like many cooks, the labels on your powders fade or fall away, and you are uncertain whether you have a bottle of turmeric or curry and don't want to risk burning your tongue in a taste test, you can try this simple test to determine the identity of a given spice. Sprinkle a little of the powder on a paper towel or plate, and spritz with Formula 409. If the powder turns red, you have turmeric. As it turns out, turmeric also can reveal the presence of alkaloids. Turmeric paper, a white paper soaked in a tincture of turmeric and then tried, can reveal the presence of alkaloids in other substances. When alkaloid-filled material hits the paper, the turmeric reacts by turning brown.

Medical Research

In addition to flavor modulation and color commentary, turmeric may offer a host of health benefits according to the standards of Western medicine—the extent of which is still under scrutiny. It is at this time inconclusive whether turmeric actually is an anti-inflammatory, but based on present medical trials in animals, it looks to be.

The chief chemical produced by turmeric, curcumin, is the subject of research for its possible benefits in treating skin and colon cancer, Alzheimer's, arthritis, diabetes, digestive issues, and topical wound care. All the research looks promising, though there is still not enough empirical data gathered to draw a conclusion.

Among the substantiated health claims, turmeric improves bile flow, reduces cholesterol levels, and makes an excellent topical and internal anti-inflammatory. There is conclusive research demonstrating its superior effectiveness in preventing plaque buildup to the more common dental care chemical, chlorhexidine hydrate.

Turmeric's external applications also have plenty of hearsay support. External use, usually in the form of a poultice or a paste smeared on the skin, has proven effective in treating insect bites such as mosquitoes and leeches, treating pink eye, and reducing infections at wound sites.

One of the persistent issues in reaching conclusions in turmeric's medical applications is that it does not stay in the human body for long.

Contraindications

As with all substances, medical professionals advise against overuse. Some people have induced ulcers from overexposure to turmeric. While plenty of folklore extolls its digestive benefits, individuals suffering from gallstones, kidney stones, and acid reflux should avoid use. Women who are pregnant or who have breast cancer should also avoid supplemental use of turmeric.

Gardening

Turmeric, while native to South Asia, can grow almost anywhere as an indoor plant. A would-be gardener just needs to obtain a rhizome, plant it in up to two inches of potting soil, and keep the soil moist but not soaked. Over time, a lily-like plant emerges; harvest the root after the plant reaches maturity.

Applications

There are several ways to use turmeric both internally and externally. Along with preparing curries, turmeric makes an excellent addition to tea—some enthusiasts swear it helps with the common cold. It is also an effective, if messy, beauty ingredient.

Turmeric Cough Drink

If you develop a persistent cough as part of a seasonal cold, try this tea for a little relief.

> 1 cup milk (non-dairy is fine)
>
> 1 teaspoon turmeric

In a pot, stir together milk and turmeric. Bring to a boil, and then reduce heat. Allow the mixture to simmer for three minutes. Drink while still warm.

Turmeric Joint Tea

Turmeric can also help in reducing joint pain because of its anti-inflammatory properties. Get some relief from aches with this tea.

> 1 cup water
>
> 1 teaspoon turmeric
>
> 2 tablespoons ginger
>
> 1 pinch cayenne
>
> 1 stick cinnamon

Combine and allow to reach boiling, then turn off the heat. Drink once it has cooled enough to feel comfortable.

Turmeric Beauty Mask

This mask exfoliates skin and reduces puffiness/swelling on blemishes. Make sure you cover up your lower body with an old towel; turmeric stains with a certain effective enthusiasm.

½ cup cornstarch

1 ½ tablespoons turmeric

1 teaspoon coconut oil (or more if needed)

1–2 teaspoons water

In a bowl, mix together, and add water one drop at a time. Stir together until the mixture forms a paste. Smooth onto skin and leave for fifteen minutes. Wash off in the shower.

Based on the appearance of present research, it looks like much of turmeric's medical fanfare may prove warranted. In this herb lies significant assistance for many of the chronic conditions plaguing us as we live longer. From cholesterol to cancer to diabetes, this root seems to have much to contribute. Yet, even without medical proof, we can enjoy this herb for its color and its seemingly magic ability to modify intense flavors into a coherent blend.

Further Reading

AltMD, "Turmeric," www.altmd.com/Articles /Turmeric--Encyclopedia-of-Alternative-Medicine.

Pandeya, N. K. "Old Wives' Tales: Modern Miracles—Turmeric as Traditional Medicine in India," *Trees for Life Journal,* December 1, 2005, www.tfljournal.org/article .php/20051201122521970.

Diana Rajchel *lives and works in San Francisco with her life partner, at least two robots, and a warren of rabbits that her neighbors insist she tolerate. Because of said warren, she uses her gardening space to grow peppers and pungent herbs that rodents are loath to raid. Diana is also a journalist, author, poet, and occasional prankster. You can read more about her at http://blog.dianarajchel.com.*

Vibrational and Flower Essences

✿ By Danu Forest ✿

Close your eyes for a moment and picture yourself walking barefoot through a rose garden at dawn at the height of summer. The sun shining on the dewy grass, glittering like diamonds scattered on emerald velvet, tiny cobwebs become glittered chandeliers, the first stirring of bird song fills you with the subtle joy of possibility, and as you pass by the roses their delicious scent enfolds you. The moist air of the morning glistens on their soft, blushing petals, the sumptuous beauty of the scene, and the sensuality of the moment fills your heart and being with the delicious joy of being alive. Your body feels divine, a god or a goddess stirring within your heart, and love surrounds you.

Can you imagine this place, this

moment in time, having a spirit, having a divine intelligence, a life of its own? Reach out your hand and touch the roses, gathering their dew onto your skin. Sorrows, fears, any sense that you are less than beautiful within and without just as you are fall away in the perfection of the moment, the wonder of nature; the roses remind you of the secret places of your heart, forgotten but stirring once again, like new love.

Essences in History

The dew of flowers and plants, and water in which flowers have been steeped have long been used for medicinal and therapeutic uses. In India the tradition of offering devotees water upon which flower petals have been scattered goes back millennia and is an excellent example of flower or vibrational essence use: to cleanse the minds and spirits of devotees, as well as restore their physical well-being. The concept of using a flowers *essence*, its "vibrational signature, pattern, or spirit," is thought to have been practiced by many cultures, including Indian, Egyptian, Chinese, and the Australian aborigines.

In Europe, the sixteenth century alchemist Paracelsus and other early chemists collected the dew from lady's mantle (*Alchemilla mollis*) for use in their potions.[1] The dew of flowers and other plants also have a long oral and folkloric history of use by wisewomen and herbal healers in Britain and Ireland. More recently, in the 1920s British Harley Street physician Dr. Edward Bach rediscovered flower essences after his work with bacteria and vaccines led him to work with homeopathy, and then extend his ideas and practice into working directly with the plants themselves. His famous thirty-eight flower remedies are still used to this day. However, since then, the whole area of flower remedies has opened up into a wider field of vibrational essences, using trees, gems, and other factors and sources along with co-creation with the plants themselves very much at the core.

Personal Stories

I first discovered flower and vibrational essences over twenty years ago. I was in a health food shop just outside London when there was a terrible, heart-wrenching cry. A small child had trapped her fingers in the door to the shop and was distraught, in pain, and in shock. Immediately, the woman behind the counter pulled out a bottle of Dr. Bach's Rescue Remedy and gave her a drop on the tongue. The effect was incredible. Within seconds the two-year-old girl calmed down. Her fingers were still clearly sore, and she held them carefully, but the shock and upset had vanished. She was clear-headed, present, and digesting what had happened to her in a way that was remarkably quick for someone her age. She walked to the tap at the back of the shop with her mother to run cold water on her hand and was smiling again within a minute. It seemed almost miraculous.

All these years later, and having made my own essences and treated clients with them for well over a decade, I must say it's a miracle I've gotten used to. A few months ago I treated another small child who'd just fallen and hurt his leg. I put a few drops of my own essences on his head as his mother comforted him, and to our amazement he calmed, sat up, and said, "That's better!" immediately.

Flower and vibrational essences don't just treat upset children; they have been used successfully for all manner of problems—emotional, spiritual, but also physical. Working with the person as a whole rather than treating an individual illness or symptom, and coming from an assumption that many illnesses and problems stem from an inner emotional, psychological, or spiritual imbalance, these essences gently treat the underlying issues that can lie at the core of many of our everyday health concerns, and can form an invaluable support to conventional or herbal medicine. However, physical changes in response to flower or vibrational essences are regularly reported, and many healers, herbalists, alternative and complementary therapists as well as those working in hospices and cancer clinics in Britain, the United States, and Australia now use vibrational essences in their daily work. They are also becoming a popular addition to the family first aid kit.

What Is a Vibrational Essence?

Vibrational essences are usually a mixture of spring water that has imbued the energetic imprint, pattern, vibration, or spirit of plants, trees, crystals, or other natural sources preserved in alcohol, glycerine, or vinegar. They are also made or added into other products such as balms, creams, and oils.

A belief in the inherent spirit of nature, or of plants, trees, and other living things, exists in many spiritual traditions around the world and is a key feature in some of the oldest religions, spiritual practices, and philosophies in the world as well as the earliest healing practices. In India the spirits of plants, and even geographical areas, are known as *devas*, meaning "shining ones." In ancient Greece the belief in the spirits of plants, especially trees, was widespread, and the name for an oak tree spirit, a *dryad*, remains with us today as a generic term for tree spirit, while the term deva now also has widespread use. In Celtic folklore the spirits of plants and trees had many names, but were also commonly understood as "the fair folk" or "the shining ones," reflecting a similarity with the devas of Hinduism and Buddhism, as well as the *genius loci*, or "spirits of place."

Modern New Age thought has also embraced the concept of tree and plant spirits, as well as quantum physics, reflecting that the spirit may be the same as a being's vibrational signature, or energetic pattern. These spirits, or energetic patterns, interact with us for our well-being.

How Do They Work?

Vibrational essences work with the higher levels of our consciousness, understood in various ways as our spirit, the positive aspects of our personality or psychology, our "higher selves," or even in shamanic terms as "the upper world" where the idea of our physical incarnation was first conceived. These interact with our rational minds and our sense of our own bodies to encourage us to change our patterns of thought or behavior to attract more well-being. Other ways of looking at it are that the energetic pattern of the plants, the part of them that is spirit, the blueprint of their being, interacts and aligns with our own spirit or energetic pattern, rebalancing, correcting, adding things that we lack or have lost, and clearing away what we no longer need.

Medical science has explored the link between our mental and emotional states for many years, and those links are now commonly acknowledged. Vibrational essences take this logic a stage further by incorporating our spirits, or vibrational pattern, into consideration, tackling physical, emotional, or psychological issues at the core—their spiritual or vibrational source—from which positive or negative influences are able to ripple through into physical effects and forms.

Scientific Studies

While there are thousands of documented positive testimonials and millions of cases of anecdotal evidence over decades of use around the world, there has been only limited scientific study into vibrational essences. However, two important studies in the United Kingdom have shown remarkable results. In 1976 Brian Forbes, a consultant who ran a cancer clinic in Bristol, found that flower essences made a notable difference in the ability of cancer sufferers to cope and come to terms with their condition. In 2007 Michael Hyland, professor of health psychology at Plymouth University, used a variety of Green Man Essences "Focus Fixes" for toddler tantrums[2] in an experiment that statistically proved that it reduced the frequency and severity of tantrums in children between two and five years old. While the matter of how vibrational essences work is still argued, the personal experience of many is that they work very well with none of the potential side effects that conventional medicine can have.

Identifying Plant Uses

In some ways, the way that certain plants, trees, and other things have been identified as useful for essences follows the lines of herbalism. The plant signature, its shape, color, smell, or other physical characteristics as well as its folklore and uses elsewhere can all help inform us of its potential uses. Oak is a good example of an essence to assist in discovering or building one's own inner strength and resilience. Rose, as described earlier, also speaks for itself. It is often used to promote inner peace, to develop our ability to feel love, and to heal our emotions. Rose is also good for helping us have a better relationship with our bodies and the physical world around us, reminding us of the joy of sensuality and the beauty of the natural world. Whatever our age, health, or relationship status, rekindle these things in someone with health problems gently adjust their attitude to life and themselves, and much of their condition can be made more comfortable at the very least.

There are many resources online as well as numerous organizations promoting the use of vibrational essences and listing directories of plants and their therapeutic essence uses. However, it is also okay to use your own sense of intuition and herbal knowledge. Many of the best practitioners use their relationship with nature, their insight, and subtle senses to help them discover which essences to use or make, while others use kinesiology or a careful study of effects together with logical deduction. As no physical plant matter is taken into the body, essences are safe to use and pose very little risk for those new to working with them.

Here Are Some Essences to Try:

Apple blossom for wholeness and general healing; good for convalescents, those with depression, and to support children.

Holly for anger and jealousy issues; feeling "prickly."

Comfrey to ease suffering from stress and prolonged trauma, or for those who feel bruised by life.

Hawthorn blossom to ease stress, broken hearts, and anxiety.

Star of Bethlehem for shock and trauma in the past or present.

Oak for strength, exhaustion, and helping the sufferer find the ability to cope.

Rose to help open the heart, bring joy and serenity back after a hard time, and find beauty once again.

Making Your Own Vibrational Essences

Making your own vibrational essences is easy and can be a wonderful way to spend a sunny day. While it's possible to buy essences, the best ones will be made in very much the same ways that you could try for yourself.

You need spring water, access to a healthy, blooming plant that you want to work with, and a sunny day. You will also need a glass bowl, a suitable bottle, sterilizing equipment, and a preservative, such as brandy, if you want your essence to keep for a while.

Some practitioners and manufacturers make their essences by cutting their chosen flower and placing it in spring water out somewhere sunny. Others will not leave the essence in the sun, but will instead take the blooms and water, and boil over a naked flame, such as a gas stove, for a few minutes. (Those who use this technique must be sure they are working with plants that are safe to imbibe.) Some may accompany their essence making with prayers, communion with the plant spirits, or other sacred activity; others simply add the flowers to the water, leave them out in the sun for a few hours, and let nature do the work. Personal beliefs, philosophy, or religion of the manufacturer seem to have little effect on the essences themselves.

Personally, I don't cut the flowers. I ask the plants themselves for their assistance, and place a bowl of water amongst the blooms to infuse their essence in this way so that no harm is done to the plant, and the most living essence is drawn into the water. I find this works best for me, and working in this way has added to my own insights about how to work with plants in various ways for healing, but I know others who work differently who also have very positive results. The best way to learn is to try it out for yourself and see what you think, see what works for you.

Finally, the blooms if used are removed, being careful not to touch them or the water with your skin, and the water is decanted into a sterilized dark glass bottle, to 50 percent. The bottle is usually topped up the remaining 50 percent with brandy or another preservative. If no preservative is used, then the essence can only be taken internally for a few days, but can still be used in a variety of other ways quite safely for some time after.

How to Take Them

The finished bottle of essence is commonly called the "master," and only a few drops of this are added to water and preservative to make a stock bottle—these are the stage and dilution commonly sold in the shops. These can be taken on the tongue or, more economically, they can be diluted further into a "dose bottle" where a few drops are put into a small bottle of water, taken over a day or two.

Vibrational essences can also be added to bath water, to plant misters to spray a room, in oil burners, in food and drink, anointed on the brow or other part of the body, or even used by placing a few drops in a bowl of water and left out somewhere in the home. As they are perfectly safe, they can be used on children, those on strong medications, and even animals and plants with positive effects. A few bottles tailored to the household's needs can make a valuable addition to the family medicine chest.

Endnotes

1. The British Flower and Vibrational Essences Association. May 2014, http://bfvea.com/resources/BFVEA_guide _to_FE__VIB_Essencesnov13.pdf.
2. Green Man Essences shop, http://www.greenmanshop .co.uk/acatalog/30mls_Focus_Fixes.html.

Resources

Danu Forest, http://www.danuforest.co.uk/individual_es-sences_23.html.

The British Flower and Vibrational Essences Association, http://bfvea.com.

The Bach Centre, www.bachcentre.com.

The Flower Essence Society, www.flowersociety.org.

Danu Forest *is a respected Wisewoman, teacher, writer, and healer. She is an Ard banDrui (Arch Druidess) of the Druid clan of Dana, and is an experienced vibrational essence practitioner making her own essences using sacred well water and traditional Celtic plants for many years. She leads her own Druid grove as well as running a thriving healing practice in Glastonbury. For more info and consultations go to www.danuforest.co.uk*

Hollies I Have Known

❧ By Linda Raedisch ❧

For the past five years I have been in a happy relationship with a ten-foot-tall *Ilex aquifolium*. If you're in the habit of receiving Christmas cards you won't need me to describe him, for he's a typical English holly. Both his height and fullness of his figure suggest he is a mature gentleman, though I would hesitate to call him old. As I write this in early September, he is busy producing clusters of pale green berries close to the bark of his outermost branches. I'm not really a holly expert, not when it comes to the botanical side of things, so I can't swear that my beloved tree is actually a "he." English hollies are *dioecious*, which is the Latinized Greek way of saying they're divided into "two houses," both alike in dignity, I'm

sure. Since males and females produce both fruits and flowers, I have no idea if my particular holly is a Romeo or a Juliet. I do, however, hope he's a stag holly, as horticulturists call the male species; with his tall stature and coat of glossy leaves he has all the look of a knight in shining armor.

Male or female, this year's crop of berries proves that it has had sexual congress, through the bees, with another holly in the neighborhood. If it is, in fact, a male specimen, then my English gentleman is also a bit of a rascal, for one male holly can easily service five females, even if they've never met.

Did I mention he likes to host parties? Whenever I pass by, his densely packed limbs are aflutter with tufted titmice, black-capped chickadees, and "little brown jobs" as they like to call them in his native Britain.

According to the Highlanders of Scotland, grass will not grow beneath a holly tree because that is where the infamous Blue Hag of Winter keeps her walking staff, but I'm pretty sure it's the white carpet of bird droppings that keeps the grass down. The birds don't come to feast on the berries; it's the dark, cavelike shelter of the boughs that attracts them. As for me, I simply enjoy the pleasure of his company.

I won't give out my beau's address because he's not, strictly speaking, mine; he resides within the tastefully and painstak-ingly landscaped grounds of a condominium complex of which I, unfortunately, am not a resident. Has this stopped me from taking a few clippings to place among my advent candles in the waning days of autumn? Not exactly. I'm afraid the same goes for the blue-berried juniper from the office park, and any pine-cone that catches my eye. Oh, the joys of the suburban jungle!

I pass the complex almost every other day on my walk into town, ogling the faux Colonial facades and brick chimneys, the network of slate paths punctuated by flowering plums, rose-begonias, and sprays of Russian sage. This quaint little village was originally built as a shopping district in the 1970s, and I suspect my valiant green knight has been there from the beginning. He would have been a much more slender chap in those days and only a few feet high, but already, I imagine, exuding Old World charm. The English holly is about as Old World as you can get. In fact, it still goes by something very close to its Anglo-Saxon name, *holegn*.

While the *Ilex aquifolium* is an immigrant, there are plenty of hollies native to the New World, and many of them thrive in my own northern New Jersey. Botanists have dubbed the American holly *Ilex opaca*, that is, "opaque," because the leaves are not as shiny as those of its English cousins. But really, the American holly will do.

I recently came across a thoroughly respectable specimen at the woodsy end of my local arboretum. This one had the unpretentious charm of a Scandinavian Christmas tree with plenty of space between the branches for birds to perch and enjoy the view. Where *Ilex aquifolium* is jovial, *Ilex opaca* is guardedly merry.

My new acquaintance certainly seemed at home there in the shadow of the towering oaks, just as *Ilex aquifolium* would have been in the primeval forests of Europe. Though a little on the scrappy side, *Ilex opaca* is every inch a holly and would not look out of place in any December window display. The thickets of the Northeast have historically been a cheap source of seasonal greenery, especially in Pennsylvania where Christmas has never gone out of style. The impoverished residents of southern New Jersey have been known to scrape their way through the winter by setting up roadside stands and hawking pinecones and sprigs of holly gathered in the wilds of the Pine Barrens. Still, I would think twice or even three times before taking a cutting from this spindly fellow.

It was by the side of a dirt path leading to Winakung, the twentieth century recreation of a seventeenth century Lenape village, that I had my first significant encounter with a native holly. Winakung means "Place of Sassafras" in Lenape, but it was the not-very-hollylike shrub with the placard bearing the name "yaupon" that caught my interest. The yaupon holly's Latin name is *Ilex vomitoria*, but that did not stop Native Americans from roasting and brewing the leaves into a caffeine-rich black tea. Later, English colonists used it to give a kick to their persimmon beer. (Just don't drink too much or it will live up to its Latin name!) In the older literature, it is sometimes spelled *japon*, but it has nothing to do with Japan; the name means "little shrubby thing" in Catawba.

Yaupon tea played a role in the rituals of the Mississipian culture of the ninth to twelfth centuries when it was drunk from incised conch shells; Cherokee and Creek tribes use it as a sacrament to this day. The Catawba, Creek, and Cherokee are Southeastern tribes, as is the tribe of *Ilex vomitoria*, so what was my plucky little friend doing so far north? I must admit I have no idea. I can only hope he's managed to survive the winters here in zone 7. As I recall, there were other, more appropriate, herbs in the Winakung healer's garden, but someone must have felt that only yaupon could bestow that hint of holiness and mystery the place needed. (Though curious writers and armchair ethnobotanists used to be welcome to wander in and out of Winakung, the village is now open only to school groups.)

I don't expect to stumble upon another yaupon here in New Jersey, but we do have plenty of other wild hollies in addition to opaca. One of my favorites is *Ilex glabra*, or inkberry. The leaves, just barely crenated, resemble bay leaves, while the lustrous black berries make it the perfect gothic Yuletide wreath. Please don't go cutting it from the wild, though! *Ilex glabra* has many cultivars that you can grow in your own backyard.

Winterberry, *Ilex verticillata*, also lacks prickles. In fact, the leaves look positively deciduous, which they are. The winterberry's leaves are shed in fall, but the scarlet fruits party on through the winter just like those of more conventional hollies.

Mountain holly, also known as catberry, doesn't look much like a holly, and it's not. True hollies have the genus name *Ilex*, and mountain holly belongs to the genus *Nemopanthus*. The mountain holly's red berries, though not exactly poisonous, are relished by neither bird nor beast, but the Potowatomi managed to make a syrup by boiling its branches. At home in the swamp, mountain holly eschews the forest's understory to form its own thickets in waterlogged soil.

It was in that same woodsy corner of the arboretum where I found the true holly, *Ilex opaca*, that I also ran into the most convincing pretender of all; a Goshiki false holly, whose mottled cream and green leaves looked to my unpracticed eye like any of a number of cultivated English hollies. But Goshiki is a cultivar of *Osmanthus heterophyllus*, a member of the olive family.

In Japan it answers to the name *hiiragi*, and hiiragi's time to shine is at the festival of Setsubun, which celebrates the last day of winter at the beginning of February. The Japanese are better attuned to the changing seasons than the rest of us and can apparently detect signs of spring when there is still snow on the ground. Setsubun is marked by the widespread throwing of parched soybeans, the goal being to pelt as many demons as you can so they won't follow you into the new year.

I had hoped to open this section on hiiragi with a quote from Basho, but it seems that the closest the beloved haiku master ever got to writing about *Osmanthus heterophyllus* is this observation of another festival, Boys' Day:

iris growing

under the eaves from a sardine's

weathered skull

Wait. Where's the hiiragi? Bear with me. One of the most potent symbols of Setsubun is a sprig of hiiragi hung on the front door. The eighteenth century silk painter Shunsho has left us with a scene of two overdressed and rather clumsy looking courtesans attempting to hoist a third courtesan high enough to fix a sprig of hiiragi to the top of a gate. At the ladies' feet is a small, red laquered stand holding more hiiragi twigs as well as three fish heads. Yes, fish heads, because no hiiragi charm is complete without a few grilled sardine heads impaled among the leaves. It's not supposed to look pretty; the painful prickles and fishy miasma are meant to prevent demons from passing through the gate and into the home. Just as many Americans allow the ghastly remains of their Christmas wreaths to collide with their Valentine decorations some Japanese apparently neglect to take their sardine skulls down before Boys' Day, which is celebrated in May.

In case you're wondering, there is such a thing as a true Japanese holly. It's *inutsuge*, also known in English as "box-leaved holly," because it makes such a nice hedge. Its Latin name is *Ilex crenata*, but the notches in its leaves are hardly perceptible, let alone prickly, and therefore no deterrent to otherworldly troublemakers.

I've used up a lot of space describing the prickliness, or lack thereof, of the leaves of various hollies. Were I to devise a prickliness scale for the genus *Ilex,* I would put the mountain winterberry, *Ilex montana,* at the very bottom, and the good old English holly at the top. I have also mentioned that birds are either not fond of holly berries or they ignore them completely. So, assuming that the plant world does not concern itself with the comings and goings of demons, where is the need for prickles at all? It must be that someone, at some time during the holly's evolution, tried to wrap their lips around those leaves and the holly didn't like it.

In the case of the American holly, the culprit was probably the white-tailed deer. *Ilex opaca's* spindliness means it does not respond well to too much pruning, so even casual browsing would have had deleterious effects. English holly looks like it could withstand a bit of nibbling, but let's not forget that English holly has long been a denizen of the hedgerows, and hedgerows mean farming, and farming means livestock.

In this case, the proof of the pudding is in the attempt to eat it. In the mid-1800s, one Mr. Daker of Barton's End in Kent noted how the uppermost leaves of his holly bushes had few or no prickles because his cows could not reach them. Factor in the insatiable sheep that have dotted English pastures for the last thousand years, and it is no wonder that *Ilex aquifolium* has armed itself so well.

Bibliography

Basho, Matsuo. *Basho: The Complete Haiku. Translated, annotated, and with an introduction by Jane Reichold.* New York: Kodansha International, 2008.

Erichsen-Brown, Charlotte. *Medicinal and Other Uses of North*

American Plants: A Historical Survey with Special Reference to Eastern Indian Tribes. New York: Dover Publications, 1989.

Great Swamp National Wildlife Refuge. *Guide to Trees and Shrubs of the Wildlife Observation Center, 3rd Edition.* Basking Ridge, NJ: Friends of the Great Swamp National Wildlife Refuge, Inc., 2011.

Kavasch, E. Barrie. *Native Harvests: American Indian Wild Foods and Recipes.* Mineola, NY: Dover Publications, 2005.

Leopold, Donald J. *Native Plants of the Northeast: A Guide for Gardening and Conservation.* Portland, OR: Timber Press, 2005.

Ordish, George. *The Living Garden: The 400-year History of an English Garden.* Boston: Houghton Mifflin, 1985.

Taylor, Raymond L. *Plants of Colonial Days.* Mineola, NY: Dover Publications, 1996.

Yoshida, Susugu. *Ukiyo-E: 250 Years of Japanese Art.* New York: Mayflower Books, 1978.

Linda Raedisch *wrote her first book at the age of six on pages cut from a brown paper bag. She has been writing professionally since 2011 and her first book for Llewellyn,* Night of the Witches: Folklore, Traditions and Recipes for Celebrating Walpurgis Night, *has been translated into French. You can learn more about holly and other seasonal greens in her second book,* The Old Magic of Christmas: Yuletide Traditions for the Darkest Days of the Year *(Llewellyn, 2013). Ethnobotany is one of Linda's favorite fields, especially when it crosses paths with the supernatural, and she has been a frequent guest on the paranormal talk radio circuit. A shoe size 9 in real life, she maintains only a miniscule digital footprint.*

Herbs and Trees of the Northwest Coniferous Forest

⇜ By Susan Pesznecker ⇝

Note: In the Pacific Northwest, where I hail from, the indigenous First People whom I know personally prefer the title of Indian to Native American. I honor this use.

I'm fortunate to live in one of the most beautiful places on earth: the United States' Pacific Northwest. I live in the Willamette Valley between the coast and Cascade Ranges, the latter with 11,000-foot-plus glaciated peaks and active volcanoes. From my home, I'm an hour from these mountains and from the Pacific Ocean. Directly east is the Columbia River Gorge, and if I drive a couple of hours southeast I'll hit Oregon's high desert, one of the least-populated places in the United States and featuring some

of the country's darkest night skies. Like I said—a beautiful place. Pretty much perfect, really. And our forests? They're the icons, the poster children of the northwest.

We Oregonians have a complex relationship with our forests, which are used by animals, people, and the logging industry alike. Oregon's forests are composed of both private and public lands and cover some 48 percent of the state's land mass. The forests are primarily coniferous / evergreen, but also contain a number of deciduous trees including the hawthorn, oak, aspen, and alder. Many of our coniferous forests are *first growth* or *second growth*, the aftermath of logging with replanting or, in some cases, of either tsunami or forest fire.

A first growth coniferous forest is characterized by small-girth trees that are all about the same size and are packed relatively closely together. There's little diversity or complexity in the first growth forest because enough time hasn't passed to allow multiple species to take hold. If the forest has been replanted, there is typically a single dominant conifer. If it's recovering from a forest fire or tsunami, alder may be the first tree to appear, followed by conifers. A second growth forest contains both young- and medium-aged conifers, along with a varied understory: different trees, shrubs, and ground cover, all fairly mature.

But an old growth forest? That's a different animal altogether. The old growth forest contains trees that are at least 200 years old, but it also hosts trees of all ages, right down to saplings. The old growth forest incorporates a dense, rich canopy with openings created when old trees die and fall to the forest floor. These openings allow sunlight to penetrate the forest floor and create the conditions needed for young trees to grow, as well as shrubs, ferns, groundcover, and other understory plants. The old growth forest also contains dead trees; if these fall horizontally they're called nurse logs. If standing vertically, they're snags. Both provide vital resources for plants and animals. Look into a pristine old growth forest, and what you'll see is immense variety in a millennial-old setting that has not been altered by humans.

The coniferous forest supports a widely diverse ecosystem, including a rich plant understory. The forest floor itself is dense, spongy, and composed of layers of composed plant material, rotting wood, and animal waste. It is rich in nutrients and provides an ideal locus for woody and herbaceous plants, and there's hardly a better place on Earth for a herbalist to go wildcrafting. Lace up those hiking boots, grab your basket, and let's explore.

Douglas Fir

West of the Cascade Range the most common northwest conifer is the Douglas fir. Despite its name, it isn't a true fir and is actually a member of the pine family, and is the second-tallest conifer in the world after the coastal redwood. According to the *Oregon Forest Facts*, if you're looking at a conifer in Oregon or Washington, eight out of ten times it's going to be a Douglas fir. The tree's leaves are arranged spirally, all around the branches, and are not sharp or prickly when brushed against the skin. The tree's topmost point—the lead—is straight, and the branches tend to sweep upward, as if the tree extends its "arms" toward the sky.

The young, green branch tips that form in the spring can be steeped in hot water for several hours to form a refreshing tea that is rich in Vitamin C. The tree's needles can be chopped and infused in a carrier oil; the resulting oil is richly scented and can be used in body oils, lotions, and balms. The resin, or pitch, was used by northwest Indians as a wound poultice, while a decoction made from the under-bark (*cambium*) treated colds, sore throats, and menstrual problems. A tea made from the needles or bark has potent antifungal properties. The green branches are often used in sweat lodge ceremonies.

> **Technique: Oil-based Infusion**. To infuse conifer needles in oil, chop them finely, place in a double boiler over simmering water, and cover with olive oil (or another high-quality carrier oil). Simmer for about 30 minutes, then turn off the heat. Repeat this process over several days, covering with a cloth (not a lid) at night. The goal is to "heat out" the moisture from the needles, while infusing the aromatics into the oil. When finished, strain and bottle.

Pine (Pinus species)

If the Douglas fir is most common west of the Cascades, the ponderosa pine holds that title on the east side. All pines have needles that grow in bunches of two to five. Ponderosa pines are strikingly tall and known for a decorative jigsaw puzzle bark. Like all pines, the ponderosa is evergreen and resinous, producing lots of what is commonly called pitch, a sticky substance that oozes out when the bark is damaged. Medicinally, pitch can be chewed or sucked on to treat a cough or sore throat—nature's lozenge. It makes a great fire starter and can be burned as an incense fumigant to treat lung disorders.

> **Technique: Incense**. To make a wild conifer incense, process needles, leaf tips, and resin/pitch by chopping or grinding with a mortar and pestle. Use the incense "loose" by burning in a thurible or atop a

charcoal pellet, or shape it into rough cones by adding more resin or a natural binder like beeswax.

Other northwest pines include the lodge pole, western white, and shore varieties. The resin, bark, and needles of all pine trees are rich in essential oils, vitamins, and natural antimicrobial compounds. An infusion made from these materials is useful for washing wounds and treating skin infections. A tea made from chopped needles and/or leaf tips is also used to treat coughs, colds, and fever.

Caution: Ponderosa pine remedies have abortifacient properties (i.e., they stimulate uterine contraction), and should not be used by women who are pregnant or may become pregnant.

Pine species have sacred uses, too. According to Moerman, the branches were used in sweat ceremonies, and the needles were smoked to bring hallucinations and for luck. The smoke is believed to repel evil spirits.

Western Red Cedar

The western red cedar is a massive tree in both girth and height, and examples have been identified that are more than 1,400 years old. The leaves are flat and waxy and tend to droop, as does the lead; twinelike "withes" hang from the branches. The tree requires a cool, wet, maritime climate, and thus tends to grow in coastal regions and west of the Cascade range.

Medicinally, needle and twig infusions can treat cough, tuberculosis, rheumatism, stomach pain, kidney trouble, and a number of other common disorders. The infusion also provides high levels of Vitamins A and C, and may be used as a tonic. Krohn describes recent research showing that western red cedar stimulates the body's white blood cell response, helping to fight infections.

Technique: Water-based Infusion. To make a water-based infusion (also known as a tea) steep aerial parts (soft leaf tips, finely chopped needles, flowers) in near-boiling water until the flavor and/or aromatics are extracted. Strain and use.

Cedar needles can be powdered and mixed with fish oil to make poultices for chest colds, arthritis, skin rashes, and to remove warts. The inner bark is mildly abortifacient and, according to Moerman, was chewed by Indians to induce menstruation and labor. The smoke from the wood (incense) is used for ritual purification and the driving away of evil spirits.

Caution: Western red cedar's essential oils are high in thujones, a type of ketone that can be toxic if taken in excess or by someone with weakened kidneys or liver. The essential oil should not be taken internally—unless with professional guidance—and should not be used during pregnancy.

Spruce

Spruces are fairly easy to identify, being known for rough, warty twigs; flaking, scaly bark; and needles that are stiff and sharp. The trees can grow to significant size, but often are more impressive in terms of diameter and "root spread" than in height. The most common northwest species is the Sitka spruce. Tea made from cambium bark, twigs, and needles is used to treat respiratory and stomach disorders, and as a laxative. The needles and powdered bark can be burned as a purifying incense, and to treat rheumatism.

As with pines, spruce's resinous pitchy gum can be used to treat sore throats and respiratory issues. The pitch was also used by local Indians to treat skin lesions and infections.

Red Alder

Alder is an important understory tree in the coniferous forest; it is a disturbance-loving species and is one of the first to reappear after anything from bulldozing to forest fire to volcanic eruption. The young alders provide the shade and moisture needed for young conifers to grow and thrive, thus helping maintain a diverse forest ecosystem. Alder prefers moist areas and can tolerate part shade; under optimal conditions, it grows with startling speed, stabilizing and reclaiming the disturbed landscape. It also enriches the landscape through nitrogen-fixing nodules on its roots.

The tree itself yields many potent medicines. Alder sap is rich in vitamins and is often consumed as a tonic. A leaf infusion is strongly antiseptic and can be used externally to treat wounds and skin infections; taken internally, the infusion treats respiratory problems. The bark, buds, and leaves can be poulticed to treat skin problems. The stem bark has strong antiemetic properties and was used by local Indians as a treatment for poisons or food poisoning.

> **Technique: Poultice**. To make a poultice chop fresh leaves, needles, bark, and/or berries finely, making a paste. Moisten if needed with a bit of neutral oil, like olive oil.

Bush Berries: Salmonberry, Thimbleberry, Huckleberry

Thimble- and salmonberries are part of the Rose family, and tend to grow best in damp, partially shaded areas in the forest understory. The red thimbleberries are both astringent and tonic, and are used to treat a wide variety of ailments, particularly stomach problems and as a tonic for weak or anemic blood.

The leaves and berries are poulticed onto wounds where they have antimicrobial properties and speed wound healing. A root decoction is useful for treating fever, influenza, and tonsillitis. According to Foster and Hobbs, research suggests that thimbleberry shortens coagulation times and thus helps control bleeding.

> **Technique: Decoction**. In a water-based infusion, a plant's delicate aerial parts are briefly steeped in water. In contrast, a decoction uses longer cooking to extract components from tougher plant materials. Place chopped bark, roots, twigs, leaves, or berries in a saucepan, cover with water, and simmer gently (do not boil) for 30 to 60 minutes. Strain and use.

Salmonberries have salmon-colored berries that are more insipid in flavor than thimbleberries. The berries are used similarly to thimbleberries, while the twigs and above-the-ground bark have pain-relieving properties. The root bark is decocted to treat stomach problems, and the roots themselves for digestive, skin, and gynecological issues. Macerated leaves have been used to pack a tooth as a toothache treatment.

Like their modern relative, the blueberry, huckleberries are members of the genus *Vaccinium*. The huckleberry's fruit is smaller, darker, and more tart than that of the blueberry. Huckleberries are found in the northwest mountainous forests. Infusions of the roots, stems, leaves, and/or berries can treat joint and lung disorders. An alcohol-based tincture of the roots and berries is strongly diuretic. Some species of huckleberry are abortifacients, inducing labor, bringing on menses, and speeding recovery after childbirth. According to Foster and Hobbs, modern research shows that huckleberry may be effective in treating the high blood sugars of diabetes.

Wild Roses

Wild roses of the northwest coniferous forest include the nootka, wood, and California wild varieties. All belong to the Rose family, and all are characterized by the production of fragrant flowers followed by the development of the plant's fruit: the rose hip. Rose hips are particularly well known for a very high Vitamin C content, as well as for high levels of antioxidants, making them valuable for treating all kinds of illnesses—especially those caused by viruses. Rose hip tea is best for this, but the hips can also be chewed whole if necessary. Gather the hips in the fall, preferably right after the first frost. When fully dried, they store well for one year and can be frozen for longer periods.

> **Technique: Drying Materials.** Dry needles, leaves, rose hips, and other plant materials on newspaper or blotting paper in a cookie sheet or other broad surface, leaving the sheet in a warm room out of direct sunlight. Most will be fully dried in a few days; heavier pieces will take longer. I recommend avoiding microwave or dehydrator drying as these drive out most of the essential oils; however, berries and large rose hips may sometimes benefit from faster drying in order to prevent molding.

Salal

Salal is a common evergreen shrub in the northwest coniferous forest, growing to several feet in height when mature and forming dense thickets. The leaves are deep green, broad, and waxy. The dark purplish-blue berries are edible, but rather insipid. A leaf tea can be used to treat gastric and respiratory problems, while a chewed leaf poultice was used by the Indians to treat wounds and skin infections. The leaves are astringent and can be chewed after meals to treat indigestion.

Enjoy working with natural herbs and medicines fresh from the coniferous forest!

Works Cited and Consulted

Foster, Steven, and Christopher Hobbs. *A Field Guide to Western Medicinal Plants and Herbs.* Boston: Houghton Mifflin, Co., 2002.

Krohn, Elise. *Evergreen Tree Medicine.* WildCraft Weekend Seminar, White Salmon, WA: 2014.

Moerman, Daniel E. *Native American Medicinal Plants: An Ethnobotanical Dictionary.* Portland, OR: Timber Press, 2009.

Pojar, Jim, and Andy McKinnon. *Plants of the Pacific Northwest Coast: Washington, Oregon, British Columbia, and Alaska.* Redmond, WA: Lone Pine, 1994.

Susan "Moonwriter" Pesznecker *is a writer, college English teacher, nurse, and hearth Pagan/Druid living in northwestern Oregon. Sue holds a master's degree in professional writing and loves to read, watch the stars, camp with her wonder poodle, and work in her own biodynamic garden. She is co-founder of the Druid Grove of Two Coasts and the online Ars Viarum Magicarum—A Magical Conservatory (http://www.magicalconservatory.com/). Sue* has authored The Magickal Retreat *(Llewellyn, 2012),* Crafting Magick with Pen and Ink *(Llewellyn, 2009), and is a regular contributor to many of the Llewellyn Annuals. Visit her on her web page (http://www.susanpesznecker.com/) and her Facebook author page (https://www.facebook.com/SusanMoonwriterPesznecker).*

Herbal Love Charms:
A Little Look at the Folklore

❧ By Laurel Reufner ☙

This article has its roots in the old medieval folk ballad "Scarborough Fair." My mother had always told me that the herbs being referenced—parsley, sage, rosemary, and thyme—were used in a love charm or potion. It got me to wondering what other plants our forebears might have linked to matters of love. And now I get to share what I've found with you.

Perhaps one of the most interesting bits of lore uncovered while researching this article was that of sowing hempseed. A young woman would scatter a handful of seeds on the ground and then run away. Once she stopped to look back, she would be able to see her future lover reaping the miraculously grown grains. The area in which a girl lived determined the best time of year for performing the divination—usually Midsummer's Eve or Day—but always at night. Sometimes the seeds would be sown in a church yard, but other times and places would have it happen in the deep woods. Oh, and an alternative time might be All Hallow's Eve.

Yarrow was believed to be sacred to Venus, goddess of love, so it makes perfect sense for the herb to have ties to the folklore of love. Simply stick it under your pillow to dream of a future lover. One source suggested adding orange blossoms to the yarrow in order to dream of your future husband. I came across a couple of different verses to be said while tucking the yarrow in.

"Good morrow, good yarrow, good morrow to thee:

I hope 'gain the morrow my lover to see,

And that he may be married to me;

The color of his hair, and the clothes he does wear;

And if he be for me, may his face be turned to me;

And if he be not, dark and surly he be,

And his back turned to me." (Vickery, 127)

Or:

"Thou pretty herb of Venus tree,

thy name is yarrow;

Now who my bosom friend must must be,

Pray tell me tomorrow."

There was also a folk tradition of greeting any yarrow plants that one might pass while on their daily travels. "Good morrow, good yarrow, good morrow to thee." (Vickery, 127)

Finally, the simplest way yarrow was used as a love charm involved placing a sprig into a buttonhole or pinning on a blossom in order to attract love your way. The beauty of much of this folklore lies in the simplicity.

Long before lavender came to be associated with chastity, it had a far more romantic reputation in the lore. Lavender sachets were carried to attract a lover (especially of the masculine variety). Lavender was burned as an incense for the same reasons. Perhaps spreading linens over the lavender bushes to dry, scenting them with the fragrance, served to keep a marriage happy.

Interestingly enough, lavender could either symbolize devotion and undying love or distrust. It all depended on which source for the language of flowers that you consulted.

I'm used to the lore on basil for prosperity, but did you know that keeping a pot of basil on your windowsill would attract love? Also, it was believed that if a young woman could get a young man to accept a sprig of basil from her hand that he would then fall in love with her.

Mandrake has a far bigger reputation with regard to lust, but according to the lore, it also has a place in love charm. Simply carry a piece of the root with you to attract someone your way. Of course, if you go far enough back in the lore, obtaining a mandrake from the wild was considered a dangerous prospect. It was believed that the root would emit a killing shriek when pulled from the ground. And if one already had a lover, then they both needed to carry a piece of the same root in order to remain together. (A branch from a bay tree, or even honeysuckle, could be used for the same purposes.)

One of my favorite flowers also plays a part in the lore—Johnny jump-ups, or violas. I'm lucky enough to live in an area where they grow wild and abundant in our yard, so I can pick my fill of them come spring. In a charming bit of lore, it's claimed that placing the flowers on the closed eyes of a sleeping person would make them, upon awakening, fall in love with the first person they saw.

Apples may very well show up more often in folklore than any other plant. One of the simplest divinatory methods to find out a lover's name was to peel an apple (an orange would also do) all in one go. Next, the peel was tossed over the shoulder and it supposedly would fall in such a way as to form the first initial of your future sweetie. In theory, this was best when done outside at night. If the peel breaks, it won't work. Actually, some sources say that a broken apple peel is a sign that the querying party wouldn't marry at all!

One could also divine information by twisting the stem of the apple while reciting the alphabet. Each twist of the stem represented one letter. Whatever letter the stem finally broke on represented the first initial of the future love.

Yet another method of apple love divination involves sleeping with an apple under your pillow. You should dream of your future love. The trick here would seem to be remembering your dream upon waking. However, considering how uncomfortable it might be to sleep on the lump made by an apple, perhaps the dreamer never fell into that sound of a sleep, making the task of remembering easier.

Want to know in which direction your future lover lived? For this one, an apple pip, or seed, was needed. Hold it between the thumb and a finger, squeezing tightly while turning in a circle and reciting the following rhyme:

"North, south, east, west,

Tell me where my love doth rest."

One final bit of apple lore before I go—not only could the number of seeds tell one how many children they would have, but it would also help divine the future for a girl and her hoped-for love. I'm assuming that the querent already had a particular young man in mind. All she had to do next was count the number of pips:

"One I love,

Two I love,

Three I love I say;

Four I love with all my heart,

And five I cast away;

Six he loves

Seven she loves

Eight they both love;

Nine he comes

And ten he tarries,

Eleven he courts

And twelve he marries."

Getting back to the "Scarborough Fair" ballad, does it really refer to a love charm? According to the relevant sources

I used for research, the answer is probably not. Some writers suggest that the song is sung by a man to his former love and that it gives a series of impossible tasks to be performed before they can reunite. They also give quite a complicated history for the song, with our better known version probably dating to the nineteenth century, so the version we know isn't even medieval.

Other sources claim that the song lists the attributes, in herbal form, necessary for a successful union. All of them draw heavily on what would be the symbolic meanings of the herbs, which it is assumed most people knew. According to the writer Beth Trissel, parsley would have represented comfort, sage was strength, rosemary was love, and thyme represented courage. I'm not sure how well I agree with it all, given the lore on parsley. It used to be considered the herb of death. However, *Cunningham's Encyclopedia of Magical Herbs* meanings for the herbs can pretty much back up Trissel's thinking. And those are certainly virtues necessary for a successful relationship, as well as the ideal ingredients for the perfect love charm.

What is surprising about my research was just how difficult it turned out to be in tracing my way through the various books, articles, and bits of lore that I came across. One would think that there would be several herbal love charms about, but that's not the case. Or at least it's not the case in any of the sources I came across. What I usually found was a line or two about this herb or that and how it was used to divine, draw, or keep love, but there was usually little mention of how it was used, which is what I find to be the most interesting part.

So, it would seem that many of the bits of lore that helped our ancestors find their mates have been lost over the course of time. If the above is any indication, many of the rituals and actions for a given culture or area were very simple and, as such, were passed around by word of mouth, which is now unfortunately lost in the past. I'll keep digging, though. It's just too interesting not to.

Select Bibliography

Cunningham, Scott. *Cunningham's Encyclopedia of Magical Herbs*. St. Paul, MN: Llewellyn Publications, 1985.

Elisabeth. "My Funny Valentine: The Herbs and Spices of Romance," *allspice*, February 10, 2012, http://tinyurl.com/nhfamvg.

Trissel, Beth. "The History and Romance Behind 'Scarborough Fair,'" *One Writer's Way*, January 23, 2011. http://tinyurl.com/loddwjc.

Vickery, Roy. *Garlands, Conkers, and Mother-Die: British and Irish Plant-Lore*. London: Continuum, 2010.

Laurel Reufner *happily calls the gorgeous hills of Athens County, Ohio, home, where she lives with her husband and two daughters. She's been earth-centered for around twenty-five years now and enjoys writing about whatever shiny topics grab her attention, especially mythology and history. She is slowly working on editing her first book and hopes to have it finished by the time you read this. Keep up with her at her blog,* Laurel Reufner's Lair *(laurelreufner .blogspot.com) or like her Facebook page Laurel Reufner.*

Moon Signs, Phases, and Tables

The Quarters and Signs
of the Moon

Everyone has seen the moon wax and wane through a period of approximately 29½ days. This circuit from new moon to full moon and back again is called the lunation cycle. The cycle is divided into parts called quarters or phases. There are several methods by which this can be done, and the system used in the *Herbal Almanac* may not correspond to those used in other almanacs.

The Quarters

First Quarter

The first quarter begins at the new moon, when the sun and moon are in the same place, or conjunct. (This means the sun and moon are in the same degree of the same sign.) The moon is not visible at first, since it rises at the same time as the sun. The new moon is the time of new beginnings of projects that favor growth, externalization of activities, and the growth of ideas. The first quarter is the time of germination, emergence, beginnings, and outwardly directed activity.

Second Quarter

The second quarter begins halfway between the new moon and the full moon, when the sun and moon are at a right angle, or a 90° square, to each other. This half moon rises around noon and sets around midnight, so it can be seen in the western sky during the first half of the night. The second quarter is the time of growth and articulation of things that already exist.

Third Quarter

The third quarter begins at the full moon, when the sun and moon are opposite one another and the full light of the sun can shine on the full sphere of the moon. The round moon can be seen rising in the east at sunset, then rising a little later each evening. The full moon stands for illumination, fulfillment, culmination, completion, drawing inward, unrest, emotional expressions, and hasty actions leading to failure. The third quarter is a time of maturity, fruition, and the assumption of the full form of expression.

Fourth Quarter

The fourth quarter begins about halfway between the full moon and the new moon, when the sun and moon are again at a right angle, or a 90° square, to each other. This decreasing moon rises at midnight and can be seen in the east during the last half of the night, reaching the overhead position just about as the sun rises. The fourth quarter is a time of disintegration and drawing back for reorganization and reflection.

The Signs

Moon in Aries

Moon in Aries is good for starting things and initiating change, but actions may lack staying power. Activities requiring assertiveness and courage are favored. Things occur rapidly but also quickly pass.

Moon in Taurus

Things begun when the moon is in Taurus last the longest and tend to increase in value. This is a good time for any activity that requires patience, practicality, and perseverance. Things begun now also tend to become habitual and hard to alter.

Moon in Gemini
Moon in Gemini is a good time to exchange ideas, meet with people, or be in situations that require versatility and quick thinking. Things begun now are easily changed by outside influences.

Moon in Cancer
Moon in Cancer is a good time to grow things. It stimulates emotional rapport between people and is a good time to build personal friendships, though people may be more emotional and moody than usual.

Moon in Leo
Moon in Leo is a good time for public appearances, showmanship, being seen, entertaining, drama, recreation, and happy pursuits. People may be overly concerned with praise and subject to flattery.

Moon in Virgo
Moon in Virgo is good for any task that requires close attention to detail and careful analysis of information. There is a focus on health, hygiene, and daily schedules. Watch for a tendency to overdo and overwork.

Moon in Libra
Moon in Libra is a good time to form partnerships of any kind and to negotiate. It discourages spontaneous initiative, so working with a partner is essential. Artistic work and teamwork are highlighted.

Moon in Scorpio

Moon in Scorpio increases awareness of psychic power and favors any activity that requires intensity and focus. This is a good time to conduct research and to end connections thoroughly. There is a tendency to manipulate.

Moon in Sagittarius

Moon in Sagittarius is good for any activity that requires honesty, candor, imagination, and confidence in the flow of life. This is a good time to tackle things that need improvement, but watch out for a tendency to proselytize.

Moon in Capricorn

Moon in Capricorn increases awareness of the need for structure, discipline, and patience. This is a good time to set goals and plan for the future. Those in authority may be insensitive at this time.

Moon in Aquarius

Moon in Aquarius favors activities that are unique and individualistic and that concern society as a whole. This is a good time to pursue humanitarian efforts and to identify improvements that can be made. People may be more intellectual than emotional under this influence.

Moon in Pisces

Moon in Pisces is a good time for any kind of introspective, philanthropic, meditative, psychic, or artistic work. At this time personal boundaries may be blurred, and people may be prone to seeing what they want to see rather than what is really there.

January Moon Table

Date	Sign	Element	Nature	Phase
1 Fri 1:41 am	Libra	Air	Semi-fruitful	3rd
2 Sat	Libra	Air	Semi-fruitful	4th 12:30 am
3 Sun 2:36 pm	Scorpio	Water	Fruitful	4th
4 Mon	Scorpio	Water	Fruitful	4th
5 Tue	Scorpio	Water	Fruitful	4th
6 Wed 1:56 am	Sagittarius	Fire	Barren	4th
7 Thu	Sagittarius	Fire	Barren	4th
8 Fri 10:07 am	Capricorn	Earth	Semi-fruitful	4th
9 Sat	Capricorn	Earth	Semi-fruitful	New 8:31 pm
10 Sun 3:23 pm	Aquarius	Air	Barren	1st
11 Mon	Aquarius	Air	Barren	1st
12 Tue 6:53 pm	Pisces	Water	Fruitful	1st
13 Wed	Pisces	Water	Fruitful	1st
14 Thu 9:48 pm	Aries	Fire	Barren	1st
15 Fri	Aries	Fire	Barren	1st
16 Sat	Aries	Fire	Barren	2nd 6:26 pm
17 Sun 12:48 am	Taurus	Earth	Semi-fruitful	2nd
18 Mon	Taurus	Earth	Semi-fruitful	2nd
19 Tue 4:13 am	Gemini	Air	Barren	2nd
20 Wed	Gemini	Air	Barren	2nd
21 Thu 8:28 am	Cancer	Water	Fruitful	2nd
22 Fri	Cancer	Water	Fruitful	2nd
23 Sat 2:21 pm	Leo	Fire	Barren	Full 8:46 pm
24 Sun	Leo	Fire	Barren	3rd
25 Mon 10:46 pm	Virgo	Earth	Barren	3rd
26 Tue	Virgo	Earth	Barren	3rd
27 Wed	Virgo	Earth	Barren	3rd
28 Thu 9:59 am	Libra	Air	Semi-fruitful	3rd
29 Fri	Libra	Air	Semi-fruitful	3rd
30 Sat 10:50 pm	Scorpio	Water	Fruitful	3rd
31 Sun	Scorpio	Water	Fruitful	4th 10:28 pm

February Moon Table

Date	Sign	Element	Nature	Phase
1 Mon	Scorpio	Water	Fruitful	4th
2 Tue 10:50 am	Sagittarius	Fire	Barren	4th
3 Wed	Sagittarius	Fire	Barren	4th
4 Thu 7:44 pm	Capricorn	Earth	Semi-fruitful	4th
5 Fri	Capricorn	Earth	Semi-fruitful	4th
6 Sat	Capricorn	Earth	Semi-fruitful	4th
7 Sun 12:59 am	Aquarius	Air	Barren	4th
8 Mon	Aquarius	Air	Barren	New 9:39 am
9 Tue 3:31 am	Pisces	Water	Fruitful	1st
10 Wed	Pisces	Water	Fruitful	1st
11 Thu 4:55 am	Aries	Fire	Barren	1st
12 Fri	Aries	Fire	Barren	1st
13 Sat 6:36 am	Taurus	Earth	Semi-fruitful	1st
14 Sun	Taurus	Earth	Semi-fruitful	1st
15 Mon 9:35 am	Gemini	Air	Barren	2nd 2:46 am
16 Tue	Gemini	Air	Barren	2nd
17 Wed 2:24 pm	Cancer	Water	Fruitful	2nd
18 Thu	Cancer	Water	Fruitful	2nd
19 Fri 9:17 pm	Leo	Fire	Barren	2nd
20 Sat	Leo	Fire	Barren	2nd
21 Sun	Leo	Fire	Barren	2nd
22 Mon 6:24 am	Virgo	Earth	Barren	Full 1:20 pm
23 Tue	Virgo	Earth	Barren	3rd
24 Wed 5:41 pm	Libra	Air	Semi-fruitful	3rd
25 Thu	Libra	Air	Semi-fruitful	3rd
26 Fri	Libra	Air	Semi-fruitful	3rd
27 Sat 6:26 am	Scorpio	Water	Fruitful	3rd
28 Sun	Scorpio	Water	Fruitful	3rd
29 Mon 6:56 pm	Sagittarius	Fire	Barren	3rd

Times are in Eastern Time.

March Moon Table

Date	Sign	Element	Nature	Phase
1 Tue	Sagittarius	Fire	Barren	4th 6:11 pm
2 Wed	Sagittarius	Fire	Barren	4th
3 Thu 5:01 am	Capricorn	Earth	Semi-fruitful	4th
4 Fri	Capricorn	Earth	Semi-fruitful	4th
5 Sat 11:22 am	Aquarius	Air	Barren	4th
6 Sun	Aquarius	Air	Barren	4th
7 Mon 2:08 pm	Pisces	Water	Fruitful	4th
8 Tue	Pisces	Water	Fruitful	New 8:54 pm
9 Wed 2:40 pm	Aries	Fire	Barren	1st
10 Thu	Aries	Fire	Barren	1st
11 Fri 2:44 pm	Taurus	Earth	Semi-fruitful	1st
12 Sat	Taurus	Earth	Semi-fruitful	1st
13 Sun 4:03 pm	Gemini	Air	Barren	1st
14 Mon	Gemini	Air	Barren	1st
15 Tue 7:57 pm	Cancer	Water	Fruitful	2nd 12:03 pm
16 Wed	Cancer	Water	Fruitful	2nd
17 Thu	Cancer	Water	Fruitful	2nd
18 Fri 2:54 am	Leo	Fire	Barren	2nd
19 Sat	Leo	Fire	Barren	2nd
20 Sun 12:39 pm	Virgo	Earth	Barren	2nd
21 Mon	Virgo	Earth	Barren	2nd
22 Tue	Virgo	Earth	Barren	2nd
23 Wed 12:23 am	Libra	Air	Semi-fruitful	Full 7:01 am
24 Thu	Libra	Air	Semi-fruitful	3rd
25 Fri 1:09 pm	Scorpio	Water	Fruitful	3rd
26 Sat	Scorpio	Water	Fruitful	3rd
27 Sun	Scorpio	Water	Fruitful	3rd
28 Mon 1:46 am	Sagittarius	Fire	Barren	3rd
29 Tue	Sagittarius	Fire	Barren	3rd
30 Wed 12:45 pm	Capricorn	Earth	Semi-fruitful	3rd
31 Thu	Capricorn	Earth	Semi-fruitful	4th 10:17 am

April Moon Table

Date	Sign	Element	Nature	Phase
1 Fri 8:37 pm	Aquarius	Air	Barren	4th
2 Sat	Aquarius	Air	Barren	4th
3 Sun	Aquarius	Air	Barren	4th
4 Mon 12:45 am	Pisces	Water	Fruitful	4th
5 Tue	Pisces	Water	Fruitful	4th
6 Wed 1:46 am	Aries	Fire	Barren	4th
7 Thu	Aries	Fire	Barren	New 6:24 am
8 Fri 1:10 am	Taurus	Earth	Semi-fruitful	1st
9 Sat	Taurus	Earth	Semi-fruitful	1st
10 Sun 12:59 am	Gemini	Air	Barren	1st
11 Mon	Gemini	Air	Barren	1st
12 Tue 3:07 am	Cancer	Water	Fruitful	1st
13 Wed	Cancer	Water	Fruitful	2nd 10:59 pm
14 Thu 8:53 am	Leo	Fire	Barren	2nd
15 Fri	Leo	Fire	Barren	2nd
16 Sat 6:23 pm	Virgo	Earth	Barren	2nd
17 Sun	Virgo	Earth	Barren	2nd
18 Mon	Virgo	Earth	Barren	2nd
19 Tue 6:24 am	Libra	Air	Semi-fruitful	2nd
20 Wed	Libra	Air	Semi-fruitful	2nd
21 Thu 7:17 pm	Scorpio	Water	Fruitful	2nd
22 Fri	Scorpio	Water	Fruitful	Full 12:24 am
23 Sat	Scorpio	Water	Fruitful	3rd
24 Sun 7:46 am	Sagittarius	Fire	Barren	3rd
25 Mon	Sagittarius	Fire	Barren	3rd
26 Tue 6:54 pm	Capricorn	Earth	Semi-fruitful	3rd
27 Wed	Capricorn	Earth	Semi-fruitful	3rd
28 Thu	Capricorn	Earth	Semi-fruitful	3rd
29 Fri 3:47 am	Aquarius	Air	Barren	4th 10:29 pm
30 Sat	Aquarius	Air	Barren	4th

Times are in Eastern Time.

May Moon Table

Date	Sign	Element	Nature	Phase
1 Sun 9:33 am	Pisces	Water	Fruitful	4th
2 Mon	Pisces	Water	Fruitful	4th
3 Tue 12:04 pm	Aries	Fire	Barren	4th
4 Wed	Aries	Fire	Barren	4th
5 Thu 12:10 pm	Taurus	Earth	Semi-fruitful	4th
6 Fri	Taurus	Earth	Semi-fruitful	New 2:30 pm
7 Sat 11:35 am	Gemini	Air	Barren	1st
8 Sun	Gemini	Air	Barren	1st
9 Mon 12:24 pm	Cancer	Water	Fruitful	1st
10 Tue	Cancer	Water	Fruitful	1st
11 Wed 4:32 pm	Leo	Fire	Barren	1st
12 Thu	Leo	Fire	Barren	1st
13 Fri	Leo	Fire	Barren	2nd 12:02 pm
14 Sat 12:52 am	Virgo	Earth	Barren	2nd
15 Sun	Virgo	Earth	Barren	2nd
16 Mon 12:33 pm	Libra	Air	Semi-fruitful	2nd
17 Tue	Libra	Air	Semi-fruitful	2nd
18 Wed	Libra	Air	Semi-fruitful	2nd
19 Thu 1:29 am	Scorpio	Water	Fruitful	2nd
20 Fri	Scorpio	Water	Fruitful	2nd
21 Sat 1:48 pm	Sagittarius	Fire	Barren	Full 4:14 pm
22 Sun	Sagittarius	Fire	Barren	3rd
23 Mon	Sagittarius	Fire	Barren	3rd
24 Tue 12:34 am	Capricorn	Earth	Semi-fruitful	3rd
25 Wed	Capricorn	Earth	Semi-fruitful	3rd
26 Thu 9:27 am	Aquarius	Air	Barren	3rd
27 Fri	Aquarius	Air	Barren	3rd
28 Sat 4:06 pm	Pisces	Water	Fruitful	3rd
29 Sun	Pisces	Water	Fruitful	4th 7:12 am
30 Mon 8:09 pm	Aries	Fire	Barren	4th
31 Tue	Aries	Fire	Barren	4th

June Moon Table

Date	Sign	Element	Nature	Phase
1 Wed 9:46 pm	Taurus	Earth	Semi-fruitful	4th
2 Thu	Taurus	Earth	Semi-fruitful	4th
3 Fri 10:01 pm	Gemini	Air	Barren	4th
4 Sat	Gemini	Air	Barren	New 10:00 pm
5 Sun 10:41 pm	Cancer	Water	Fruitful	1st
6 Mon	Cancer	Water	Fruitful	1st
7 Tue	Cancer	Water	Fruitful	1st
8 Wed 1:47 am	Leo	Fire	Barren	1st
9 Thu	Leo	Fire	Barren	1st
10 Fri 8:46 am	Virgo	Earth	Barren	1st
11 Sat	Virgo	Earth	Barren	1st
12 Sun 7:33 pm	Libra	Air	Semi-fruitful	2nd 3:10 am
13 Mon	Libra	Air	Semi-fruitful	2nd
14 Tue	Libra	Air	Semi-fruitful	2nd
15 Wed 8:18 am	Scorpio	Water	Fruitful	2nd
16 Thu	Scorpio	Water	Fruitful	2nd
17 Fri 8:34 pm	Sagittarius	Fire	Barren	2nd
18 Sat	Sagittarius	Fire	Barren	2nd
19 Sun	Sagittarius	Fire	Barren	2nd
20 Mon 6:55 am	Capricorn	Earth	Semi-fruitful	Full 6:02 am
21 Tue	Capricorn	Earth	Semi-fruitful	3rd
22 Wed 3:08 pm	Aquarius	Air	Barren	3rd
23 Thu	Aquarius	Air	Barren	3rd
24 Fri 9:30 pm	Pisces	Water	Fruitful	3rd
25 Sat	Pisces	Water	Fruitful	3rd
26 Sun	Pisces	Water	Fruitful	3rd
27 Mon 2:08 am	Aries	Fire	Barren	4th 1:19 pm
28 Tue	Aries	Fire	Barren	4th
29 Wed 5:03 am	Taurus	Earth	Semi-fruitful	4th
30 Thu	Taurus	Earth	Semi-fruitful	4th

Times are in Eastern Time.

July Moon Table

Date	Sign	Element	Nature	Phase
1 Fri 6:44 am	Gemini	Air	Barren	4th
2 Sat	Gemini	Air	Barren	4th
3 Sun 8:20 am	Cancer	Water	Fruitful	4th
4 Mon	Cancer	Water	Fruitful	New 6:01 am
5 Tue 11:28 am	Leo	Fire	Barren	1st
6 Wed	Leo	Fire	Barren	1st
7 Thu 5:41 pm	Virgo	Earth	Barren	1st
8 Fri	Virgo	Earth	Barren	1st
9 Sat	Virgo	Earth	Barren	1st
10 Sun 3:32 am	Libra	Air	Semi-fruitful	1st
11 Mon	Libra	Air	Semi-fruitful	2nd 7:52 pm
12 Tue 3:52 pm	Scorpio	Water	Fruitful	2nd
13 Wed	Scorpio	Water	Fruitful	2nd
14 Thu	Scorpio	Water	Fruitful	2nd
15 Fri 4:14 am	Sagittarius	Fire	Barren	2nd
16 Sat	Sagittarius	Fire	Barren	2nd
17 Sun 2:33 pm	Capricorn	Earth	Semi-fruitful	2nd
18 Mon	Capricorn	Earth	Semi-fruitful	2nd
19 Tue 10:10 pm	Aquarius	Air	Barren	Full 5:57 pm
20 Wed	Aquarius	Air	Barren	3rd
21 Thu	Aquarius	Air	Barren	3rd
22 Fri 3:35 am	Pisces	Water	Fruitful	3rd
23 Sat	Pisces	Water	Fruitful	3rd
24 Sun 7:33 am	Aries	Fire	Barren	3rd
25 Mon	Aries	Fire	Barren	3rd
26 Tue 10:37 am	Taurus	Earth	Semi-fruitful	4th 6:00 pm
27 Wed	Taurus	Earth	Semi-fruitful	4th
28 Thu 1:17 pm	Gemini	Air	Barren	4th
29 Fri	Gemini	Air	Barren	4th
30 Sat 4:09 pm	Cancer	Water	Fruitful	4th
31 Sun	Cancer	Water	Fruitful	4th

August Moon Table

Date	Sign	Element	Nature	Phase
1 Mon 8:12 pm	Leo	Fire	Barren	4th
2 Tue	Leo	Fire	Barren	New 3:45 pm
3 Wed	Leo	Fire	Barren	1st
4 Thu 2:34 am	Virgo	Earth	Barren	1st
5 Fri	Virgo	Earth	Barren	1st
6 Sat 11:57 am	Libra	Air	Semi-fruitful	1st
7 Sun	Libra	Air	Semi-fruitful	1st
8 Mon 11:51 pm	Scorpio	Water	Fruitful	1st
9 Tue	Scorpio	Water	Fruitful	1st
10 Wed	Scorpio	Water	Fruitful	2nd 1:21 pm
11 Thu 12:24 pm	Sagittarius	Fire	Barren	2nd
12 Fri	Sagittarius	Fire	Barren	2nd
13 Sat 11:11 pm	Capricorn	Earth	Semi-fruitful	2nd
14 Sun	Capricorn	Earth	Semi-fruitful	2nd
15 Mon	Capricorn	Earth	Semi-fruitful	2nd
16 Tue 6:52 am	Aquarius	Air	Barren	2nd
17 Wed	Aquarius	Air	Barren	2nd
18 Thu 11:34 am	Pisces	Water	Fruitful	Full 4:27 am
19 Fri	Pisces	Water	Fruitful	3rd
20 Sat 2:18 pm	Aries	Fire	Barren	3rd
21 Sun	Aries	Fire	Barren	3rd
22 Mon 4:19 pm	Taurus	Earth	Semi-fruitful	3rd
23 Tue	Taurus	Earth	Semi-fruitful	3rd
24 Wed 6:40 pm	Gemini	Air	Barren	4th 10:41 pm
25 Thu	Gemini	Air	Barren	4th
26 Fri 10:06 pm	Cancer	Water	Fruitful	4th
27 Sat	Cancer	Water	Fruitful	4th
28 Sun	Cancer	Water	Fruitful	4th
29 Mon 3:11 am	Leo	Fire	Barren	4th
30 Tue	Leo	Fire	Barren	4th
31 Wed 10:22 am	Virgo	Earth	Barren	4th

Times are in Eastern Time.

September Moon Table

Date	Sign	Element	Nature	Phase
1 Thu	Virgo	Earth	Barren	New 4:03 am
2 Fri 7:55 pm	Libra	Air	Semi-fruitful	1st
3 Sat	Libra	Air	Semi-fruitful	1st
4 Sun	Libra	Air	Semi-fruitful	1st
5 Mon 7:38 am	Scorpio	Water	Fruitful	1st
6 Tue	Scorpio	Water	Fruitful	1st
7 Wed 8:20 pm	Sagittarius	Fire	Barren	1st
8 Thu	Sagittarius	Fire	Barren	1st
9 Fri	Sagittarius	Fire	Barren	2nd 6:49 am
10 Sat 7:55 am	Capricorn	Earth	Semi-fruitful	2nd
11 Sun	Capricorn	Earth	Semi-fruitful	2nd
12 Mon 4:28 pm	Aquarius	Air	Barren	2nd
13 Tue	Aquarius	Air	Barren	2nd
14 Wed 9:23 pm	Pisces	Water	Fruitful	2nd
15 Thu	Pisces	Water	Fruitful	2nd
16 Fri 11:22 pm	Aries	Fire	Barren	Full 2:05 pm
17 Sat	Aries	Fire	Barren	3rd
18 Sun 11:58 pm	Taurus	Earth	Semi-fruitful	3rd
19 Mon	Taurus	Earth	Semi-fruitful	3rd
20 Tue	Taurus	Earth	Semi-fruitful	3rd
21 Wed 12:53 am	Gemini	Air	Barren	3rd
22 Thu	Gemini	Air	Barren	3rd
23 Fri 3:33 am	Cancer	Water	Fruitful	4th 4:56 am
24 Sat	Cancer	Water	Fruitful	4th
25 Sun 8:48 am	Leo	Fire	Barren	4th
26 Mon	Leo	Fire	Barren	4th
27 Tue 4:43 pm	Virgo	Earth	Barren	4th
28 Wed	Virgo	Earth	Barren	4th
29 Thu	Virgo	Earth	Barren	4th
30 Fri 2:52 am	Libra	Air	Semi-fruitful	New 7:11 pm

October Moon Table

Date	Sign	Element	Nature	Phase
1 Sat	Libra	Air	Semi-fruitful	1st
2 Sun 2:43 pm	Scorpio	Water	Fruitful	1st
3 Mon	Scorpio	Water	Fruitful	1st
4 Tue	Scorpio	Water	Fruitful	1st
5 Wed 3:26 am	Sagittarius	Fire	Barren	1st
6 Thu	Sagittarius	Fire	Barren	1st
7 Fri 3:40 pm	Capricorn	Earth	Semi-fruitful	1st
8 Sat	Capricorn	Earth	Semi-fruitful	2nd 11:33 pm
9 Sun	Capricorn	Earth	Semi-fruitful	2nd
10 Mon 1:33 am	Aquarius	Air	Barren	2nd
11 Tue	Aquarius	Air	Barren	2nd
12 Wed 7:43 am	Pisces	Water	Fruitful	2nd
13 Thu	Pisces	Water	Fruitful	2nd
14 Fri 10:08 am	Aries	Fire	Barren	2nd
15 Sat	Aries	Fire	Barren	Full 11:23 pm
16 Sun 10:04 am	Taurus	Earth	Semi-fruitful	3rd
17 Mon	Taurus	Earth	Semi-fruitful	3rd
18 Tue 9:30 am	Gemini	Air	Barren	3rd
19 Wed	Gemini	Air	Barren	3rd
20 Thu 10:28 am	Cancer	Water	Fruitful	3rd
21 Fri	Cancer	Water	Fruitful	3rd
22 Sat 2:34 pm	Leo	Fire	Barren	4th 2:14 pm
23 Sun	Leo	Fire	Barren	4th
24 Mon 10:16 pm	Virgo	Earth	Barren	4th
25 Tue	Virgo	Earth	Barren	4th
26 Wed	Virgo	Earth	Barren	4th
27 Thu 8:51 am	Libra	Air	Semi-fruitful	4th
28 Fri	Libra	Air	Semi-fruitful	4th
29 Sat 9:01 pm	Scorpio	Water	Fruitful	4th
30 Sun	Scorpio	Water	Fruitful	New 12:38 pm
31 Mon	Scorpio	Water	Fruitful	1st

Times are in Eastern Time.

November Moon Table

Date	Sign	Element	Nature	Phase
1 Tue 9:43 am	Sagittarius	Fire	Barren	1st
2 Wed	Sagittarius	Fire	Barren	1st
3 Thu 10:05 pm	Capricorn	Earth	Semi-fruitful	1st
4 Fri	Capricorn	Earth	Semi-fruitful	1st
5 Sat	Capricorn	Earth	Semi-fruitful	1st
6 Sun 8:55 am	Aquarius	Air	Barren	1st
7 Mon	Aquarius	Air	Barren	2nd 2:51 pm
8 Tue 4:45 pm	Pisces	Water	Fruitful	2nd
9 Wed	Pisces	Water	Fruitful	2nd
10 Thu 8:45 pm	Aries	Fire	Barren	2nd
11 Fri	Aries	Fire	Barren	2nd
12 Sat 9:24 pm	Taurus	Earth	Semi-fruitful	2nd
13 Sun	Taurus	Earth	Semi-fruitful	2nd
14 Mon 8:23 pm	Gemini	Air	Barren	Full 8:52 am
15 Tue	Gemini	Air	Barren	3rd
16 Wed 7:57 pm	Cancer	Water	Fruitful	3rd
17 Thu	Cancer	Water	Fruitful	3rd
18 Fri 10:14 pm	Leo	Fire	Barren	3rd
19 Sat	Leo	Fire	Barren	3rd
20 Sun	Leo	Fire	Barren	3rd
21 Mon 4:34 am	Virgo	Earth	Barren	4th 3:33 am
22 Tue	Virgo	Earth	Barren	4th
23 Wed 2:42 pm	Libra	Air	Semi-fruitful	4th
24 Thu	Libra	Air	Semi-fruitful	4th
25 Fri	Libra	Air	Semi-fruitful	4th
26 Sat 3:01 am	Scorpio	Water	Fruitful	4th
27 Sun	Scorpio	Water	Fruitful	4th
28 Mon 3:46 pm	Sagittarius	Fire	Barren	4th
29 Tue	Sagittarius	Fire	Barren	New 7:18 am
30 Wed	Sagittarius	Fire	Barren	1st

December Moon Table

Date	Sign	Element	Nature	Phase
1 Thu 3:52 am	Capricorn	Earth	Semi-fruitful	1st
2 Fri	Capricorn	Earth	Semi-fruitful	1st
3 Sat 2:44 pm	Aquarius	Air	Barren	1st
4 Sun	Aquarius	Air	Barren	1st
5 Mon 11:31 pm	Pisces	Water	Fruitful	1st
6 Tue	Pisces	Water	Fruitful	1st
7 Wed	Pisces	Water	Fruitful	2nd 4:03 am
8 Thu 5:15 am	Aries	Fire	Barren	2nd
9 Fri	Aries	Fire	Barren	2nd
10 Sat 7:41 am	Taurus	Earth	Semi-fruitful	2nd
11 Sun	Taurus	Earth	Semi-fruitful	2nd
12 Mon 7:41 am	Gemini	Air	Barren	2nd
13 Tue	Gemini	Air	Barren	Full 7:06 pm
14 Wed 7:09 am	Cancer	Water	Fruitful	3rd
15 Thu	Cancer	Water	Fruitful	3rd
16 Fri 8:15 am	Leo	Fire	Barren	3rd
17 Sat	Leo	Fire	Barren	3rd
18 Sun 12:52 pm	Virgo	Earth	Barren	3rd
19 Mon	Virgo	Earth	Barren	3rd
20 Tue 9:40 pm	Libra	Air	Semi-fruitful	4th 8:56 pm
21 Wed	Libra	Air	Semi-fruitful	4th
22 Thu	Libra	Air	Semi-fruitful	4th
23 Fri 9:32 am	Scorpio	Water	Fruitful	4th
24 Sat	Scorpio	Water	Fruitful	4th
25 Sun 10:19 pm	Sagittarius	Fire	Barren	4th
26 Mon	Sagittarius	Fire	Barren	4th
27 Tue	Sagittarius	Fire	Barren	4th
28 Wed 10:12 am	Capricorn	Earth	Semi-fruitful	4th
29 Thu	Capricorn	Earth	Semi-fruitful	New 1:53 am
30 Fri 8:29 pm	Aquarius	Air	Barren	1st
31 Sat	Aquarius	Air	Barren	1st

Times are in Eastern Time.

Dates to Destroy Weeds and Pests

Dates	Sign	Quarter
Jan 6, 1:56 am–Jan 8, 10:07 am	Sagittarius	4th
Jan 23, 8:46 pm–Jan 25, 10:46 pm	Leo	3rd
Jan 25, 10:46 pm–Jan 28, 9:59 am	Virgo	3rd
Feb 2, 10:50 am–Feb 4, 7:44 pm	Sagittarius	4th
Feb 7, 12:59 am–Feb 8, 9:39 am	Aquarius	4th
Feb 22, 1:20 pm–Feb 24, 5:41 pm	Virgo	3rd
Feb 29, 6:56 pm–Mar 1, 6:11 pm	Sagittarius	3rd
Mar 1, 6:11 pm–Mar 3, 5:01 am	Sagittarius	4th
Mar 5, 11:22 am–Mar 7, 2:08 pm	Aquarius	4th
Mar 28, 1:46 am–Mar 30, 12:45 pm	Sagittarius	3rd
Apr 1, 8:37 pm–Apr 4, 12:45 am	Aquarius	4th
Apr 6, 1:46 am–Apr 7, 6:24 am	Aries	4th
Apr 24, 7:46 am–Apr 26, 6:54 pm	Sagittarius	3rd
Apr 29, 3:47 am–Apr 29, 10:29 pm	Aquarius	3rd
Apr 29, 10:29 pm–May 1, 9:33 am	Aquarius	4th
May 3, 12:04 pm–May 5, 12:10 pm	Aries	4th
May 21, 4:14 pm–May 24, 12:34 am	Sagittarius	3rd
May 26, 9:27 am–May 28, 4:06 pm	Aquarius	3rd
May 30, 8:09 pm–Jun 1, 9:46 pm	Aries	4th
Jun 3, 10:01 pm–Jun 4, 10:00 pm	Gemini	4th
Jun 20, 6:02 am–Jun 20, 6:55 am	Sagittarius	3rd
Jun 22, 3:08 pm–Jun 24, 9:30 pm	Aquarius	3rd
Jun 27, 2:08 am–Jun 27, 1:19 pm	Aries	3rd
Jun 27, 1:19 pm–Jun 29, 5:03 am	Aries	4th
Jul 1, 6:44 am–Jul 3, 8:20 am	Gemini	4th
Jul 19, 10:10 pm–Jul 22, 3:35 am	Aquarius	3rd
Jul 24, 7:33 am–Jul 26, 10:37 am	Aries	3rd

Dates to Destroy Weeds and Pests

Dates	Sign	Quarter
Jul 28, 1:17 pm–Jul 30, 4:09 pm	Gemini	4th
Aug 1, 8:12 pm–Aug 2, 3:45 pm	Leo	4th
Aug 18, 4:27 am–Aug 18, 11:34 am	Aquarius	3rd
Aug 20, 2:18 pm–Aug 22, 4:19 pm	Aries	3rd
Aug 24, 6:40 pm–Aug 24, 10:41 pm	Gemini	3rd
Aug 24, 10:41 pm–Aug 26, 10:06 pm	Gemini	4th
Aug 29, 3:11 am–Aug 31, 10:22 am	Leo	4th
Aug 31, 10:22 am–Sep 1, 4:03 am	Virgo	4th
Sep 16, 11:22 pm–Sep 18, 11:58 pm	Aries	3rd
Sep 21, 12:53 am–Sep 23, 3:33 am	Gemini	3rd
Sep 25, 8:48 am–Sep 27, 4:43 pm	Leo	4th
Sep 27, 4:43 pm–Sep 30, 2:52 am	Virgo	4th
Oct 15, 11:23 pm–Oct 16, 10:04 am	Aries	3rd
Oct 18, 9:30 am–Oct 20, 10:28 am	Gemini	3rd
Oct 22, 2:34 pm–Oct 24, 10:16 pm	Leo	4th
Oct 24, 10:16 pm–Oct 27, 8:51 am	Virgo	4th
Nov 14, 8:23 pm–Nov 16, 7:57 pm	Gemini	3rd
Nov 18, 10:14 pm–Nov 21, 3:33 am	Leo	3rd
Nov 21, 3:33 am–Nov 21, 4:34 am	Leo	4th
Nov 21, 4:34 am–Nov 23, 2:42 pm	Virgo	4th
Nov 28, 3:46 pm–Nov 29, 7:18 am	Sagittarius	4th
Dec 13, 7:06 pm–Dec 14, 7:09 am	Gemini	3rd
Dec 16, 8:15 am–Dec 18, 12:52 pm	Leo	3rd
Dec 18, 12:52 pm–Dec 20, 8:56 pm	Virgo	3rd
Dec 20, 8:56 pm–Dec 20, 9:40 pm	Virgo	4th
Dec 25, 10:19 pm–Dec 28, 10:12 am	Sagittarius	4th

Times are in Eastern Time.